SOUTH-SOUTH MIGRATIONS AND THE LAW FROM BELOW

This book explores the narratives and experiences of people in the Global South as they encounter the impact of international law in their lives. It looks specifically at approaches to international migrations and the law, as states in the Global South confront migration-related challenges.

Taking a case study approach, drawn from the experiences of undocumented and displaced migrants in China and Nigeria, the book shows how informal justice systems not only exist but are upheld. With an innovative analysis drawing both on intersectionality and Third World Approaches to International Law (TWAIL), it moves away from the classic international versus regional and domestic law approach to reveal the experience of the Third World in relation to the law.

This fascinating study will appeal to international law, human rights and immigration scholars, as well as those in the field of development studies.

Volume 90 in the series Studies in International Law

Studies in International Law

Recent titles in this series

Judicial Deference in International Adjudication: A Comparative Analysis
Johannes Hendrik Fahner

Human Rights Commitments of Islamic States: Sharia, Treaties and Consensus
Paul McDonough

Intervention in Civil Wars: Effectiveness, Legitimacy, and Human Rights
Chiara Redaelli

General Principles as a Source of International Law: Art 38(1)(c) of the Statute of the International Court of Justice
Imogen Saunders

The Law of Humanity Project: A Story of International Law Reform and State-making
Ukri Soirila

Extraterritoriality and Climate Change Jurisdiction: Exploring EU Climate Protection under International Law
Natalie L Dobson

International Law and the War with Islamic State: Challenges for Jus ad Bellum and Jus in Bello
Saeed Bagheri

Private Actors as Participants in International Law: A Critical Analysis of Membership under the Law of the Sea
Armando Rocha

Truth and Transitional Justice: Localising the International Legal Framework in Muslim Majority Legal Systems
Alice Panepinto

State Responsibility for Non-State Actors: Past, Present and Prospects for the Future
Richard Mackenzie-Gray Scott

International Agreements between Non-State Actors as a Source of International Law
Melissa Loja

Judicial Decisions in International Law Argumentation: Between Entrapment and Creativity
Letizia Lo Giacco

South-South Migrations and the Law from Below: Case Studies on China and Nigeria
Oreva Olakpe

For a complete list of titles in this series
see www.bloomsbury.com/uk/series/studies-in-international-law/

South-South Migrations and the Law from Below

Case Studies on China and Nigeria

Oreva Olakpe

•HART•
OXFORD • LONDON • NEW YORK • NEW DELHI • SYDNEY

HART PUBLISHING

Bloomsbury Publishing Plc

Kemp House, Chawley Park, Cumnor Hill, Oxford, OX2 9PH, UK

1385 Broadway, New York, NY 10018, USA

29 Earlsfort Terrace, Dublin 2, Ireland

HART PUBLISHING, the Hart/Stag logo, BLOOMSBURY and the Diana logo are trademarks of Bloomsbury Publishing Plc

First published in Great Britain 2023

A catalogue record for this book is available from the British Library.

A catalogue record for this book is available from the Library of Congress.

Library of Congress Control Number: 2023930226

ISBN: HB: 978-1-50995-818-4
ePDF: 978-1-50995-820-7
ePub: 978-1-50995-819-1

Typeset by Compuscript Ltd, Shannon

Acknowledgements

THIS BOOK IS the product of work that started in 2014 and so many people have enriched the process of researching and writing it. I am thankful to my family – to Christian Akioja Olakpe, my father, for inspiring and supporting my research, to my siblings Ufuoma, Uzoezi, Udhedhe, Mazino and Mano for cheering me on, and to my spouse Uyi Ogunseri for succour. I am exceedingly grateful to my phenomenal friends Rafeeat Aliyu, Amaka Vanni and Mirella Manhombo for always uplifting me, giving me feedback and proof reading, and editing my drafts.

I also want to thank all the participants in Nigeria and China who gave their valuable time, resources, shared their personal stories with me and trusted me to document their stories.

My sincere gratitude to Yamini, Gary, Kate, Nicole, Sarah, Mrs Eyo-Ita, Dee, Adeola, Professor Maduagwu, Professor Obafemi, Sheila, Jyothi, Mr Ishola, Nnamdi, Ikenna, Minhua, Professor Liu, the Chinese in Africa-China in Africa Research Network, contacts in UNHCR and IOM Beijing, the School of Social Sciences and the Social Management Academy of Beijing Normal University, the Black Women in Beijing network, and the many people who opened doors for me in China and Nigeria.

This book would not exist without the support and fantastic supervision of Professor Gina Heathcote and Professor Lutz Oette, the needed encouragement and advice from Professor Anna Triandafyllidou, Dr Amaka Vanni, Professor Luis Eslava, and Dr John Carlaw- Thank you for your kindness, for reading the volume, and offering important guidance to me.

Finally, to my mother, Justina Oberuru Olakpe, I render my deepest appreciation for her tireless effort to support all my dreams and push me to see them to fruition. This book is the outcome of her hard work.

This book is dedicated to all the people who were involved in any way in the research and writing process, especially the communities whose daily struggles against injustice and hegemony inspired this volume.

Contents

1

The Case for Research on South-South Migration and the Law from Below

> Nobody cares about our struggles even though we gave up our rights to placate Nigeria, Cameroon and the international community to ensure there is peace in West Africa. We legitimised the UN system and international law, setting precedents and creating history on the implementation of an ICJ judgement but because we do not bear arms, we are ignored. One day, our goodwill will expire.[1]

> The Nigerian community contributes money to pay for the tickets of Nigerians who overstay to return home. The community has judges that settle issues between Nigerians. The Nigerian community is doing the job of the Embassy. The former Ambassador caused a lot of problems for the community, he wanted to dissolve the community. He created so many problems and destroyed the structures that had taken so long to build here. Nobody knows how hard it has been to build this community and all the work we have been doing nor the progress we made.[2]

I. UNPACKING SOUTH-SOUTH MIGRATIONS

As a child raised in the Niger Delta region of Nigeria, I often heard about the Bakassi Peninsula and the dispute between Cameroon and Nigeria from my father. He spoke about the Bakassi people and how their lives were upended by some distant court in a place called The Hague. As I grew older, I noticed more news reports in Nigeria about the Bakassi people, mostly about their displacement and abandonment. These stories never made it to the international news networks, and I often wondered why. Those discussions with my father sparked my interest in international law. I pursued that goal of furthering my education, eager to learn about the Bakassi Peninsula in particular. During my master's level training in international law in Geneva, we studied everything about the case – excluding the legal implications and the impact of the decision of the international court on the Bakassi people.

[1] Listening session at Ikang Returnee Camp, Cross Rivers State, Nigeria, June 2016, on file with the author.

[2] Personal interview with Mr B in Baiyun District, Guangzhou, China, March 2016, on file with the author.

Pedagogy did not seem to concern itself with what came after the decision of the court in The Hague. What happened to the people who lived in the Peninsula after Cameroon was given ownership? How did the judgment impact their lives? What does this tell us about the state of international law? All these details were missing. Having heard so much about the impact of the court's decision on the everyday lives of people discussed over home-cooked meals and in the local news, I realised that something crucial was missing in how we discuss international law.

My encounters as a student travelling in China raised similar questions. There I met Africans who were seeking asylum or living without recognised migrant status. They told stories of building community, finding justice outside the protections of the state, and of their struggles against discrimination and exclusion within a state that does not recognise international migrant and refugee protections. These stories were again missing in discussions about how international legal norms and practices – including citizenship, refugee and undocumented status – shape the daily lives of people in the Global South.

Third World Approaches to International Law (TWAIL), a movement that concerns itself with writing the Third World into international law, provided answers to my questions and curiosity over the missing voices in international law. TWAIL is defined by Antony Anghie as a dialectic of opposition to international law rooted in identifying and challenging the oppressive characteristics of the law that stem from Western norms and practices. This became my guiding tool as I delved deeper into these two separate yet similar cases. I wanted to understand how specific communities in their paths to justice demonstrate the 'law of the everyday' and the 'law from below' in the Global South. In the words of Hilary Charlesworth, the 'law of the everyday' here refers to 'issues of structural justice that underpin everyday life'.[3] These issues stem from the violent, exclusionary or harmful practices of states that manifest themselves economically, politically, and in laws and policies that impact the daily lives of people. The law from below has been described as law from informal, subaltern, local sources that stem from ordinary people and social movements in the Global South.[4]

Critical scholars like Charlesworth and Balakrishnan Rajagopal argue that a refocus of international legal scholarship is necessary in order to challenge the status quo. This is a status quo that maintains the dominance of Eurocentric and/or Western narratives in international law and the erasure of Global South experiences and contributions.[5] My book contributes to the refocusing of international law through studying expressions and interpretations of and encounters with international law in the Global South. People in the Global South grapple

[3] See Hilary Charlesworth, 'International Law: A Discipline of Crisis' (2002) 65 *MLR* 377.

[4] See Balakrishnan Rajagopal, 'International Law and Social Movements: Challenges of Theorizing *Resistance*' (2003) 41 *Columbia Journal of Transnational Law* 397.

[5] See James Thuo Gathii, 'TWAIL: A Brief History of its Origins, its Decentralized Network, and a Tentative Bibliography' (2011) 3 *Trade Law & Development* 26, at 29.

with the impact of international legal norms, decisions and practices in their daily lives. Through the course of my research, I encountered communities in China and Nigeria, both at the fringes of the state and the comforts of citizenship, yet fighting to create a space for themselves. These encounters inspired this book. Here, I deliberately centre the experiences of the law of everyday 'from below'.[6] More comprehensively, this book is a study on how China and Nigeria engage with international law issues without looking to Europe and North America as the point of reference in understanding international law. Nigeria and China are regional hegemonies that influence international relations and human rights in both Asia and Africa.[7] With these two states as case studies, I compare how these powerful non-Western countries interpret their role and position in the international community in relation to the people and communities engaged in South-South migrations.

Many aspects of South-South migrations are still largely underexplored, and this is particularly true in international legal scholarship.[8] I derive an understanding of international law from the experiences and narratives of undocumented or displaced communities and state practice in the Global South – specifically using China and Nigeria as case studies. Critical legal scholars have discussed the law of the everyday and the importance of learning how conceptual and spatial boundaries are materialised by the law.[9] My interrogation delves deep into what migration within the Global South exposes about communities at the fringes of international, regional and domestic society. Undocumented and displaced communities exhibit complex manifestations of empowerment and marginality simultaneously. These are significant in terms of understanding the impact of international law on people in the Global South.

My case studies intentionally encompass and reflect narratives of migrants who may be at the fringes of the state in the Global South. Some are undocumented migrants, who in my understanding are migrants without legal permission to reside in the host country. Displaced migrants on the other hand are stuck

[6] I will discuss terminology in more detail below in section I.B.

[7] See Shahar Hameiri and Lee Jones, 'Rising Powers and State Transformation: The Case of China' (2016) 22(1) *European Journal of International Relations* 72; Qingjiang Kong and Xiaojuan Ping, 'International Law in International Institutions: Implications for a Rising China' (2015) 1 *Chinese Journal of Global Governance* 157; Olusola Ogunnubi and Ufo Okeke-Uzodike, 'Can Nigeria Be Africa's Hegemon?' (2016) 25(2) *African Security Review* 110. The case study backgrounds will be discussed in more detail in ch 2.

[8] See Philippe de Lombaerde, Fei Guo and Helion Neto, 'Introduction to the Special Collection: South-South Migrations: What is (Still) on the Research Agenda?' (2014) 48 *International Migration Review* 103; Catherine Wihtol de Wenden, 'New Migrations' (2016) 23 *SUR – International Journal on Human Rights* 17. Campillo-Carrete gives an in-depth review of the growing literature on South-South migrations across history, economics, anthropology, sociology, development etc. In international legal scholarship, South-South migration is still a budding area of focus and missing in Campillo-Carrete's review. See Beatriz Campillo-Carrete, 'South-South Migrations: A Review of the Literature' (2013) International Institute of Social Studies, Erasmus University of Rotterdam, https://www.iss.nl/sites/corporate/files/Campillo_WP_South-South_migration_Lit-reviewannotated-bibly_22July_2013.pdf.

[9] See Charlesworth (n 3) 392; Annelise Riles, 'A View from the International Plane: Perspective and Scale in the Architecture of Colonial International Law' (1995) VI(1) *Law and Critique* 39.

between borders and border disputes. These migrants could be refugees fleeing persecution in accordance with Article 1 of the United Nations (UN) Refugee Convention, asylum seekers who are seeking refuge in a state in the Global South, or those termed 'economic migrants' who migrate primarily for better work or life opportunities.[10] Narratives of these variations of migration question the concept of marginality and how different groups experience it on their path to justice and in their experience of South-South migration.[11] Marginality is framed around exclusion from the benefits of citizenship and formal law, and these exclusions shape experiences of the law in the Global South.

China disrupts many stereotypes as an economically powerful state with a permanent seat on the UN Security Council. It has numerous internal inequalities and power asymmetries, and like many developing countries, sovereignty in the Chinese context is shaped by a past of Western domination and interference in its internal affairs. China sees itself as a leader of the developing world and strategically utilises its position in the Security Council to defy perceived Western domination. It also wields enormous economic power in Africa, offering itself an alternative to the West.[12] This has created a power differential between China and African states, similar to the power differentials during colonial times.[13] Sino-African relations are a complex site of hierarchies, power struggles and hegemony in the Global South which must be unpacked and analysed. This is particularly significant as migrations and contact between China and Africa are increasing exponentially and will shape the configurations of power in the Global South.[14]

There has been significant anthropological, sociological, historical and economic research on African migrants in China, but there is almost no research on the relationship between the law and this group of migrants.[15] Scholars

[10] See Convention Relating to the Status of Refugees (adopted 28 July 1951, entered into force 22 April 1954) 189 UNTS 137 (Refugee Convention), art 1. The definition of migrant in this book refers to people who move within or outside a state, notwithstanding their legal status or their reasons for migrating.

[11] I use the term 'marginalised groups' as a term to describe these groups who are on the fringes of the state and/or formal law.

[12] See Christopher Alden and Dan Large, 'On Becoming a Norms Maker: Chinese Foreign Policy, Norms Evolution and the Challenges of Security in Africa' (2015) 221 *China Quarterly* 123; and Lowell Dittmer and George T Yu (eds), *China, the Developing World, and the New Global Dynamic*' (Boulder, Lynne Rienner, 2010) 251.

[13] See Karen Foerstel, 'China in Africa: Is China Gaining Control over Africa's Resources?' (2008) 2(1) *CQ Global Researcher* 8.

[14] See Padraig Carmody and Peter Kragelund, 'Who is in Charge: State Power and Agency in Sino-African Relations' (2016) 49 *Cornell International Law Journal* 1.

[15] For example, see Adams Bodomo, 'The African Trading Community in Guangzhou: An Emerging Bridge for Africa-China Relations' (2010) 203 *China Quarterly* 693; Daouda Cisse, 'South-South Migration and Trade: African Traders in China' (2013) 15(1) *Centre for Chinese Studies at Stellenbosch University*, https://www.african-review.com/journal/v5(1)december2013/Cisse_South-South%20Migration%20and%20Sino-African%20Small%20Traders.pdf; Paul-Henri Bischoff, 'African Transnationalism in China: At the Interface of Local, Transnational, Bilateral and Multilateral Responses' (2017) 52(7) *Journal of Asian and African Studies*; B Sautman, 'Anti-Black

such as Lili Song[16] and Jennifer Yip[17] have carried out research on non-Chinese asylum seekers and refugees in China. Chinese legal scholar Guofu Liu provides a comprehensive Chinese legal approach to external immigrations; however, this does not unravel the nuances of the experience of law among migrants from non-Chinese and non-Asian developing countries.[18] China's historical conception of migration, particularly of asylum seekers, refugees and other undocumented migrants, has been shaped by the 'returning Chinese' identity.[19] China's permissiveness towards migration into its territory has been based on the idea of welcoming or receiving back its 'lost' nationals. This concept has shaped its policies and acceptance or rejection of international migration law. However, from the early 2000s, new forms of migration such as undocumented, asylum and refugee migrations began to challenge this stance. In this work, I focus on migrations into China that have taken place from the late 2000s to date, specifically on asylum seeking and undocumented African migrants.

Nigeria is a colonial creation with a very complicated national identity and contentious national borders. This colonialism-induced fragmentation has shaped Nigeria's perception of what sovereignty is and the constant struggle between identity, nationalism, and borders (and indeed that of many other African states).[20] Nigeria, like China, views itself as a regional leader and also seeks to assert itself in international relations, particularly in relation to the African continent.[21] As an economic powerhouse on the continent, it has started to grapple with new issues relating to migrations. Traditionally, it has experienced economic migrations from other West African countries, as well as internal migrations. However, there are notable changes that are occurring contemporarily, such as forced migrations stemming from the Boko Haram insurgency and the Cameroon Anglophone crisis. The 2002 International Court of Justice (ICJ) boundary dispute settlement of the Bakassi Peninsula, which

Racism in Post-Mao China' (1994) 138 *China Quarterly* 413; Lavinia Lin et al, 'Health Care Experiences and Perceived Barriers to Health Care Access' (2014) 17(5) *Journal of Immigrant and Minority Health* 1509.

[16] ibid. See also Lili Song, 'China and the International Refugee Protection Regime: Past, Present, and Potentials' (2018) 37(2) *Refugee. Survey Quarterly* 139.

[17] See J Yip, 'Stranded amidst Resettlement Applications: A Case Study of Pakistani Refugees in China' (thesis, Budapest, Central European University, 2011).

[18] See Guofu Liu, *Chinese Immigration Law* (Farnham, Ashgate, 2011); Guofu Liu, 'Legislation, Impacts and Deficiencies of the Law of Exit and Entry Administration of China 2013' (2014) 4(4) *International Journal of Public Law and Policy* 381; Guofu Lui and Tanjirul Islam, 'Illegal Immigrant Policy in China: Comparative Study with Australia and Canada' (2010) 11(2*) Beijing Law Review* 489.

[19] See Lili Song, 'Who Shall We Help? A Refugee Definition in a Chinese Context' (2014) 1 *Refugee Survey Quarterly* 44.

[20] See Okonkwo C Eze, Alexander Elimian and Uchenna Chinwuba, 'The Politics of State Creation and National Integration in Nigeria' (2015) 8 *Journal of Politics and Law* 113.

[21] See Jason Warner, 'Nigeria and "Illusory Hegemony" in Foreign and Security Policymaking: *Pax-Nigeriana* and the Challenges of Boko Haram' (2017) 13(3) *Foreign Policy Analysis* 638.

transferred contested territory to Cameroon and changed Nigeria's borders, has created a new group of migrants from the Peninsula.[22] Nigeria perceives the loss of the Peninsula as an infringement on its sovereignty by Cameroon and the international community, and this may have shaped its response to the Bakassi migrants.[23]

Available research on the international dispute between Cameroon and Nigeria focuses on the legitimacy of colonial treaties versus pre-colonial realities.[24] My research is vital in discussing the impact of a Eurocentric international law on indigenous peoples and the crucial role that Third World approaches to international law may have in correcting or avoiding injustices created by this system. The impact of the decision on the Bakassi community (in particular, those identifying as Nigerian), their displacement from the Peninsula, and subsequent changes on their perception and encounters with the law in their community are examined in the forthcoming chapters. This approach shifts the discussion beyond the dispute and the settlement at the ICJ, taking it into the lives and experiences of the Bakassi migrant community in real time.

The cases of China and Nigeria raise questions pertaining to how both countries define and approach 'non-traditional' migrants[25] in relation to domestic, regional and international law. How do both states utilise and/or misuse international norms, laws, and policies to deal with new challenges? I will be using the case studies as part of my methodology and will go into further contextual analysis in the following chapters using TWAIL as my theoretical and methodological framework.[26] I will take a deeper dive into the use of TWAIL ideas, arguments, and methodologies in Chapter 2.

A. Connecting China and Nigeria

China and Nigeria appear distant and unrelated if we are thinking about geographical location, history, culture, or even political or social norms.

[22] This will be discussed in more detail in ch 2.

[23] See Mohamed A El-Khawas and J Ndumbe Anyu (eds), *Case Studies of Conflict in Africa: The Niger-Delta, the Bakassi Peninsula and Piracy in Somalia* (Lewiston, NY, Edwin Mellen Press, 2012).

[24] ibid. See also JR Bassey, 'Anglo-German Treaty of 1913 and its Influence on World Court Decision in the Nigeria vs Cameroon Case Concerning Bakassi' (2014) 6(11) *International Journal of Current Research* 9832; Njinkeng Bekong, 'International Dispute Settlement: Land and Maritime Boundary between Cameroon and Nigeria – Origin of the Dispute and Provisional Measures' (1997) 9 *African Journal of International and Comparative Law* 287; United Nations Security Council Press Release, 'Security Council Press Statement on Bakassi Peninsula Developments', SC/11094 AFR/2680 (2013).

[25] Here I am referring to migrants who fall out of the discourse on international migration law and its protections as well as protections in national legislation and policy due to their specific characteristics.

[26] See Makau Mutua and Antony Anghie, 'What is TWAIL?' (2000) 94 *Proceedings of the Annual Meeting, American Society of International Law* 31. For further discussion of TWAIL, see chs 2–5.

However, there is more than meets the eye. Beyond being in the Global South, both my case studies centre on African undocumented migrants, asylum seekers or refugees with links to Nigeria. With little research available on South-South migrations in China and Nigeria within international law discourse, I suggest that import gained from analyses on the case studies far outweighs their correlation.

Most importantly, TWAIL indicates that there ought to be different types of understandings and encounters with the law.[27] Two dissimilar case studies achieve the goal of truly looking for diverse understandings and interpretations of the law in all spaces and at all levels of society. At any rate, juxtaposing the case studies makes their similarities more apparent. For example, the case studies reveal almost identical approaches in China and Nigeria towards different types of migrants without status, as well as the parallel challenges of intersectionality and injustice. Choosing to focus on case studies in the Global South is a step towards the beginning of the unravelling and unpacking of knowledge embedded therein.

Both case studies also deal with communities grappling with the impact of internationally created norms and practices of states including migrant status, the privilege of citizenship and the protections of formal law. The case studies also show us the ways in which these communities contribute to the law through acts of resistance, contestation, and the creation of their own legal and/or political frameworks to address the injustices created by the international system. To understand understudied narratives of South-South migrations, it is useful to juxtapose different systems to draw critiques, meaning and conclusions about Third World approaches to and encounters with the law. It is for this reason that I chose to use case studies; to do a fine-grained examination of different communities engaging in different forms of South-South migrations and their paths to justice.

I employ case studies as a tool to analyse and understand different approaches to the law. It is through making comparisons that the gaps in these approaches become evident for critique and discussion. In other words, case studies create room to discuss the limitations of my methodological approach (discussed further in Chapter 2) because through a side-by-side juxtaposition of two different cases, the grey areas become more evident for critique. Consequently, this book studies the narratives of communities involved in South-South migrations in both case studies and their impact on domestic, regional and international law. These narratives shift the attention from the state to the migrants who engage in South-South migrations, and highlight the significance and impact of their daily encounters with the law and the state. Using these juxtapositions, I analyse similarities and divergences between the case studies on South-South migrations and what the commonalities or differences say about international

[27] Gathii (n 5).

law, justice, human rights, etc. I also use the case studies to question my own perceptions and assumptions of international law by studying legal cultures that reflect 'different patterns of order that shape people, institutions, and the society in a jurisdiction'.[28]

On the surface, studying the cases of China and Nigeria side by side might seem like comparing apples to oranges; however, both case studies share the commonality of understudied narratives of undocumented, asylum and refugee migrations in the Global South. In both case studies, migrant communities have established themselves by necessity and have either tried to assimilate cultural and legal norms or struggle against the power of sovereignty and the privilege of citizenship. It is by looking at different approaches, hierarchies and narratives that an understanding of South-South migrations is achieved as it is unfolding.

TWAIL is one of the critical legal models that seek to incorporate non-Western narratives into international legal scholarship as a way of challenging and enriching international legal discourse.[29] TWAIL as a theory is similar to feminist approaches to international law, which argued that international law is structurally biased against women and called for reforms that address the oppression and inequality of women in interaction with the state.[30] The idea of intersectionality, which is concerned with studying the intersection of identity with domination and discrimination, is rooted in the work of US critical race feminisms. The term 'intersectionality' was coined by Kimberlé Crenshaw in the 1980s to conceptualise the institutionalisation of discrimination and oppression due to how legal systems erase, ignore or overlook the multidimensional nature of Black and female identities in America.[31] This theory has

[28] Edward J Eberle, 'Comparative Law' (2007) 13 *Annual Survey of International & Comparative Law* 93, at 94.

[29] For example, see Makau Mutua, 'Critical Race Theory and International Law: The View of an Insider-Outsider' (2000) 45 *Villanova Law Review* 841; Luis Eslava and Sundhya Pahuja, 'Between Resistance and Reform: TWAIL and the Universality of International Law' (2011) 3 *Trade Law and Development* 103; Obiora Chinedu Okafor, 'Critical Third World Approaches to International Law (TWAIL): Theory, Methodology, or Both' (2008) 10 *International Community Law Review* 371; Luis Eslava, *Local Space, Global Life: The Everyday Operation of International Law and Development* (Cambridge: Cambridge University Press, 2015); Zoran Oklopcic, 'Beyond Empty, Conservative, and Ethereal: Pluralist Self-Determination and a Peripheral Political Imaginary' (2013) 26 *Leiden Journal of International Law* 509; E Tendayi Achiume, 'Reimagining International Law for Global Migration: Migration as Decolonization' (2017–18) 111 *American Journal of International Law Unbound* 142. Other critical attempts to incorporate diverse narratives into international law include the Marxist approach, legal pluralism and post-colonial theories.

[30] See Hilary Charlesworth and Christine Chinkin, *The Boundaries of International Law: A Feminist Analysis* (Manchester: Manchester University Press, 2000); Karen Knopp, 'Re/Statements: Feminism and State Sovereignty in International Law' (1993) 3 *Transnational Law and Contemporary Problems* 293; Patricia Collins, 'The Tie That Binds: Race, Gender and US Violence' (1998) 21(5) *Ethnic and Racial Studies* 917.

[31] Intersectionality will be discussed in greater detail in ch 4. See Kimberlé Crenshaw, 'Demarginalizing the Intersection of Race and Sex: A Black Feminist Critique of Antidiscrimination Doctrine, Feminist Theory and Antiracist Politics' (1989) 1 *University of Chicago Legal Forum* 139, at 140; Leslie McCall, 'The Complexity of Intersectionality' (2005) 30(3) *Signs* 1771; Jennifer Nash, 'Rethinking Intersectionality' (2008) 89 *Feminist Review* 1.

resonated with and inspired TWAIL scholars such as Makau Mutua, because intersectionality presents a lens through which we can also understand identity (such as race, gender and class) as a legal reality in international law.[32] TWAIL as a movement has expanded its themes and its scope beyond formal imperialism and deals with complex forms of informal imperialism in the Global South – ranging from international criminal law, environmental issues and transitional justice, for example.[33] However, there is still limited engagement with migration law and refugee law within the existing TWAIL work. My research on South-South migrations expands the discussion on Third World approaches not only into the sphere of migration law and refugee law, but also into other aspects of migrations in the Global South that are not evident on the surface, such as the role of informal justice mechanisms, how intersectionality affects discrimination, and the space between the law and its application.

I study the narratives of migrant communities in these spaces in order to gain a deeper understanding of what the law means to non-traditional migrant groups, as well as the practice of states to understand their approach towards South-South migrations and international law. Within TWAIL, there has been less focus on the day-to-day experiences and perceptions of international law in the Global South, particularly at a more cellular/local level.[34] Anghie states that in order for international law to be truly universal and for international justice to be compelling, legal theory must draw from a variety of legal systems, traditions and understandings.[35] Obiora Chinedu Okafor argues that TWAIL centres the Global South both in theoretical discourse and in research methodology.[36] Mutua holds that tools like intersectionality should be used to understand how law impacts people at the local level.[37] Sundhya Pahuja and Luis Eslava argue that a methodology that focuses on international law as a material project is vital for TWAIL to press towards the universal promise of international law.[38] However, none of these works delves into the application of these methodological approaches in research in the Global South. Eslava's

[32] Mutua (n 29).

[33] See Luis Eslava, 'TWAIL Coordinates', *Critical Legal Thinking*, 2 March 2019, http://criticallegalthinking.com/2019/04/02/twail-coordinates. See also Asad G Kiyani, 'Third World Approaches to International Criminal Law' (2015) 109 *American Journal of International Law Unbound* 255; Julia Dehm, 'Post-Paris Reflections: Fossil Fuels, Human Rights and the Need to Excavate New Ideas for Climate Justice' (2017) 8(2) *Journal of Human Rights and the Environment* 280; Corri Zoli, 'Islamic Contributions to International Humanitarian Law: Recalibrating TWAIL Approaches for Existing Contributions and Legacies' (2015) 109 *American Journal of International Law Unbound* 271; Vasuki Nesiah, 'Theorizing Transitional Justice' in Anne Orford and Florian Hoffman (eds), *Oxford Handbook of International Legal Theory* (Oxford, Oxford University Press, 2016).

[34] The work of Eslava particularly focuses on the everyday encounters with and expressions of international law in the Global South. See Eslava (n 29).

[35] Antony Anghie, *Imperialism, Sovereignty and Making International Law* (Cambridge, Cambridge University Press) 320.

[36] Okafor (n 29).

[37] Mutua (n 29).

[38] Eslava and Pahuja (n 29).

TWAIL-based work on Latin America, on the other hand, relies on legal ethnography to understand the impact of international law and development on the daily lives of people there.[39] My case studies on South-South take a similar path. There are great lessons to learn about the law from undocumented or displaced communities in the Global South; these lessons can give insight into the realities and the issues of structural justice that underpin everyday life.

Annelise Riles reflects on how certain issues are elevated over others to the international level out of the domestic or regional, arguing that understandings of what is international or local is based on perceptions of size and scale; the international is larger than the local.[40] Riles believes that this is what gives international law its cosmopolitan design and that though international law may be different in scale from the local, it is at the local level that we see its real manifestations.[41] This book brings the discussion on non-Western understandings and/or contributions to aspects of the law to a local level. The motivation for this intention is that in the real world, though law at the international level is still mainly created and interpreted by states, at other levels the experience and interpretation of the law is just as significant because it reflects the gaps or efficiencies, justice or injustice and hierarchies created by the law as it impacts marginalised people.[42] International law does not exist at the international level only; it seeps into the daily lives of human beings and communities, impacting even those communities that seem to live outside the law due to a lack of documentation or 'illegality' created by norms and rules on borders and citizenship that have become globalised. Without understanding the law at these levels, unravelling the gaps and critiquing expressions and interpretations, we cannot expect international law to be reformed in a way that creates a balance between the Global South and the Global North. An understanding of the law's impact at a local level will assist in balancing out inequalities because with that understanding, international law can begin to address the issues that have been overlooked because of the innate imperialistic nature and history of international law, which Anghie argues has operated to 'exclude and subordinate people on account of their gender, race and poverty'.[43] Communities and individuals challenge injustices that stem from international norms and rules in their daily lives, and international law is lacking the richness of the knowledge from those encounters and contributions. An understanding of the law of everyday goes hand in hand with Anghie's vision 'that law that can play its ideal role of limiting and resisting power'.[44]

[39] Eslava (n 29).
[40] Riles (n 9) 40.
[41] ibid 49.
[42] Throughout this book, marginality will be used in reference to people or communities who live outside of the benefits of citizenship and formal law.
[43] Anghie (n 35) 318.
[44] ibid.

B. On Terminology and Power

Throughout this book, I use specific terminology to indicate scales of asymmetries of power and perspective. The Third World or Global South as terminologies are not negative in and of themselves, but are a medium to understand the context of imperialism and colonialism in the world.[45] I use the terms 'Third World' and 'Global South' not as geographical locations or fixed contexts, but to refer to places where asymmetries of power in the international system have impacted law, economy and politics, and have created various hierarchies and exclusions in the daily lives of people in those spaces. The Global North is not the perfect opposite of the Global South, but is instead conceptualised as spaces that have been centred as sources of power, norms, rules and hierarchies, as well as knowledge. This conceptualisation shapes my use of terms like 'marginalisation', which I employ to refer in the context of migration, to individuals or groups who are excluded from the formal, legal regime and its protections, as well as the benefits of citizenship. I also use the term 'periphery' to indicate scales of marginality/exclusion. This conceptualisation is limited because power and marginalisation are fluid; there are peripheries in the Global North and there is privilege and power in the Global South. However, these terminologies are essential in order to show the gaps created where international laws and norms often originate and how it applies to different people in real life. Finally, I use both 'Africa' and 'African' as umbrella terms because while my case studies are linked to Nigeria and Nigerians, I also encountered and interviewed other nationalities in China, for example. Additionally, I see African and Black identity as a reflection of labels that apply to people from Africa in the diaspora (in this case, in China). I will discuss this in more detail in Chapter 4. The research in this book does not take a rigid approach to geographical locations and focuses more on the ways in which asymmetries of power affect specific groups of people engaging in South-South migrations, while still recognising the state as the primary subject of international law.

II. THE RESEARCH PROBLEM

This book sets out to examine the gap in knowledge concerning experiences, interpretations and expressions of the law in the everyday lives of marginalised communities in the Global South. Comprehensively, it problematises the lack of understanding of the dynamic and diverse postcolonial international landscape. In other words, I question why international legal scholarship is neglecting significant developments happening outside of Europe and North America by focusing on subaltern sources in the Global South. The Global North exerts

[45] Anghie (n 35).

more influence on the development of international law – a good example is in situating the international refugee law regime in Europe, as opposed to Africa, despite the latter hosting more refugees and displaced people than all European countries.[46] Both Asia and Africa have undergone numerous developments in the sphere of refugee laws that remain relatively underexplored or ignored.[47] There are responses to international law in these spaces that are packed with lessons about the impact of the law and how it is experienced, understood and challenged in marginalised communities.

Since the end of colonialism, the positions and narratives in the Global South have transformed. Yet the West remains the centre and the point of reference in discourse on the international law experience. In the period immediately after decolonisation, the dichotomy and hierarchies between the West as the architect of international law and the new states as 'subjects' of international law was glaring and deep. Non-Western peoples had no say in the colonial formations of statehood and power, and after decolonisation, the only option available for states in the Global South was to accept the international legal order along with the rules and norms that came with it or face exile from the international community.[48] Mutua argues that concepts of international law, including self-determination, though liberating to non-Western states, were born out of European struggles and narratives. He uses the case of Biafra's attempt at self-determination from Nigeria to show that within the international system, self-determination is determined by the approval of the Western states that created it.[49] Anghie asserts that even though self-determination influenced decolonisation, it was perceived as a threat to the stability of established international law.[50] As a result, most non-Western states have accepted this legal order in order to belong to the international community of states. In fact, these states have often evolved over time to use international law in the same ways that Western states do; to bolster their power both internally and externally, to protect agendas, and to challenge and change international law. However, this acceptance of international law and participation in international community

[46] See also UN Refugee Agency, Global Trends: Forced Displacement in 2017', 19 June 2018, at https://www.unhcr.org/5b27be547.pdf. See also Glen Peterson, 'The Uneven Development of the International Refugee Regime in Post-war Asia: Evidence from China, Hong Kong and Indonesia' (2012) 25(3) *Journal of Refugee Studies* 326. Peterson in his analysis on the refugee law regime in China argues that the United Nations High Commissioner for Refugees (UNHCR) in the 1940s was a 'colonial-era institution'; it was based on and aimed at settling only European asylum seekers.

[47] For example, China's migration law and approach towards refugees has been undergoing massive changes, but these changes have not yet been widely discussed and unpacked. China is in the process of transforming from being completely disengaged with international refugee law to increasing engagement with it. See Song (n 16). China's refugee and migration context and developments will be discussed in detail in Chapters Two and Three.

[48] Mutua (n 29) 849–50.

[49] ibid 850.

[50] See Antony Anghie, 'Finding the Peripheries: Sovereignty and Colonialism in Nineteenth Century International Law' (1999) 40 *Harvard International Law Journal* 1, at 3–4.

has not reflected significant changes because the West remains the benchmark for international law rules, norms and legal discourse and research. The overarching structure of state consent allows the prioritisation of the Western-centric model of law and Western state practice (and *opinio juris*) to remain the benchmarks for establishing customary international law today.

In the Global North, ongoing securitisation and criminalisation of migration shape law and policy. Migration is a controversial topic in Western countries, and this has influenced international law in a way that does not fully reflect other realities outside that context. Although considerable research has gone into international migration and the law generally, the focus has been centred on the developments and challenges in the West.[51] South-South migration is misconceived to be more of a humanitarian or porous border issue that does not affect the Global South in the same way as it affects the Global North.[52] Generally, knowledge on South-South migrations is lacking for numerous reasons, ranging from the perception of a lack of significance or impact of knowledge of South-South migrations at the international level to a lack of resources and access to a body of knowledge with which to draw significance from. This is the challenge of TWAIL for scholars from the Global South and is the research problem my book aims to address.

A. The Historical Underpinnings of International Migrations

Economics has impacted the regulation of international migrations more than any other factor.[53] Thomas Schindlmayr's analysis of international migrations frames the discussion on historical and colonial experiences.[54] Schindlmayr utilises the example of Britain's justified migrations between colonies in the mid-nineteenth century for cheap labour.[55] Schindlmayr creates a timeline of international migration, showing the role that the West has played in shaping migrations throughout history.[56] This is very important in understanding migrations from a TWAIL perspective and brings in a much-needed alternative understanding of international migrations – it discusses the colonial history of migrations and how international law has developed around it.

[51] See Stephanie J Nawyn, 'Migration in the Global South: Exploring New Theoretical Territory'(2016) 46(2) International *Journal of Sociology* 81.

[52] Mahir Saul and Michaela Pelican, 'A New Research Perspective on Contemporary African Migration' (2014) 43(1–3) *Urban Anthropology and Studies of Cultural Systems and World Economic Development* 2.

[53] Thomas Schindlmayr, 'Sovereignty, Legal Regimes and International Migration' (2003) 41(2) *International Migration* 109.

[54] ibid.

[55] ibid 113.

[56] ibid 112.

During the colonial era, migrations from Europe to the Global South functioned as a tool of colonial conquest, obtaining territories, subordinating indigenous peoples and accessing resources. Sovereignty was used to justify the legitimisation of these migrations for colonial purposes.[57] Between 1914 and 1945, Europe began to look inward with its own internal problems and outwardly facing the wave of decolonisation. Migration from Europe to the Global South as a tool of colonial power was no longer popular.[58] This era was the beginning of curtailed migration.[59] After decolonisation, the privilege of sovereign equality and self-determination, once limited to the West, spread to the rest of the world. The proliferation of independent states increased the number of physical boundaries that were strengthened and maintained through norms like *uti posseditis*, which emerged as an international law prior to the acceptance of many states as sovereign entities. As physical boundaries strengthened, so did the need for migration control between states. Self-determination and sovereign equality did not translate into economic or political equality between the Global South and the Global North. For example, prior to the United Kingdom Act of 1962, subjects of the Commonwealth could migrate to and reside in the UK without restrictions. However, the 1962 Act provided residency rights only for those with British ancestry (ie, grandparents). In other words, only white Commonwealth subjects had residency rights from 1962 onwards, effectively creating a two-tier immigration structure that accorded greater privileges to those from white settler colonies.

After 1945, international human rights and economic interdependence expanded, destabilising the colonial power imbalance between the West and the Global South. However, the pre-existing hierarchical traditions of centring the West and peripheralising the Global South continued. This has resulted in an international law that is paradoxically emancipatory as well as oppressive; while international law is rooted in hierarchical traditions, decolonised states are to some degree, empowered by the changes in the international system. Consequently, migrations from the peripheries to the West becomes politicised contemporarily because of the West's perceived hierarchy in relation to the rest of the world. International migrations have been shaped by international law's imperial past, and the politics and struggles of the West.[60] In discussing these historical underpinnings briefly, it is clear why legal scholarship on international migrations and discourse has been focused on the West. The importance of understanding, deconstructing and unpacking the uses of international law for racialised hierarchies in the international system is equally apparent.

[57] Mutua (n 29) 33.
[58] Schindlmayr (n 53) 114.
[59] ibid 114–15.
[60] Mutua and Anghie (n 26) 31.

Zoran Oklopcic, in his analysis of pluralist self-determination and a peripheral political imaginary, asserts that contemporarily, pluralist approaches (which he identifies in the ideologies of Leopold Senghor and Edvard Kardelj) to international law based on political theories have sought to challenge the hierarchies and power imbalances in the system, but have not succeeded.[61] Oklopcic's analysis utilises the example of France, whose extremely intrusive colonial policies affected internal politics and cultures within Francophone West Africa. However, when Leopold Senghor, who led the Negritude movement, demanded a French Union, where Francophone Africans would be equal to French citizens, there was a fear in France that Africans would migrate en masse to Paris and 'dilute French political domination'.[62] As a result, this constitutional proposal was not accepted by the French state.

Oklopcic's example reveals the link between colonialism, migration and the perceived threat that migrants from the Global South become in the West. This precedent may be the reason why contemporary migrations are politicised in the West: a fear of heterogeneity and of the Other. Many laws and policies have been built around this politicisation of migrations. This has shaped the international legal system and created the trends in research today. International refugee law emerged to address the crises of political and religious refugees in Europe during the World Wars initially. However, the creation of multiple vulnerable states and borders imposed by *uti possidetis* meant that migration and refugee laws anchored in inter-European experiences were and still are not fit for purpose. The Bakassi Peninsula dispute between Nigeria and Cameroon (which will be discussed in Chapter 2) is a good example of the failure of international law to uphold Africa's pre-colonial configurations, regional migrations and movements. The Bakassi case also shows the role that the law plays in upholding the legacy of colonialism and Eurocentric solutions to problems in the Global South.

Tendayi Achiume, like Oklopcic, analyses the historical underpinnings of the centring the Global North in the study of international migrations. Achiume describes colonialism aptly as 'migration from Europe to the rest of the world' that created 'asymmetrical benefits structures of co-dependence in contemporary global order'.[63] In calling colonialism migration, Achiume centres migration in the discussion of colonialism and its impact on contemporary international law, an important contribution to the literature on international migration. This presents a new way of understanding colonialism and its effects on international law, as well as the hierarchies and co-dependencies in the world today that can be seen in international migration patterns.[64] Achiume identifies that colonisation institutionalised an advantage to different national hegemons

[61] Oklopcic (n 29).
[62] ibid 524.
[63] Achiume (n 29) 143.
[64] ibid 142–43.

in the West and shaped the development of international law.[65] Achiume argues that although international law pretends colonialism has ended, it supports and protects the status quo, which is the dominance of former colonial powers and other powerful actors at the international level to the detriment of the Global South.[66] International law does very little to challenge the hierarchies. It is for this reason that I focus on case studies where hierarchies created by the international system are confronted and challenged at the local level, and where groups and individuals are doing this work of change and resistance in their everyday encounters and experiences.

Achiume adds to the discussion on recentring the Global South by identifying decolonisation as any means (including migration) that 'responds to the asymmetrical benefits of co-dependence in the contemporary global order and seeks to achieve a more equitable relationship between centre and periphery'.[67] This perspective is striking. To Achiume, migration of people in the Global South across any borders is an act of decolonisation and resistance to the status quo, which has severely limited the power and the space in which people from the Global South can move. It is a 'rebalancing of the asymmetrical system initiated by many of the same state sovereigns that now self-righteously seek the exclusion of these migrants'.[68] This is a radical approach to understanding international migration and South-South migration specifically; people in the Global South recentre themselves and decentre the Global North when they migrate. My case studies explore the ways in which migrant communities challenge different forms of oppression as well as the ways in which they outmanoeuvre the limitations of the state and of asylum, undocumented or displaced statuses.

B. The Politicisation of Migration in International Migration Discourse

Since as early as the 1990s, migration in the West has undergone a process of politicisation due to geopolitical shifts after the fall of the Berlin Wall, economic transformations like the Schengen agreements and an increase in migration. As previously homogeneous societies and communities began to diversify, communal hostilities emerged at local levels, while legal and policy changes ensued at national, regional, and international levels.[69] These ongoing changes can be observed in constitutional changes in Germany, Pasqua laws in France, and the current debate on migration legislation in the UK and the US, among many numerous instances.[70]

[65] ibid 144.
[66] ibid 145.
[67] ibid 143
[68] ibid.
[69] See Catherine Dauvergne, *Making People Illegal: What Globalization Means for Migration and Law* (Cambridge, Cambridge University Press, 2008) 14.
[70] ibid.

Following the 9/11 attacks in the US, migration became important within the security and political agendas of many Western states and migration controls have increasingly become normalised as a means to control security threats.[71] The US-led 'War on Terror' (and later, under Barack Obama, the global 'war against terrorist actors') has led to the categorisation of migration as among the threats to national security due to the role that the movement of people, information and goods have played in facilitating terrorism.[72] The securitisation of Africa by virtue of the presence of US military bases is changing African border practices, disregarding and uprooting the history of cross-border migrations on the continent, and importing US narratives and practices on terrorism and security into Africa.[73]

Catherine Dauvergne, who focuses on the intersection of globalisation and migrations in international law, points out that territory is necessary for sovereignty to be viable and that if nationality is tied to borders, migrations will affect sovereignty.[74] From this point of view in the current international system, borders are exclusive and citizenship a privilege defined by the state. This automatically makes migration a destabilising factor. Migration activates state power since interception, detention and deportation are all within the jurisdiction of the state. Since both documented and undocumented migrations affect the make-up of the state, it brings to the fore questions of citizenship, the identity of the state itself, and the state's control of power and its borders.[75] When undocumented migration is rife, it may be an indication that the state is not in control of its borders and that its sovereignty is weakening, according to Dauvergne. Nevertheless, undocumented migration can be used to bolster and protect the interests of the state when politicised – this is when the state uses migration and border control as the basis for the development of anti-migration laws and policies. Dauvergne sees migration law as a national assertion of power and identity, and she states that migration is a central issue of sovereignty in the West as Western states are closer to the ideal of 'nation' than other states.[76] Dauvergne further points out

[71] ibid 115; see also Susan Ginsburg, 'Counter Terrorist Mobility: Shaping an Operational Strategy', Migration Policy Institute (2006), https://www.migrationpolicy.org/research/countering-terrorist-mobility-shaping-operational-strategy; Mary A Young, 'Smuggling and Trafficking of Refugees and Asylum Seekers: Is the International Community Neglecting the Duty to Protect the Persecuted in the Pursuit of Combating Transnational Organized Crime?' (2004) 27 *Suffolk Transnational Law Review* 101, at 106.

[72] See Sharon Pickering, 'Border Terror: Policing, Forced Migration and Terrorism' (2004) 16(3) *Global Change, Peace & Security* 211; Patricia Mallia, *Migrant Smuggling at Sea: Combating a Current Threat to Maritime Security through the Creation of a Cooperative Framework* (Leiden, Martinus Nijhoff, 2010) 18.

[73] See Victor Ojarukotu and Sabelo J Ndlovu-Gatsheni, 'Surveillance over a Zone of Conflict: Africom and the Politics of Securitisation of Africa' (2010) 3(6) *Journal of Pan African Studies* 94; Horace Campbell, 'Remilitarisation of African Societies: Analysis of the Planning behind Proposed US Africa Command' (2008) 3(1) *International Journal of African Renaissance Studies* 6.

[74] Catherine Dauvergne, 'Sovereignty, Migration and the Rule of Law in Global Times' (2004) 67 *MLR* 588, at 594.

[75] ibid 592.

[76] Dauvergne (n 69) 7.

that migration is important in the construction of the mythic foundations of these 'desirable' nations and that it plays an important role in silencing and marking the absence of indigenous populations. Dauvergne maintains that migration is the last bastion of state sovereignty, meaning that migration is the last tool that states will use to protect and uphold their sovereignty due to the impact of globalisation on migration and politics.[77] This statement assumes that the interaction between migration and sovereignty in the Global North is enough to make deductions about migration in the rest of the world. Dauvergne asserts that while refugee populations are predominantly located in Africa and Asia, 'prosperous Western nations have led the development of refugee law from the onset and continue to do so'.[78] Nevertheless, Dauvergne points out that the current Europeanisation of international refugee law is because of the current legislative developments in Europe.[79] She also identifies the hierarchical arrangements of sovereign power highlighted in the global politics of migration laws, stating that the migration laws that matter are only those of 'prosperous Western states' due in part to their greater capacity to attempt enforcement of their laws.[80] Finally, for Dauvergne, a sovereign state controlling its borders is a powerful image that negates any other method of regulating migration and draws parallels between overthrowing the concept of sovereignty to an attempt to overthrow the Christian God.[81] While Dauvergne makes very important discoveries and assertions on the impact of globalisation and migrations on sovereignty, this focuses only on 'prosperous Western states' and Global South to Global North migrations. This analysis does not question why the international refugee law regime is Europeanised or why the Global South is missing in the research. The focus on the Global North is illustrative of the scholarship in the field of international migration law and I choose to centre Dauvergne's work as an example here for this reason. These assumptions reflect the trends in international legal discourse that create exclusiveness in the international system and ignore the contributions and struggles of non-Western countries and peoples to international law. Therefore, there is a need for an inclusive discussion on international law that takes a plurality of approaches into consideration.

It has been argued by scholars such as Christian Joppke, Saskia Sassen and David Jacobsen that globalisation has impinged on areas that originally were in the sphere of sovereignty (such as trade, access to information, human rights and migrations).[82] According to this argument, state sovereignty is *waning* due

[77] ibid 47.
[78] ibid 65.
[79] ibid 165.
[80] ibid 173.
[81] ibid 174.
[82] See Christian Joppke, *Challenge to the Nation State: Immigration in Western Europe and the United States* (Oxford, Oxford University Press, 1998). See also Saskia Sassen, *Losing Control? Sovereignty in an Age of Globalization* (New York, Columbia University Press, 1996); David Jacobson, 'New Border Customs: Migration and the Changing Role of the State' (1998) 3(2) *UCLA Journal of International Law and Foreign Affairs* 443.

to these factors. Consequently, issues like migration that further undermine the state's control over its territory have become a high priority. There is an opposing argument that a *waxing* of sovereignty has taken place as a response to the 'threat' of migration. An example of this can be found in practices of externalising migration control measures in remote locations or neighbouring countries.[83] However, these arguments have been based on developments in Europe and North America only. In analyses by these scholars, there is no reference to the impact of globalisation on state sovereignty in Asia or Africa. Emerging scholarship on South-South migrations is largely not concerned with international law. South-South migrations have been discussed in economics, anthropology, development, and sociology more than in law.[84] Also, legal research on South-South migrations tends to be focused on Asia, for example, the migration and terrorism nexus in Bangladesh and North Korean refugees in China.[85]

Other scholars including Virginie Guiraudon and Gallya Lahav argue that states are constantly creating new ways to circumvent the impact of the development of human rights law.[86] Guiraudon and Lahav hold that states have adopted a 'shifting up', 'shifting down' or 'shifting out' policy to address the problem of migration. 'Shifting up' refers to a multiplication of intergovernmental cooperation at the international level (for example, the Schengen Group, which Lahav and Guiraudon envision as state responses to international migration) to regain some of the sovereignty/control lost over migration flows. 'Shifting down' is described as engaging local authorities (for example, city halls) and 'shifting out' involves non-state actors (like airlines) in monitoring and implementing migration law.[87] Again, Guiraudon and Lahav utilise examples from Europe and North America to buttress their arguments on the impact of international

[83] See Ronaldo Munck, 'Globalisation, Governance and Migration: An Introduction' (2008) 29(7) *Third World Quarterly* 1227; Arjun Appadurai, *Modernity at Large: Cultural Dimensions of Globalization* (Minneapolis, University of Minnesota Press, 1996); Stephen Castles and Mark J Miller, *The Age of Migration: International Population Movements in the Modern World* (Basingstoke, Palgrave Macmillan, 2003).

[84] For example, see Oliver Bakewell, 'South-South Migration and Human Development: Reflections on African Experiences' (2009), International Migrations Institute, University of Oxford, MPRA Paper No 19185; Emma Mawdsley, 'Human Rights and South-South Development Cooperation: Reflections on the Rising Powers as International Development Actors' (2014) 36 *Human Rights Quarterly* 630.

[85] For example, see Mubashar Hasan, 'South-South Migration and Security Risks: Political Islam and Violent Extremism in the Shadow of Globalisation in Bangladesh' (2017) 73(3) *India Quarterly* 312; Song (n 16).

[86] See Virginie Guiraudon and Gallya Lahav, 'A Reappraisal of the State Sovereignty Debate: The Case of Migration Control' (2000) 33 *Comparative Political Studies* 163. See also Louis Henkin, 'That "S" Word: Sovereignty, and Globalization, and Human Rights, et Cetera' (1999) 68(1) *Fordham Law Review* 1. Henkin argues that state sovereignty is just as strong as it used to be in the past, regardless of the development of the human rights regime. His analysis of sovereignty differs because he centres his question on what sovereignty can do for human rights rather than what human rights is doing to sovereignty.

[87] ibid 181–88.

migration on sovereignty.[88] Work on South-South migration exists, but mainstream scholarship sees this as being at the peripheries of the discipline.

The commonality in these arguments is the concentration of analysis on Global South to Global North migrations, with the Global North being imagined as the centre of the discussion and the destination of migrations. All destination states utilised in mainstream accounts tend to be liberal European or North American democracies. While these studies are vital as they provide necessary insight, they fail to draw any perspectives from states outside of that axis and as a result, they indirectly contribute to the disconnectedness of international law with non-Western narratives and experiences. They reinforce the space between the Global South and the Global North, with the former regarded as the sending states and the latter the desirable destination. This reinforces the image of the Global South as poor and undesirable, and the West/Global North as inherently desirable. The problem of centring the Global North is not only in the field of international law and migration, but other fields as well. Sociologist Stephanie Nawyn holds that:

> [M]ost theoretical and methodological development, as well as most identified empirical patterns, within the field of migration studies relies on research conducted on South-to-North migration … Focusing on South-South migration allows for the testing and either affirmation or modification of existing theories that migration scholars have for why people migrate, who migrates, where they choose to migrate to and why.[89]

Here, Nawyn highlights not only the huge knowledge gap due to the one-sided nature of research on international migrations, but also that research on South-South migrations is important in critiquing existing theories therein. I take a similar approach in looking at intersections between South-South migrations and law. Using TWAIL to study South-South migrations allows for the testing and affirmation of existing legal norms but most importantly, it allows Third World citizens to be at the centre of this test. It is not enough to increase the study (or studies) of the Global South to create a balance of knowledge about international law; it is just as important for this knowledge to come from the perspectives, critiques and analysis of people from the Global South. As such, this book's research problem takes the Global South as the start and end point of migration, while also moving beyond legal doctrine to build a legal ethnography.

Additionally, Nawyn discusses why research on South-South migrations is important. The assumptions guiding research on South-North migrations have been made plain already; the Global North has sturdy frameworks of rights, laws and norms as well as exclusions that have developed around migrations from the Global South. The benefits of citizenship, or the lack thereof, in the

[88] Virginie and Lahav (n 86).
[89] Nawyn (n 55) 81.

Global North is evident. However, there is insufficient research into how non-citizenship affects migrants in states where citizens may also be limited in their access to rights.[90] What kind of knowledge will be unravelled in studying migrations within the Global South that challenge existing social (in Nawyn's case) and legal categories? There is still much that remains unknown, overlooked or ignored in the Global South and due to these knowledge gaps, harmful assumptions and generalisations have guided the understandings of the Global South. The case studies on Nigeria and China will show the impact of non-citizenship and exclusions on migrant communities in those spaces, the impact of migrant identity on experiences of the law, and how undocumented and displaced migrants in the Global South challenge and resist marginalisation and oppression by creating their own laws and/or forms of justice.

An analysis on South-South migrations and the implication for international law destabilises harmful constructs that minimise or disregard experiences in the Global South. There is a need for research that shifts focus to the Global South and what is happening in numerous spaces where marginalised migrant groups challenge rules, norms and categories. Excluding the impact of South-South migrations in legal research feeds into the systemic silencing of narratives. It also feeds into the mythic foundations of the desirability of the West as the core, and the irrelevance of the others as the periphery.[91] The foundations of the desirability are perhaps rooted in the racism of colonialism. This myth was the inspiration for the goal of 'civilising' indigenous populations in the past. Contemporarily, this myth is reinforced in the story of international migrations. Western states are perceived to be desirable because of the influx of migrants seeking a better life, many from former colonies that are usually developing countries, ignoring the fact that most migrations occur outside of the West and do not have the West as the destination, even more so if internally displaced persons (IDPs) are included. At the same time, Western states have built policies and laws around the politics of migrations. This politicisation of South-North migrations has also influenced the trends in international legal research on migrations and migration policy in the Global South, through both colonial and contemporary legal transplants.[92]

The focus of research on international law and related cases and jurisprudence in the West feeds into the demarcation in the experience and practice of international law. As a result, there is a need for an approach specifically targeting understudied developments in the Global South that are just as relevant experiences and practices of international law. Consequently, there are two layers of silencing and two types of peripheralisations in international discourse on South-South migrations and law: the silencing of the

[90] ibid 81–84.
[91] Dauvergne (n 69).
[92] Henkin (n 86) 18.

non-Western state and that of the individuals and groups who migrate to these non-Western states. These layers of silencing perpetuate an oversimplification of the non-Western experience of international law. This in turn creates new and hidden layers of marginalisation and further potential for the exploitation and dehumanisation of asylum seekers and other migrants outside of the Western context as their experiences are not documented or highlighted. The non-Western state is silenced because its developments and experiences of international law are often perceived to be limited to domestic or regional confines. Non-Western individuals involved in South-South migrations are silenced because their narratives are confined to a very limited space of discussion and analysis. At the level of international law, it is more common to discuss, for example, the African refugees in Greece than the Somali refugees in China or Cameroonian refugees in Nigeria. This research problematises the elevation of some migrants into international and global dialogues and the neglect of others, in particular the South-South migrants and their encounters with law.

Scholars in the West like Megan Ryburn,[93] Patrick von Berlo[94] and Achiume are now discussing the intersection of South-South migrations with international law. Ryburn focuses on Bolivian migrants in Chile and the impact of non-citizenship on them,[95] whereas von Berlo and Ryburn, together focus on the idea of 'crimmigration' or the merging of criminal law and migration and attrition through enforcement as the processes that have led to the exclusion of migrants.[96] Nevertheless, both Ryburn and von Berlo do not seek to draw significance from the intersection of these issues in the Global South at the international level. Ryburn and von Berlo's research highlights problems in those spaces, not looking for interpretations of and encounters with the law as indicators of what the law means to migrants in the Global South. A TWAIL perspective takes research beyond identifying the problems in South-South migrations into knowledge of how South-South migrants and states in the Global South contribute to the operation and mechanics of the law and to the operation of international law generally.

Achiume argues that contemporarily, international law allows for violence against and exclusion of certain types of migrants because the law – which is still rooted in the Western concept of territorial sovereignty – permits the exclusion of non-citizens, primarily migrants from the Global South.[97] However, Achiume expands beyond the Global North to include the elites of postcolonial

[93] See Megan Ryburn, 'Living the Chilean Dream? Bolivian Migrants' Incorporation in the Space of Economic Citizenship' (2016) 76 *Geoforum* 48.

[94] Megan Ryburn and Patrick von Berlo, 'South-South Migration: Law, Procedure, and Exclusion in Under-explored Contexts', *Leiden Law Blog*, 16 November 2016, http://leidenlawblog.nl/articles/south-south-migration.

[95] Ryburn (n 93) 51–52.

[96] Ryburn and von Berlo (n 94).

[97] Achiume (n 29) 143.

nations, non-state actors and those involved in different imperial projects, like China, as part of those who benefit from a colonial advantage.[98] This is significant because it recognises that spaces in the Global South now embody the same hegemonic influences and practices as the Global North. It is important not only to focus on the Global South for new understandings of the law, but also to discuss the ways in which hegemonic influences in those spaces contribute to hierarchies and exclusions. This understanding is the reason why in addition to centring the Global South in international migration and legal order, I discuss the power stratifications that lead to exclusions amidst migrants engaging in South-South migrations. I shift the focus of research to the mainstream of the Global South, inspired by the centring of the Global North, as well as the politicisation of migration and the securitisation of borders and its impact on legal scholarship, as discussed above. This is aimed at contributing to the growing work on engagement with and contributions to the law from marginalised communities in the Global South.

III. RESEARCH QUESTIONS

In commencing my research, I sought to answer the following question: how are migrant communities and individuals in the Global South encountering the law at their level and what are the ramifications of these encounters for international law? Through my case studies, the following subquestions arose:

- (i) Why is it important to discuss experiences of the law in the Global South from a local level?
- (ii) What hierarchies and exclusions are perpetuated because of the current system of international law and within local communities? What do these hierarchies say about Third World experiences of the law?
- (iii) What are the regional and domestic laws and policies affecting migrations, and what do they say about approaches and interpretations of international law in China and Nigeria?
- (iv) How are legal processes informing the application of international human rights/refugee law and procedures in these countries and beyond?
- (v) What does the evidence gathered imply for international law and what impact does it have on changing the discourse?

Through these questions, I expose the myths and exclusions perpetuated in South-South migrations, as well as the potential such migrations have to reform and enrich law at the international level. In researching and answering these questions, it is possible to gain a better understanding of the impact of the struggles and challenges of Third World peoples in the development of international law and human rights.

[98] ibid 144–45.

IV. RESEARCH OBJECTIVES AND SIGNIFICANCE

As mentioned above, my first research objective was to study the narratives and experiences of people in the Global South as they encounter the impact of international law in their lives in order to understand why and how they encounter the law and how they respond to it (ie, whether they challenge it, reject it or accept it). This aims to critique the idea that people in the Global South (particularly marginalised groups and communities) are irrelevant to the law. I contend that even the most marginalised communities make numerous contributions to the law that have significance at the international level – if only they are unravelled, discussed and elevated beyond the confines of colonial boundaries and definitions of citizenship and space. This book argues that in order for international law to be reformed and for the law to be truly international, these narratives, encounters and experiences must become just as significant as the developments and experiences of the law in the West.

The second aim of this book is to explore approaches to international migrations and the law from the viewpoint of communities and states in the Global South. As states in the Global South confront new migration-related challenges, how they interpret international norms (by either accepting or rejecting them) and their interaction with communities and people involved in these migrations indicates their approach to international law and norms. Utilising regional and national/local realities for contextualisation, I highlight the practices and role of non-Western states in the development of international law and human rights. Additionally, I bring the discussion of South-South migrations into international law. The impact of the ongoing securitisation and criminalisation of migration, and the discrimination against foreign migrants that is shaping law and policy in many Western countries has been well studied. Research that contextualises approaches to law and South-South migrations in the Global South is vital. As mentioned above, research on both Nigeria and China is still either sparse or even non-existent as aspects of South-South migrations remain outside of the discussion in international law and in discussions on TWAIL. Dialogue on migrations within the Global South often focuses on conflict, refugee migration, remittances or brain drain, whereas there are other dimensions.[99] I reveal these hidden nuances of South-South migrations with my case studies. In this book, I argue that case studies are vital because they allow us to study more than one example; one cannot discuss approaches to international law without looking at different locales and using these tools to critique and analyse both approaches to the law in the Global South and the international system. This work brings migration and informal justice into the TWAIL discussion with the aim of opening spaces for new discussions about the law in the Global South by looking closely at local encounters with the law for significance at the international level.

[99] Saul and Pelican (n 52).

V. OUTLINE OF THE BOOK

In Chapter 2, I will discuss why a legal study of international migrations is an important element of TWAIL scholarship. Chapter 3 will show my research methodology and methods, including the general research background and design, the background of the case studies, the data collection process, the research participants and ethical considerations. It will discuss the limitations to the research, as well as my positionality and personal reflection on the research process.

In Chapter 4, I study the experiences of different types of migrants and the law at regional and national levels, using the first set of findings from my research in China and Nigeria. The chapter analyses how and why states detach themselves from international human rights and legal obligations when dealing with non-citizens. It reflects on the impact of Western hegemonic practices on the international system, and particularly on the Global South and how migrants experience law because of this detachment. Western hegemonic practices permit states to avoid legal obligations such as the requirement to abide by human rights standards when dealing with certain types of migrants. The two case studies will be discussed separately and then juxtaposed to see how undocumented, asylum seeking and displaced migrants in both cases are experiencing the disconnection between responsibility and rights. This chapter analyses the legal frameworks in place to protect refugees and asylum seekers at the international and regional levels as a way of understanding the approaches that Nigeria and China have towards the migration of these groups of people. It will discuss the ways in which the communities and individuals in both case studies encounter refugee laws and policies, as well as their perceptions of the spaces they occupy in the states they are migrating to. Finally, it draws conclusions on the impact of state responsibility (or the lack thereof) to protect the human rights of undocumented and asylum-seeking groups and individuals engaging in South-South migrations.

In Chapter 5, I discuss the concept of intersectionality, identity (legal, social, economic etc) and how the intersection of the multiple and complex identities of the migrants in both case studies demonstrates the hierarchies and power stratifications in South-South migrations and the experience of the law in the Global South. This chapter analyses the way in which intersectionality shapes national or state-level approaches towards undocumented, displaced or asylum-seeking migrants and how these migrants understand their position in relation to the state and the hierarchies and power structures therein. It first discusses identity as it relates to non-citizens who are undocumented or asylum seeking, then examines why identity is important in understanding how marginalised people engage with the law and the way it shapes state implementation of laws and policies. Second, it discusses the fascinating link between an intersection of identities, TWAIL approaches and South-South migrations – identity is central in the discussion on South-South migrations and TWAIL because of the history of colonialism, borders and how these factors shape who we are and how we see ourselves within national, regional and international stratifications. I analyse the impact this has on resilience or victimhood in South-South migration narratives and experience of the law. Third, it discusses identity in the case studies and the role it plays in shaping the ways in which both the state and migrant groups or individuals are behaving. What happens because of how the state and the undocumented or displaced migrant understand identity and what does this say about Third World experiences of the law? This study draws some conclusions on intersectionality and identity (or identities) of migrant communities in the Global South, the complexity and dynamism of intersections, myths and hierarchies perpetuated in these spaces as a result of the current system of international law where citizenship is still very central to the migration narrative and what this means for the future.

Chapter 6 analyses the third set of findings from my research; local-level informal justice mechanisms in communities engaging in South-South migrations. This chapter will first seek to understand informal justice systems, looking into the meaning of the terminology and the arguments surrounding it. I assess the link between informal justice and TWAIL concepts as well as whether there is a link between informal justice, South-South migrations and excluded migrant communities. The chapter examines the case studies in Nigeria and China separately and again makes a juxtaposition to understand the informal justice frameworks in the Global South and their significance as sources of alternative knowledge about law, marginalisation, empowerment, legal consciousness and mobilisation. Finally, it will explore the role of local level informal justice mechanisms in reinforcing or dismantling hierarchies and exclusions in Nigeria and China, as well as the Global South and what significance this holds at the international level.

Chapter 7 concludes the book and revisits the questions I originally raised and whether there were gaps and inconsistencies or strong links between my original assumptions and my discoveries. The conclusion discusses the implications of Third World approaches or solutions to migration challenges in the Global South, drawing on both its benefits and drawbacks for a better understanding of how Third World approaches can contribute significantly to a truly international law to the advantage of people in developing countries. This chapter also infers what both case studies show about the rule of law and how it is both a limitation and an emancipator to marginalised migrants in the Global South. Finally, this chapter discusses how both cases destabilise or reinforce understandings of marginality and power in the Global South, coming to a comprehensive conclusion on the importance of South-South migrations and Third World approaches to international law.

2

Methods and Methodology

Researching the Law from Below

I. PLURAL APPROACHES TO UNDERSTANDING: THEORETICAL CLARIFICATIONS ON TWAIL AND THE PERIPHERY

THE CURRENT SYSTEM of international law and international relations is based on Western domination of the world over time.[1] The path to understanding of the international legal system is coloured by the West-centric history of international law, the practices of powerful states and institutions that dictate custom and norms, and the dominant discourses and location of international legal academe in the West. This has resulted in institutionalised hierarchies and dichotomies that can be destructive and oppressive by erasing or rewriting non-Western histories, experiences and contributions. Many scholars have taken up the challenge of changing the production of knowledge about international law, analysing what the law means to different people in the Global South, how it impacts different communities and the ways in which they contest the oppressiveness of the system.

TWAIL scholars argue that international law needs to be reformed and rethought. For example, Makau Mutua draws ideas from Critical Race Theory (CRT) where CRT – a primarily American school of thought that emerged from the Civil Rights Movement, focused on studying the struggles of Black and other subordinated groups within the American system through multidimensionality and intersectionality.[2] Multidimensionality is a method focused on unpacking the many intertwined belongings that individuals or groups have in their daily lives. Similarly, intersectionality is a method used to analyse the ways in which different labels or identities intersect to reproduce asymmetries of power in the lives of minority groups. Both methods allow researchers to analyse structures/structural violence in societies. In my research, these methods reflect on the ways in which migrant communities substantiate the law

[1] Makau Mutua, 'Critical Race Theory and International Law: The View of an Insider-Outside' (2000) 45 *Villanova Law Review* 841, at 841.

[2] See Patricia Collins, 'Social Inequality, Power and Politics: Intersectionality and American Pragmatism in Dialogue' (2012) 26(2) *Journal of Speculative Philosophy* 442.

from below and confront the issues of structural justice that underpin their everyday lives.

Multidimensionality, intersectionality and TWAIL produce a refined understanding of identity as a legal reality and are all tools that enable an unpacking and rethinking of identity and the law. Identity is central to how individuals see and experience power or justice; belonging to a certain group or community has an impact on access to certain protections and privileges. Migrant identity (particularly undocumented, refugee, asylum-seeking or displaced status) stems from international law and shapes how individuals and groups encounter justice and asymmetries of power in the minutiae of their daily lives. Unpacking and rethinking involves focusing on the narratives of migrants engaging in South-South migrations and the non-Western state as the interpreter and author of its own response and practice of international law, and feeding that into the discourse and critique of international law. In the words of Obiora Chinedu Okafor, the purpose of TWAIL is 'to write the Third World into international legal analysis, focusing on understudied narratives of Third World peoples in international law'.[3] A plurality of approaches and narratives of international migrations are needed in the analysis and discussions on the development and evolution of international migration laws.[4]

CRT tools of analysis could be useful in international law because of their emancipatory potential.[5] TWAIL and CRT are connected because the international system is based on a false concept of the 'universal' and the domination and subordination of many by a few. The system's origins are in Eurocentric norms and principles of Christianity, which rationalised colonialism, conquest and domination historically, leading to the creation of new states and the concept of sovereignty, among other things.[6] Therefore, according to Mutua's analysis, having these roots in European culture, biases, existence and struggles, international law is inherently Eurocentric. International refugee law is Europeanised not merely because Europe has the most developed refugee law system and enforcement capabilities, but also because refugee law itself originated from European struggles and norms.[7] In this sense, international law is

[3] See Obiora Chinedu Okafor, 'Critical Third World Approaches to International Law (TWAIL): Theory, Methodology, or Both?' (2008) 10 *International Community Law Review* 371.

[4] See Megan Ryburn and Patrick van Berlo, 'South-South Migration: Law, Procedure, and Exclusion in Under-explored Contexts', *Leiden Law Blog*, 16 November 2016, http://leidenlawblog.nl/articles/south-south-migration. However, in fields like anthropology, there have been numerous studies on South-South migrations. For example, see Bruce Whitehouse, 'Overcoming the Economist Fallacy: Social Determinants of Voluntary Migration to the Sahel from the Congo Basin' in Abdoulaye Kane and Todd Leedy (eds), *African Migration Patterns* (Bloomington, Indiana University Press, 2013) Mahir Saul and Michaela Pelican, 'A New Research Perspective on Contemporary African Migration' (2014) 43(1–3) *Urban Anthropology and Studies of Cultural Systems and World Economic Development*, Special Issue: Global African Entrepreneurs.

[5] Mutua (n 1) 845.

[6] ibid.

[7] ibid at 841.

not universal, even though the universality of the international system is embodied in the United Nations.

Furthermore, Mutua adopts a stance that international law aggravates human suffering. I do not completely agree with Mutua on this, as international law through international human rights has shielded individuals from the oppressiveness of sovereignty to a certain extent.[8] However, it is evident that the current system of international law creates a false universality, silencing those experiences and identities that do not conform to the pre-set hierarchies and power structures in the international system. The CRT method of multi-dimensionality and intersectionality is about identifying and highlighting the silencing and marginalising factors.[9] Antony Anghie's article on sovereignty asserts that the colonial encounter, far from being peripheral to the making of international law, has been central to the formation of the discipline.[10] The Westphalian system of sovereignty was created by powerful colonial states, and non-Western states inherited this legacy through decolonisation and self-determination. States in the Global South have adhered to these inherited definitions of statehood and sovereignty and have thrived on them. Anghie states that international lawyers awoke to the existence of a multicultural world only because of decolonisation. His central argument is that the character and nature of international law cannot be understood without what he terms 'colonial confrontation'.[11] This perspective points to the interaction between the Global South and the West as essential to shaping notions of sovereignty and positivism. The 'periphery' and the 'centre' are co-constitutive of one another. This perspective could be understood to mean that the Global South has contributed considerably to the development of international law; however, this was not a contribution based on consent, equality or mutual benefit. Even though the colonial encounter has shaped international law and the Global South has had a role to play, these power differentials and racialised hierarchies are still reinforced, hence the need for a plurality of approaches.

Marxist approaches to international law influence, and are influenced by, TWAIL because they study oppression based on class and call for a reform of international law. Scholars like Bhupinder Chimni argue that international law institutionalises inequalities in the international system that reflect the oppressiveness of the bourgeoisie to the detriment of the working class and the poor in developed and developing countries.[12] Chimni also uses a Marxist

[8] ibid at 845.

[9] According to Mutua, TWAIL is counterhegemonic, anti-hierarchical and suspicious of universal creeds or truths. Anghie adds that it is a coalitionary movement. See Makau Mutua and Antony Anghie, 'What is TWAIL?' (2000) 94 *Proceedings of the Annual Meeting, American Society of International Law* 35–37.

[10] See Anthony Anghie, 'Finding the Peripheries: Sovereignty and Colonialism in Nineteenth Century International Law' (1999) 40 *Harvard International Law Journal* 1.

[11] ibid at 6.

[12] See Bhupinder Chimni, 'Marxism and International Law: A Contemporary Analysis' (1999) 34(6) *Economic and Political Weekly* 337.

perspective in his analysis on Third World approaches to international law, which focuses on the impact of globalisation and the growing gap in wealth between the Global South and the Global North as a system that perpetuates discrimination and oppression, as well as how the elite in all states benefit from participation in the international system.[13]

Chimni captures the real inequalities of the international system in both the developed and the developing world due to the Marxist/TWAIL approach. It is only when these inequalities are exposed that they can be addressed. TWAIL aims to expose the disparities and injustice in the international system so that it can be reformed. The arguments from Mutua and Chimni above show that some scholars juxtapose these approaches to analyse the impact of international law on people in the Global South. These approaches are linked by a common attention to how international law contributes to a system of inequalities that needs reform.

Arguments made by some international legal jurists state that international law would be better off if it reflected particularistic rather than universal norms. Amongst such scholars are Jose Alvarez, a former Judge at the International Court of Justice (ICJ), who advocated for a 'new' international law because society and international life are in a state of constant change.[14] Alvarez advocated for an 'American International Law' that would specifically address a body of problems and situations that could only arise on the American continent due to its historical, geographical and political situation.[15] According to this conceptualisation, international law would be based on regional realities, cultures and sensibilities, as opposed to a universal body of rules and norms. This could make international law more streamlined and perhaps more effective at addressing regional issues. However, Alvarez assumes that the American continent is a monolith and that there are no dichotomies and hierarchies that would hinder this equality; particularistic international law will not address marginalisation if it does not also engage the peripheries within that context. Chimni argues that there is a need to recognise different transnational groups and classes; the use of 'undifferentiated classifications' foists universality or homogeneity that creates variations in the experiences of different transnational groups and classes. Chimni further argues that this approach enables the identification of dominant groups that benefit from international legal regimes, but also illustrates the limits of international human rights law by highlighting the exclusions in the system.[16]

[13] See Bhupinder Chimni, 'Third World Approaches to International Law: A Manifesto' (2006) 8 *International Community Law Review* 3.

[14] See Arnulf Becker Lorca, 'Alejandro Alvarez Situated: Subaltern Modernities and Modernisms that Subvert' (2006) 19 *Leiden Journal of International Law* 879.

[15] ibid.

[16] See Bhupinder Chimni, 'Prolegomena to a Class Approach to International Law' (2010) 21(1) *European Journal of International Law* 57 at 75 and 82.

Taslim Elias Olawale, another former Judge at the ICJ, focused on the *sui juris* character of African nations in the international legal system.[17] According to him, Africans had their own unique ideas of right and wrong, and legal and moral liability that should be weighed equally with that of Europeans and Americans. He held that the current international legal system led to the 'peripheralisation' of African and Asian countries and as a result needed reform, an opinion that was similar to that of Alvarez.[18] This analysis, like that of Alvarez, questions the homogeneity of the international legal system and its erasure of African contributions and experiences. However, again African experiences are not monolithic; different factors ranging from class, ethnicity etc create variations in experiences. Therefore, TWAIL scholars like Mutua see the value of CRT tools like intersectionality in the analysis of international law and the Global South.

On the other hand, Arnulf Becker Lorca's analysis of international law argues that international law universalised when jurists from semi-peripheral polities, such as Japan, the Ottoman Empire and Latin American states, appropriated European international legal thought.[19] He further argues that classical international law only recognised sovereign equality between states belonging to the 'family of civilised nations', while sovereign autonomy and equality were denied beyond the West.[20] He claims that the elites of semi-peripheral polities, facing pressures to sign unequal treaties, realised the stakes of learning the international legal language, which led to a doctrinal appropriation or, in other words, a particularistic universalism.[21] This position breaks the international system into more defined hierarchies with the West at the centre as the origin of international law and semi-peripheral states in the middle as successful transplants of the ideas and norms of the centre, thus coming closer to equality. The peripheral states still developing in the system are left out of the equation entirely.

All these arguments pre-suppose that a cohesion exists among peripheral states and semi-peripheral states. There are hierarchies between nations in the Global South and even within a state. Hierarchies exist between citizens and migrants (both documented and undocumented), and between nationals and stateless persons or refugees in the current international system. Great power differentials, discriminations and exclusions are not confined to the colonialism-rooted interaction between the West and the Global South, but are also present in other interactions. The links between TWAIL and international migrations

[17] See Carl Landauer, 'Things Fall Together: The Past and Future Africas of T.O. Elias's Africa and the Development of International Law' (2008) 21 *Leiden Journal of International Law* 351.

[18] See Chin Leng Lim, 'Neither Sheep nor Peacocks: T. O. Elias and Post-colonial International Law' (2008) 21 *Leiden Journal of International Law* 295.

[19] See Arnulf Becker Lorca, 'Universal International Law: Nineteenth-Century Histories of Imposition and Appropriation' (2010) 51 *Harvard International Law Journal* 475.

[20] ibid.

[21] ibid at 478.

exposes the unevenness of the system even in the periphery. Some scholars like Karin Michelson point to the fact that the idea of the periphery is very fluid and not as static as imagined. This is based on the arguments that the international system has transformed to give the Global South a voice in the international system. In other words, while the inequalities between the West and developing countries exist, over time, developing countries have been able to canvas for the protection of their interests in international law rather than being silent and powerless.

Karin Michelson encapsulates these changes in her analysis of Third World voices in international discourse.[22] She highlights the contributions that non-Western states have made to move towards greater democracy in the system and to reorient beyond the marginalisation of their narratives and experiences. She looks to movements like the New International Economic Order in the 1970s, which was an attempt to correct the predatory nature of the economic order.[23] She also examines the clamour for an international right to development, championed by non-Western states to counter the utilisation of international development aid by powerful Western states to create divisions and alliances.[24] And, finally, she points to the clashes between the Global North and the Global South in relation to the regulation of international environmental laws that conveniently forgot the impact of colonialism on the environment.[25] This elucidates the changes that have occurred in the way in which the Global South positions itself in the international system. Going beyond identifying the Global South as weak and exploited in the colonial history of international law, it signifies a shift to proactivity. On a more material level, non-Western states now have their individual interpretations of international law and sovereignty, and this informs their actions, both domestically and at the international level.[26] James Thuo Gathii asserts that Third World states have mobilised state sovereignty to reify state power at the expense of individual rights and freedoms.[27] For example, China utilises the idea of sovereignty to rationalise enforcing the control over Tibet and Tibetan people, even though it historically fought against the control of the West and Japan. This reflects how the impact of colonialism and the idea of sovereignty in international law have affected the Global South. In fact, it is possible that wholesale co-opting of sovereignty has led to the oppressiveness of many states in the Global South towards their peoples.[28]

[22] Karin Michelson, 'Rhetoric and Rage: Third World Voices in International Legal Discourse' (1997) 16 *Wisconsin International Law Journal* 353.

[23] ibid at 370.

[24] ibid at 375.

[25] ibid at 387–91.

[26] For example, China has refused to ratify the Migrant Workers Convention because it perceives that there is a clash between the realities in the domestic context of migration in China and the responsibilities of the Convention.

[27] James Thuo Gathii, 'TWAIL: A Brief History of its Origins, its Decentralized Network, and a Tentative Bibliography' (2011) 3 *Trade, Law and Development* 26 at 41–42.

[28] ibid at 43.

According to Bonaventura de Sosa Santos, international law can be emancipatory due to globalisation and human rights.[29] The emancipatory potential of international law involves identifying points through which international law breaks away from its Eurocentric and colonial past, and acknowledges the struggles and narratives of non-Western peoples in the international legal process. Within the context of migrations, an international legal scholarship that connects globalisation and migration to racial power, silence and irrelevance, and that examines processes that produce racial stratifications of migrants would tap into the emancipatory potential of international law. In his analysis of TWAIL and CRT, Mutua does not focus on globalisation and the state, yet his view on the potential of international law is similar to that of de Sosa Santos. He holds that the liberating potential of international law will be possible if TWAIL and CRT are utilised as tools of reform in international law. In Gathii's opinion, international law is transformative yet retrogressive, and he asserts that due to this messy nature, TWAIL is necessary to 'expand or open up new conceptual spaces for international legal scholarship and praxis'.[30]

Pahuja and Eslava root the distortions of international law in issues of material distribution and imbalances of power.[31] They argue that it is crucial to review the ways in which international law manifests on a mundane and quotidian plane. In my understanding, this means going beyond the historically Eurocentric confines of international law and looking at contemporary and material sites for resistance to this Eurocentrism. Pahuja and Eslava allude to the transformative potential of international law, which can only be activated when international law is analysed beyond false universalism. They state that TWAIL rejects the idea of the 'universal' because the 'universal' is impossible and has led to exclusions. Instead, a plurality of approaches could be more fruitful.[32] This is possible by closing the discursive, normative and institutional distance from national realities in international law;[33] in other words, bringing the narratives that have been confined to regional or national spaces into international legal spaces. This idea is at the very core of my research. Pahuja and Eslava call for an extension of the spatial scope of analysis of international law into areas that are also embodiments of international law, but are not within the restricted body of norms and institutions of international law which have subordinated

[29] Catherine Dauvergne, *Making People Illegal: What Globalization Means for Migration and Law* (Cambridge, Cambridge University Press, 2008) 36. De Sousa Santos argues for a cosmopolitan globalisation in order for international law to be emancipatory. See Boaventura de Sousa Santos and César A Rodríguez Garavito (eds), *Law and Globalization from Below: Towards a Cosmopolitan Legality* (Cambridge, Cambridge University Press, 2005).

[30] Gathii (n 27) 40.

[31] See Luis Eslava and Sundhya Pahuja, 'Between Resistance and Reform: TWAIL and the Universality of International Law' (2011) 3 *Trade, Law and Development* 103 at 105.

[32] ibid at 122

[33] ibid at 123.

the Global South. Pahuja and Eslava give examples of the domestic level of work on undocumented migration as an example.[34]

I examine the materialisation of TWAIL in international law by looking at non-Western experiences of international migrations and the law through case studies. This takes the interrogation beyond those locales that are traditionally discussed as 'international'. Gathii asserts that the purpose of TWAIL is to produce underrepresented and alternative knowledge about international law; this is the purpose that frames my research.[35] My research on South-South migrations produces alternative knowledge on different aspects of the law and goes a step further than the theoretical conceptualisations of TWAIL by studying the law from below within communities engaging in South-South migrations. I also employ Pahuja and Eslava's conceptualisation of resistance to Eurocentrism in material sites by looking into how migrant communities experience intersectionality, struggle against hegemony and create their own structures to counter those that institutionalise their marginalisation.

II. TWAIL AS METHODOLOGY

As a student of international law, I often wondered how to situate myself in what I was studying. Dominant discourses usually engage with the Global South as merely a source of case law, places where international law's legitimacy is proved or tested for legal dissection. Being of African descent, it was odd to study law in such a clinical manner. International legal norms and decisions have serious consequences in the daily lives of people in the Global South. For me, centring the narratives and struggles of people's everyday lives was the only way to understand, critique and improve international law. As a result, I needed to explore research methodologies and methods that would give me epistemological and empirical freedom.

Okafor identifies TWAIL as not just a theory, because it 'describes the behaviour of a related set of social phenomena',[36] but as a set of theories with a central set of ideas.[37] TWAIL revolves around writing the Third World into international legal analysis and producing alternative knowledge about international law.[38] Okafor also identifies TWAIL as a methodology because it is a body of methods that insists on writing the Third World into international legal analysis, identifying 'continuities and discontinuities' and focusing on the understudied narratives of the Third World.[39] Similarly, Eslava identifies that TWAIL analyses

[34] ibid at 127.
[35] Gathii (n 27) 38.
[36] Okafor (n 3) 373.
[37] ibid at 375.
[38] ibid.
[39] ibid at 377.

the continuities and discontinuities of international law, politics and economics as it affects people in the Global South and delineates it as a methodology. Here, TWAIL pays attention to different and dynamic accounts of history and imperialism, drawing from local specificities and regional trends and fights to alter legal understanding.[40] Situating my research in view of Eslava's delineation, this project is not part of the historical project of TWAIL per se, but more about documenting ongoing struggles against forms of hegemony, imperialism and power asymmetries, drawing from local specificities and regional trends.

A TWAIL methodology consists of the following:

(a) 'trans-disciplinarity', which entails drawing from other critical approaches like CRT and feminism into legal scholarship'
(b) placing subalternity at the centre of international legal scholarship; and
(c) using anthropological methods to understand the impact of the law on the lives of people in the Third World and using analysis based on 'historical sensibility' for people of the Third World and a distrust about narratives that claim to be universal.[41]

TWAIL employs the use of empirical evidence drawn from real Third World narratives and experiences of historical developments and injustices in international law created by contemporary international law. It further uses what Andrew Sunter calls the 'hermeneutics of suspicion', which aims to find meaning from people (rather than their expressions) in order to reduce generalisations, universalisation and biases.[42] Using TWAIL as my methodological framework, my research uses empirical evidence through case studies and legal ethnographies, centres on subalternity and utilises a trans-disciplinary approach to both critique and draw meaning about the law from South-South migrations.

Pahuja and Eslava argue that international law has traditionally disconnected itself 'discursively, normatively and institutionally from national realities'. TWAIL methodologically challenges this disconnection[43] because it places emphasis on the material life of international law as it unfolds in the everyday.[44] Eslava and Pahuja add that TWAIL is essential as a methodological tool because it enables people from developing countries to find the international in national and regional spaces that are usually ignored but affect numerous populations

[40] Luis Eslava, 'TWAIL Coordinates', *Legal Critical Thinking*, 2 April 2019, http://criticallegalthinking.com/2019/04/02/twail-coordinates.

[41] Michelle Burgis-Kasthala, 'Scholarship as Dialogue? ICL, TWAIL and the Politics of Methodology' (2016), RegNet Research Papers, No 103, Regulatory Institutions Network at 13–14.

[42] See Andrew F Sunter, 'TWAIL as Naturalised Epistemiology' (2007) 20(2) *Canadian Journal of Law and Jurisprudence* 475 at 489 and 498. Sunter defines hermeneutics as a systemic inquiry into meaning according to a specific set of philosophically grounded principles, which sets a foundation for methodological analysis (at 498).

[43] Eslava and Pahuja (n 31) 123.

[44] ibid at 125.

in developing countries.[45] TWAIL is the most appropriate methodology to frame my research on South-South migrations as an issue in international law, as my research deliberately raises questions, and draws meaning on international law out of local and micro-level interactions between people engaging in South-South migrations.

TWAIL as a methodology focuses on using alternative histories and narratives to challenge dominant approaches in international law.[46] In the study of international migrations, the dominant approach is to draw knowledge, meaning and standards from Western norms, narratives, practices and experiences, and make them universal, as discussed in Chapter 1. My research disrupts this approach by using case studies on South-South migrations to draw alternative observations, critiques and conclusions on international law. Within the context of migrations, a TWAIL methodology means that my research focuses on communities engaging in South-South migration, the narratives of the individuals and communities in these spaces, their encounters with the law and concepts of international law like the rule of law and informal justice, borders, human rights, refugee law, citizenship and identity. My goal is to contribute to the accumulation of knowledge about the impact of the law on Third World peoples that has been previously unknown and to contribute to the discourse on the law of the everyday, which was expanded by Eslava.[47] In addition, my aim in using TWAIL as a lens to look at migrations is to challenge exclusions and marginalisation occurring within the Global South because of hegemonic approaches to international law. My positionality is shaped by a desire for the recognition of the important role that the Global South plays in international law. I am a scholar from the Global South, from Nigeria, a country with relatively powerful regional influence. This, along with my Western education, shapes my view of the co-constitutive relationships between core and peripheries, as well as the heterogeneity within the Global South. This is why it is necessary to document the variations of experience, of privilege and marginality in my research.

III. CASE STUDIES AND LEGAL ETHNOGRAPHIES AS TWAIL METHODOLOGIES

According to Eslava and Pahuja, legal ethnographies are the next frontier of TWAIL scholarship.[48] I agree with this point of view and adopt it in my research. This is similar to Okafor's claim that TWAIL is a methodology in addition to being a school of thought. What this means is that in order for

[45] ibid at 129.

[46] Pooja Parmar, 'TWAIL: An Epistemological Inquiry' (2008), 10 *International Community Law Review* 363 at 367.

[47] See Luis Eslava, *Local Space, Global Life: The Everyday Operation of International Law and Development*' (Cambridge, Cambridge University Press, 2015).

[48] Eslava and Pahuja (n 31) 126.

Third World approaches to be centred, TWAIL scholars must take their interrogation beyond theoretical arguments into the crystallisation of the law in the daily lives of people in the Global South. To do this, TWAIL scholars rely on methods that give us the flexibility to study the law from below by listening to the narratives and experiences of individuals and communities in the Global South.

Sujith Xavier argues in favour of TWAIL-based ethnographies that facilitate understanding of the material realities of people in the Global South and, as such, are both tools of emancipation from and resistance to the status quo.[49] According to this conceptualisation, it is the ethical responsibility of international law scholars to affirm the material reality of the Global South and to give accurate portrayals of how international law affects the lives of people there.[50] I understand this to mean that ethnography – which enables understanding of the material realities of people in the Global South – is crucial to any research about the Global South. Therefore, I employ ethnography as part of my research method to ethically portray how international migration regimes impact migrant communities engaging in South-South migrations. Many TWAIL scholars focus on theoretical analysis, questions and discussions. Eslava highlights that they have:

> [E]ngaged in an exploration of international law in terms of the historical and material relations from which it emerges and which it generates. In particular, these authors have studied international law in terms of its relation with the expansion of European empires and their ontological structures, economies and cultural and legal frames through the colonial process and the daily disciplines that this process unleashed, as well as the global spread of the nation-state form, the expansion of the international institutional realm, especially from the second half of the twentieth century onwards, and the channelling of these historical events and their problematic political and economic effects through contemporary international normative discourses, in particular the idea of development.[51]

TWAIL scholarship mainly revolves around theoretical discussions, failing to do legal ethnography and to go to the lowest levels to understand the law from below. This failure to incorporate legal ethnography may be because the law of the everyday is not black letter law, but is found in informal spaces and mundane experiences, or due to a preference to focus on the historical as a source of alternative legal accounts. Both historical accounts offering alternative contexts and ethnographies cannot work in isolation. It is for this reason that I give regional histories and contextualisation for each case study below, in addition to the ethnographic work documenting experiences of the law of the everyday to

[49] Sujith Xavier, 'Learning from Below: Theorising Global Governance through Ethnographies and Critical Reflections from the Global South' (2016) 33 *Windsor Yearbook of Access to Justice* 229 at 248.

[50] ibid at 245.

[51] Eslava (n 47) 26–27.

balance alternative legal accounts. The use of ethnography is a purposeful reaction to what I believe is the continuing lack of TWAIL work from below. TWAIL as a school of thought and a methodology still has not done enough listening to the narratives at the lowest level, even informal, ordinary and local sources of knowledge in the Global South. Even though Eslava and Pahuja among others have done this work, there is room for more ethnography. If TWAIL aims to 'reduce the distance of the world of international law from the lives of ordinary peoples', it follows that TWAIL work must be done at the level of the 'ordinary people'.[52] One cannot see the local level and the issues of structural justice that underpin everyday life without completely engaging at that level. Without ethnographic research, TWAIL risks remaining stuck in the rigidity that it seeks to cast aside: that international law is found only at the international level, that it is intangible and that there is no alternative understanding of the law.

Eslava is a TWAIL scholar who uses legal ethnography extensively to analyse international law and international development as they manifest at the local level in Bogota, Colombia.[53] He understands legal ethnographies as necessary for research that addresses 'a multiplicity of geographies, levels of governance and the plethora of norms and administrative mechanisms, mundane things and subjective formations'.[54] I agree very much with this and take this same approach in my research. Migration, like development, relates to many geographical locations, norms, administrative mechanisms etc, and, as such, legal ethnography is the most appropriate to reflect these multiplicities. My research, like that of Eslava, seeks to make a methodological intervention of a more close-to-the-ground study of the law, which is only possible through ethnography. My specific methodological intervention upholds the study of migration and the law from below. My research aims to fill the gap in knowledge on how global migration mechanisms affect the daily lives of migrants in the Global South.

Utilising ideas on international law from below, my research tests TWAIL beyond theory through a fine-grained ethnography of the spaces of informal law within migrant communities in the Global South. Legal ethnography allows me to map existing realities, relying on data based on observations of the everyday of migrant communities in Nigeria and China to capture the social meanings of daily occurrences of the law. Taking things a step further, it allows me to learn about how the law is created and experienced from below, reaching into new spaces like informal justice that would not be possible if the interrogation were not ethnographic in nature. Ethnography frees my research from the rigidity of international rules and norms, and grants me flexibility of sources of information because I can draw significance from local sources, events, subjects and experiences.

[52] Bhupinder Chimni, 'The World of TWAIL: Introduction to the Special Issue' (2011) 3(1) *Trade, Law and Development* 14 at 20.

[53] Eslava (n 47) 27.

[54] ibid at 24.

According to Eva Burton, in order for any intercultural legal research to be meaningful, it must be interdisciplinary; for example, legal research must employ anthropological tools to have a balanced view of a study where different cultures are interacting.[55] In my case studies of South-South migrations, multiple cultures come into play. Using ethnographic interviewing as a tool, I aggregated different perceptions of the law, of injustice and how it is remedied, different approaches to refugee and asylum rights and different perceptions of marginalisation. This is exemplified in my two case studies. The use of case studies is TWAIL-ian because it acknowledges that the universal does not exist; differences between two case studies offer greater knowledge on the Global South, which the research aims to uncover and critique. I have chosen to use two case studies as part of my methodology in order to highlight the fact that there are different claims of marginalisation and power in spaces within the Global South in the research and to apply TWAIL at a local level. This strategy focuses not only on Third World narratives but also on their nuances – that there are variations based on historical, political and economic contexts coupled with challenges that make these narratives important tools of knowledge on what the law means to different peoples of the world.

In addition, I analyse how two non-Western regional hegemon states – China and Nigeria – engage with new types of international migrants by looking at how states respond to these new groups of migrants through either accepting or rejecting international norms. Contrasting state responses with a socio-political analysis of domestic and regional realities, I unpack the complex interaction between migration, human rights and state responsibility in both contexts. Case studies add specificity to my project on how the law unfolds at a material level in a non-Western context. I present a deeper analysis of how these understudied aspects of law impact the narratives of different groups of people in developing countries and its implications.

Pierre Legrand holds that in comparative analysis such as those of my Chinese and Nigerian case studies, one cannot focus on rules and categories because this will produce research that is a miscomprehension of the encounters with the law that are under scrutiny and the ways in which the encounters are perceived and achieved.[56] Legrand links case studies to research methods that go beyond the traditional approach to law and instead lean on observations conducted in other fields that are of direct significance to the cross-cultural approach of the researcher.[57] This is the reason why ethnographies and case studies are an appropriate method of compiling data to be used for comparative legal analysis; they are methods that enrich comparative analysis because they

[55] See Eva Burton, 'Why We Need Comparative Legal Studies' (1984) 8 *Resource News* 9.

[56] Pierre Legrand, '*A Modern Approach to Comparative Law* by Peter de Cruz' (1995) 58(2) *MLR* 262 at 272.

[57] ibid.

support the aggregation of different perceptions of justice, marginalisation, rights and obligations, instead of looking strictly at the differences between rules and categories as the data.

IV. METHODOLOGICAL LIMITATIONS

As a scholar from a developing country, I try to identify aspects of the discussion about international law that derive meaning from the Third World. My purpose as a scholar is to truly understand how people in developing countries impact and are impacted by international law. I recognise that my approach is limited by the fact that being a scholar from a developing country does not necessarily mean that I understand the contexts and realities of other Third World peoples. As a scholar trained in the West, I cannot claim to have the same narratives or to encounter the same laws as the people in the spaces in which I carried out my research. Nothing captures the emotion of the 'insider but outsider' more aptly than Mutua's analysis of CRT when he states that:

> Though an outsider to CRT and international law, I am in a very real sense an insider to both. I am part of an international elite that personally benefits from the norms and structures of international law. My reality is not that of marginal and down trodden citizens in Latin America, Africa, Asia, or, for that matter, North America. I do not strain under the daily avalanche of the cruelties of globalization, state repression and abuse … I am also an outsider because of that other consciousness that I carry, the consciousness of the historical, political and cultural realities of the Africa that I am a part of, indeed of the Third World to which I belong, as distinct from the West. In international law, I see a system of ordering and understanding the world, a system and normative edifice that makes me accurately aware of my subordinate and marginal place in it as an 'other'.[58]

In researching the realities of communities, groups and individuals that are oppressed and marginalised in the Global South, it is important for the researcher to be aware of where they stand, to own up to it, and to be able to see how it impacts their interaction with and perceptions of the truths of the participants of their research. To avoid overly projecting my perceptions and opinions in my research, I used a mixture of methods. In the early stages of my research, I noticed that interviews tended to be shaped by my perceptions of what was on the ground. As a result, during my research, I prioritised listening and allowed people to lead conversations. This helped me take a back seat, giving participants the centre stage to own their stories about migration and the law. There were listening sessions where people talked for hours, and I listened without interrupting them. These interviews were semi-structured and informal to allow participants to discuss their experiences of injustice and the law in ways

[58] Mutua (n 1) 846.

they were comfortable with. This enabled me to document experiences as they were lived, to see things from their perspective as much as possible and to learn by listening, not speaking. For the ethical purposes of preserving the safety of the identities of those who I interacted with and interviewed during my field research, I have taken steps to anonymise all names. As a result, in all the subsequent chapters, interviewees will have single-letter names.

Another limitation on my research methodology is the risk of neglecting theory in favour of ethnographic data. Ethnographic data on its own requires detailed processing, contextualisation, analysis etc. In order to balance my analysis of the data, I chose themes that I drew from the field research and then grounded the data in the theoretical discussions surrounding those themes. For example, narratives of informal justice kept coming up in both my case studies and so became one of the themes on which I chose to focus. The data I documented on the field were situated within and juxtaposed alongside theoretical conceptualisations of informal justice, which, as a result, opened up the discourse on informal justice to TWAIL analysis. There is scope for further discussions on the relationship between TWAIL and other critical theories beyond CRT and feminism in relation to the law of the everyday and the narratives of undocumented or displaced migrants on issues like informal justice.[59]

One of the challenges with case studies is attempting to discuss wide historical contexts together in one project. There was always the risk of missing something significant due to the sheer size of each case study. Due to this limitation, I included contextual analysis in all the following chapters. For example, in addition to the contextualisation of the two case studies here, Chapter 3 provides international, regional and national contexts for both case studies specifically under the theme of that chapter – state responsibility towards the migrant communities I encountered. While it made the book lengthy context-wise, this was necessary to present an analysis that was as balanced as possible. A future research prospect may be to focus solely on the contexts of these case studies and to discuss them from a historical point of view. My project was not about the history, but rather about the narratives of the daily struggles of South-South migrants happening in real time.

Another possible risk that could arise from my research on the narratives of migrant communities is that of fetishising and idealising the local. This is a challenge for research focusing on alternative knowledge, narratives or histories. In order to overcome the temptation of fetishisation, my research does not conceptualise the Global South as a utopia or the local as the ideal. The

[59] See David W Kennedy, 'New Approaches to International Law Bibliography' (1994) 35 *Harvard International Law Journal* 417; Annalise Riles, 'The View from the International Plane: Perspective and Scale in the Architecture of Colonial International Law', Cornell Law Faculty Publications, Paper 1072 (1995); Hilary Charlesworth, Christine M Chinkin and Shelley Wright, 'Feminist Approaches to International Law' (1991) 85 *American Journal of International Law* 613; Chantal Thomas, 'Critical Race Theory and Postcolonial Development Theory: Observations on Methodology' (2000) 45 *Villanova Law Review* 1195.

local is presented as what it is: a space where exclusion and empowerment are both possible. Understanding the ways in which both exclusion and empowerment happen at the local level is crucial for a more dynamic international law in the Global South. In Chapter 3, I discuss national and regional legal frameworks shaping approaches towards the migrant communities in my case studies, rather than focusing only on narratives from below. TWAIL methodology does not conceptualise the Third World as a utopia, but centres it in the discourse and scholarship of international law. I use my case studies as my way of understanding the good and the bad in international law and international migration. Recalling the thoughts of Eslava and Pahuja, the aim of looking at the law of the everyday and the local is to be able to see realities beyond what has been portrayed simply as areas of 'anthropological curiosity or simply disaggregated expressions of people's agency or false consciousness' and presenting them as what they truly are: valid and significant expressions of resistance to international and developmental interventions.[60] Future research expanding the areas that my research does not cover will open up further opportunities to map out international law's manifestation in the everyday realities in the Global South.

[60] Eslava and Pahuja (n 31) 129.

3

Contexts and Sites

The Background to the Case Studies

I. A BRIEF CONTEXT FOR THE CHINA CASE STUDY

CHINA EMBODIES MULTIPLE identities in the international system: it is paradoxically an economically powerful state and, as mentioned earlier in Chapter 1, it breaks numerous stereotypes while simultaneously fitting into many others.[1] Historically, China's concept of sovereignty was shaped by the West's interference in its internal affairs.[2] While the scale of China's colonial experience is small compared to other states in the Global South, it experienced internal strife caused by the presence of Western influence on its territory (resulting in wars like the Boxer Rebellion and the Sino-Japanese wars). As a result, China's stance has been anti-colonial and 'anti-Western', even going as far as supporting African countries in the fight for decolonisation under Mao Zedong.[3]

Contemporarily, China sees itself as a leader of the developing world and has positioned itself as the voice that speaks against the West. Internally, China has the largest population in the world and has had to enforce strict laws regulating the movement of its citizens within its borders, these same population pressures restrict the migration of foreigners.[4] In addition, China's internal dynamics uphold a culturally and politically homogeneous environment, even to the detriment of Chinese minority groups. This cultural homogeneity is further threatened by international migrations, especially from non-Chinese regions

[1] In 2016, at the Nuclear Security Summit, President Xi Jinping described China as being 'the world's biggest developing country'. See 'President Xi Attends Nuclear Security Summit, Visits Europe', *China Daily*, 2 April 2016, www.chinadaily.com.cn/world/2016xivisitczech/2016-04/02/content_24246632.htm. As of 2022, China sees itself as a developing and a developed country. See Foreign Ministry Spokesperson Mao Ning's Regular Press Conference, 13 October 2022, Ministry of Foreign Affairs of the People's Republic of China, www.fmprc.gov.cn/mfa_eng/xwfw_665399/s2510_665401/2511_665403/202210/t20221013_10782991.html.

[2] See Diane Preston, *The Boxer Rebellion: The Dramatic Story of China's War on Foreigners That Shook the World in the Summer of 1900* (New York, Berkley Books, 2001).

[3] See Sun Yun, *Africa in China's Foreign Policy* (Washington DC, Brookings Institute, John L Thornton China Center, 2014) at 6.

[4] See Kean Merril, 'China's National Resident Identity Card: Identity and Population Management in Transition' (2005) 23 *UCLA Pacific Basin Law Journal* 212.

because it visibly clashes with the assumed homogeneity of the Chinese people.[5] Economically, China is stretching its influence into the African continent, resulting in migrations from Africa to China and vice versa. With the increasing power that China wields and its foray into the African continent and the impact on Africans, it has been compared to colonial Europe in its brutal search for resources, trade and alliances.[6]

Studying China's interaction with the 'other' is particularly necessary in order to see how China's perception of migrants from a region considered to be different impacts China's legal and socio-political processes, whether there are discriminations and exclusions, and what these discriminations and exclusions are. This dynamic of shapeshifting between being a ruthless, resource-hungry power and a benevolent alternative to the West makes China a very significant study for TWAIL approaches. Not only does China have a great influence on regional developments (through the Association of Southeast Asian Nations (ASEAN), for example), but its internal realities are also unique and have shaped its approach to migration laws and policies both domestically and internationally.

As was mentioned in Chapter 1, historically, China's conception of migration, and particularly the acceptance of asylum seekers, refugees and migrants without status, has been based on the 'returning Chinese' identity.[7] In other words, China's permissiveness of migration into its territory has been tailored more to the idea of welcoming back its 'lost' nationals than welcoming foreign migrants.[8] In his analysis on the refugee law regime in China, Glen Peterson argues that the UNHCR in the 1940s was a 'colonial-era institution': it was based on and aimed at settling only European asylum seekers.[9] As a result, when there was persecution of Indonesians with Chinese ancestry in Indonesia in 1959, the UNHCR did not attempt to protect or resettle them.[10] China accepted Indonesian refugees and resettled them in China due to their Chinese

[5] My research does not focus on the regulation of internal migrations in China, but on international migrations. However, the impact of the problems of internal migrations on the law and policy on international migrations are significant. China is faced with millions of internal migrants who are challenging the limitations of internal migration control and access to social services. For many Chinese citizens, migration within China is a Herculean task. In addition to the challenges of population control, there is generally an unfavourable outlook on foreign migration, particularly if these are refugee, asylum or undocumented migrations. These issues will be discussed in more detail in ch 5. See also Tiejun Cheng and Mark Selden, 'The Origins and Social Consequences of China's Hukou System' (1994) 139 *China Quarterly* 644; and Wu Ling, 'Decentralization and Hukou Reforms in China' (2013) 32(1) *Policy and Society* 33.

[6] Karen Foerstel, 'China in Africa' (2008) 2(1) *CQ Global Researcher* 1 at 8.

[7] See Lili Song, 'Who Shall We Help? A Refugee Definition in a Chinese Context' (2014) 33(1) *Refugee Survey Quarterly* 44.

[8] See Glen Peterson, 'The Uneven Development of the International Refugee Regime in Post-War Asia: Evidence from China, Hong Kong and Indonesia' (2012) 25(3) *Journal of Refugee Studies* 326.

[9] ibid at 327.

[10] ibid at 328.

ancestry. In addition to Indonesians, China accepted migrants from countries such as Vietnam and Cambodia and offered them asylum in the 1980s, which was also due to the concept of a shared ancestry known as 海外华人 or hǎiwài huárén.[11] Although this has been China's practice in accepting asylum-seeking migrants in the region, it has not applied to all neighbouring countries – for example, China has turned a blind eye for political reasons to migrants from North Korea and Myanmar.[12] There were very few migrations from countries with no Chinese ancestral ties of the same magnitude as that which occurred in the 1980s (except the European migrants resettled by the UNHCR) and during the Cultural Revolution. As a result, China did not really develop an approach both in terms of law and policy towards non-Chinese asylum seeking or undocumented migrants, particularly from countries in the Global South for a long time.[13]

Since the Deng Xiaoping reforms of the 1980s, which focused on the economy and development, China has relaxed its migration policies and, as a result, has begun to see greater migrations from countries that have no ancestral or cultural ties to China.[14] From the 2000s, Africans began migrating to China in greater numbers, some for business, education or tourism, as well as to seek asylum.[15] This accelerated due to China's contemporary Sino-African development policies, in which it made promises in terms of investments, scholarships and infrastructure in exchange for natural resources and trade in Africa.[16] More than at any time in history, Africans and other non-Chinese peoples from developing countries are migrating to China. The undocumented and asylum-seeking Africans in China do not fit China's policy of accepting 'returning Chinese' migrants. There are no official numbers of how many African migrants are in China, but there have been estimates of up to 500,000.[17] There are no estimates of how many refugees are in China.[18] This information is not documented by the Chinese government or the UNHCR.

[11] See Guofu Liu, *Chinese Immigration Law* (Farnham, Ashgate, 2011).

[12] See Song (n 7).

[13] China did receive many non-Chinese students during Mao Zedong's anti-colonial campaigns in Africa. China offered scholarships to Africans and other peoples to study in Beijing as a means of encouraging the fight against colonialism and the spread of communism. However, this did not end well, particularly for the Africans, because their presence was not accepted by the Chinese and eventually led to protests in Nanjing and was also part of what spurred the Tiananmen Square incident. See Barry Sautman, 'Anti-Black Racism in Post-Mao China' (1994) 138 *China Quarterly* 413.

[14] See Song (n 7).

[15] See Heidi Ostbo Haugen, 'Nigerians in China: A Second State of Immobility' (2012) 50(2) *International Migration* 65.

[16] See Zhiqun Zhu, 'China's New Diplomacy in Africa' (2007), Conference Paper, International Studies Association 48th Annual Convention, Chicago, at 15.

[17] See Adams Bodomo, *Africans in China: A Socio-cultural Study and its Implications on Africa-China Relations* (New York, Cambria Press, 2012).

[18] Liu (n 11) 89.

China has ratified certain international migration law instruments showing that it is willing to engage with migration through international law.[19] Notable among these are the Refugee Convention,[20] the Transnational Organised Crime Convention,[21] the Convention against Torture,[22] the Convention on the Elimination of Racial Discrimination,[23] the Vienna Convention on Consular Relations[24] and the Vienna Convention on Diplomatic Relations.[25] However, this willingness to engage with international law has not resulted in the inculcation of these norms in China's approach towards foreigners. It is important to note that China does accept asylum seekers, but mainly if they are seeking asylum for *political reasons*, according to Article 32 of China's Constitution (Zhōnghuá Rénmín Gònghéguó Xiànfǎ).[26] This element of the Constitution was created with refugees from specific parts of Asia (like Cambodia and Vietnam) in mind.[27] Therefore, these political reasons are often based on identity and nationality (acceptance of returning Chinese versus rejection of North Koreans and no approach towards non-Chinese peoples from the Global South). In terms of undocumented migrations, China, like other countries, does not offer any protections for undocumented migrants and considers their presence to be a breach of the law, incurring punishments such as fines, imprisonment and deportation.[28] According to Guofu Liu, one of the main reasons why China has no approach in relation to non-Chinese asylum-seeking migrations from the Global South is that the migration of foreigners to China is at a fairly early stage and the number of asylum seekers is low.[29] On the other hand, China has a more defined approach towards undocumented migrants because Chinese rules also prohibit and penalise undocumented migrations.

[19] China also ratified the Convention against Torture (in 1988), the Convention on the Eradication of All Forms of Racial Discrimination (in 1982), the Convention to Eradicate All Forms of Discrimination against Women (in 1980), the International Convention on Economic, Social and Cultural Rights (in 2001), the Child Rights Convention (in 1992), the UN Convention against Transnational Crime (in 2003), the Vienna Convention on Consular Relations (in 1979), the Vienna Convention on Diplomatic Relations (in 1975) and the Convention Relating to the Status of Refugees and its Protocol (in 1982). However, there has been hesitation to ratify the Migrant Workers Convention, the Stateless Persons Convention and the Convention on Civil and Political Rights. There is no absolute right to enter China's territories. Many of the rights in the Migrant Workers Convention might not be viable in China due to population pressures. Chinese nationals within Chinese territory are also considered migrants and acceding to the rights within the Migrant Workers Convention might lead to many problems in terms of policy and implementation.

[20] 189 UNTS 137, [1954] ATS 5.

[21] (2001) 40 ILM 335.

[22] 1465 UNTS 85, [1989] ATS 21.

[23] 660 UNTS 195, [1975] ATS 40, (1966) 5 ILM 32.

[24] 596 UNTS 261, 21 UST 77, TIAS 6820.

[25] 500 UNTS 95, 23 UST 3227, (1961) 55 AJIL 1064.

[26] Constitution of the People's Republic of China of 1982 (Zhōnghuá Rénmín Gònghéguó Xiànfǎ, 1982).

[27] Liu (n 11).

[28] China, Law of 2012, Exit and Entry Administration Law of the People's Republic of China, Order No 57, 1 July (2013), arts 59, 62, 78, 79 and 80.

[29] Liu (n 11).

There were no unified administrative authorities in China focused on migration (immigration administration was divided between the Ministry of Foreign Affairs, the Ministry of Public Security and Border Control) and, as a result, China did not develop a specific position on migration for a long time.[30] Finally, Liu states that there are no rules for the application of refugee status and no rules concerning humanitarian status; there are also no regulations to determine the temporary protection status of asylum seekers in China.[31] In his analysis of the implementation of human rights by Chinese courts, Sanzhuan Guo asserts that in China, even the most fundamental of human rights in the Chinese Constitution, like the right to education, require citizens to bear obligations in order to enjoy them. In other words, in the Chinese context, protections are limited even for Chinese nationals.[32] It follows that as a result, when it comes to protections for foreigners, like asylum seekers or even undocumented migrants, there is a gap in the domestic legal regime, and this explains the context of the domestic realities that are affecting migrations in China.

A. Geographical Location and Description of Research Subjects in China

There are over 1,000 UN-registered asylum seekers and over 300 recognised refugees currently in China (from various states across Africa, South Asia and Southeast Asia) and these numbers are on the rise.[33] It is unknown how many asylum seekers are non-Chinese. My study focuses on communities of African undocumented migrants and asylum seekers in Beijing and Guangzhou. Because Nigerians constitute the highest number of both asylum-seeking and undocumented African migrants in China, my study focuses primarily on the Nigerian community.

China sends all its asylum seekers, from countries like Pakistan, Afghanistan, Somalia, Ethiopia, Nigeria and Sudan, to Yanjiao, a town with a sizeable population of over 250,000 people under the administration of the city of Sanhe, close to Beijing (about 25 km away) and located east of Tiananmen Square. South of Beijing, the port city of Guangzhou is one of China's commercial hubs and has the highest concentration of African migrants, particularly undocumented migrants and communities who have been present since the late 1990s. Unlike the type of migrants in Beijing, most of the migrants in Guangzhou are merchants and businesspeople. As with the number of African asylum seekers, the exact number of undocumented African migrants in Guangzhou is unknown; however,

[30] ibid.
[31] ibid.
[32] See Sanzhuan Guo, 'Implementation of Human Rights Treaties by Chinese Courts: Problems and Prospects' (2009) 8 *Chinese Journal of International Law* 161.
[33] Interview with Mr H at the UNHCR in Beijing, December 2015, on file with the author. See also the UNHCR China profile, https://www.unhcr.org/china.html#:~:text=About%201%2C160%20persons%20of%20concern,facto%20integrated%20pending%20Government%20regularization.

the number of African undocumented migrants in Guangzhou is high, especially with concentrations in areas like Xiaobei. African communities have developed in Guangzhou over time and the Nigerian community is the largest and the most organised. As a result, Guangzhou is central to understanding the narratives of African migrants in China, including those who are undocumented.

i. Research Execution

a. Summary of Interviews Conducted

I interviewed asylum seekers and undocumented migrants in Beijing and Guangzhou (a total of 36 people, all of them West African), support groups in Beijing and Guangzhou working with migrants (one non-Chinese and two Chinese ones), as well as[34] international organisations working with foreign migrants in China (the UNHCR, International Organization for Migration (IOM), and the United Nations Development Programme (UNDP)). I also interviewed some members of religious groups (the Beijing International Christian Fellowship and the African Women's Fellowship) with insight on migrant status and Chinese academia and locals (Professor Guofu Liu and legal scholars at the Beijing Institute of Technology, the only university in China where the law programme has a focus on migration). This research took place between November 2015 and March 2016.

I used group observation, interviews, listening to narratives, social interaction, as well as conducted volunteer work with NGOs that worked with my focus group. I communicated with research subjects in person, through email, phone and using tools like WeChat and Skype. I utilised tools like WeChat to network and to get research leads because WeChat is one of the foremost mediums of communication in China. I used Skype calls (with or without video) and email to connect to people who were uncomfortable with face-to-face encounters. I used observation, listening and social interaction when I encountered large groups of people; these tools were more effective than one-to-one interviews as people were more open to sharing information about themselves in an informal and less structured manner. Observing and listening to groups helped me to understand group dynamics before selecting people who I would contact for one-to-one interviews.

b. Field Report

I observed the dynamics in the Beijing International Christian Fellowship,[35] the largest African fellowship in Beijing and the place where almost all African Christians in Beijing converge. I met a fellowship leader through them and was

[34] I have some proficiency in the Mandarin language, which was useful during this stage of my field research.

[35] Beijing International Christian Fellowship: www.bicf.org.

able to make other connections with a foreign support group for asylum seekers. Beijing is the only place in China where refugees can legitimately seek asylum, so the church has become a resource for African migrants (both documented and undocumented, as well as asylum-seeking refugees). I interviewed two workers of the foreign support group and was able to get names of people in the UNHCR who I could interview about migration in China. I also established an arrangement to volunteer for the support group to observe and understand their role in assisting migrants. The support group focuses on helping asylum seekers apply for refugee status, as well as providing support with necessities like food, accommodation and education for those with children. My affiliation with the fellowship and the support group did not lead to many one-to-one encounters with asylum seekers and undocumented migrants, but it enabled me to understand the community better. I observed the community for two months. I was able to interview and/or observe 17 asylum seekers and undocumented migrants in Beijing. Those I observed did not disclose their status, while those I interviewed were often in the process of applying for asylum and were more open to sharing their experiences. I was able to interview asylum seekers from Liberia, Sierra Leone, Nigeria and Mali.

I interviewed immigration expert Gary Chodorow about his knowledge of African asylum seekers and undocumented migrants, and found out that even within foreign migration law circles, there was little knowledge or understanding of non-Chinese asylum seekers and undocumented migrants.[36] In addition, I was able to talk to seven Chinese law scholars at the Beijing Institute of Technology about the Chinese approach to African asylum-seeking refugees. This was made possible by Professor Guofu Liu, who is currently one of the few academics in China focusing on refugee law and migration. I interviewed five UN workers about the role of the UN in China with regard to non-Chinese and non-Asian asylum seekers and undocumented migrants in China. Among them were two senior staff members of the IOM and the UNHCR.[37]

The findings from my research in Beijing can be summarised as follows:

(i) Churches are a resource for African asylum seekers from all over the continent. Any African (undocumented or asylum seeking) who comes to the church for support and assistance is attended to. Members of the church come from all walks of life, from UN and diplomatic staff to businesspeople, educators, students etc. This variety creates a support group that helps with things like food and shelter.

(ii) Non-Christian undocumented and asylum seekers often form their own close-knit communities of support. For example, the Somali refugee community is a solid resource for any refugee coming from the refugee camps in Kenya.

[36] Gary Chodorow profile, Chodorow Law Offices: http://lawandborder.com/gary-chodorow.

[37] Both IOM and UNHCR staff preferred to be anonymous.

(iii) In order to seek asylum in Beijing, many African asylum seekers need passports. As a result, there is a thriving underground passport business that cuts across African networks in some of the big cities in China to provide this service to them.

(iv) The UNHCR and other UN agencies are severely limited in terms of what they can do in China. China prohibits collaboration between UN agencies in the country – for example, the UNHCR cannot work with the IOM in China. The UNHCR in Beijing is charged solely with providing 'soft services' to asylum seekers (as with the church). Because undocumented migration is illegal in China, and China does not acknowledge refugee law in a traditional sense, there is very little protection for asylum seekers. For example, if an application for asylum fails, the UNHCR must report the failure to the Chinese authorities, which exposes the asylum seeker to imprisonment or deportation. UN agencies in China cannot pool their resources together to work with refugees because the government is suspicious of foreign interference with internal issues. Therefore, there is no engagement of refugees/asylum seekers in a capacity that would help them. There are no means for the UNHCR to provide for all the refugees in China, even though the UNHCR office in Beijing is the only place where they can seek asylum.

(v) The UNHCR does not receive any support from the Chinese government to take care of the influx of refugees into China and its assistance budget in China is dwindling.

(vi) The asylum seekers who make it to Beijing are often trying to find a way out of China (except those who are from a region facing a crisis, like Somalia). Most of them seek asylum in China based on a lack of understanding of Chinese migration laws.

(vii) The UNHCR does not have access to airports, borders and other access points because China limits its sphere of influence. Refugees are limited as they must travel to the UNHCR office in Beijing to seek asylum. Most of the people I spoke to had relied on a smuggler to procure passports for them so that they could get to Beijing.

c. Seeking Refuge from the Ebola Epidemic: A Snapshot of Mr S

Mr S is from Liberia. He left Liberia for China before the Ebola epidemic. He arrived with a two-week tourist visa at the city of Dalian, where he had some friends who were studying at a university. His visa ran out, but he could not return to Liberia because the epidemic was escalating. He was not properly informed of Chinese immigration laws, so he did not register at the Public Security Bureau when he arrived in China. Without this registration, he was not able to extend his visa. He sought the help of his university friends, who helped to connect him with foreign support organisations. They offered him advice and support, and he was able to quickly travel to the UNHCR in Beijing to seek asylum. He was screened by the UNHCR to verify his asylum claims and was registered as an asylum seeker in China. In 2015, even though the Ebola epidemic was over, he wanted to remain in China and enrol at a Chinese university.

d. A Summary of the Asylum Procedure in China

It takes two weeks to get an interview date/appointment with the UNHCR and 14–16 months to be registered as an asylum seeker in China and obtain an identity card. If the case succeeds, the asylum seeker will be assigned refugee status. There is no stipend for refugees, so refugees are often forced to investigate alternative sources of income, even though there are no provisions in the Constitution or the Entry and Exit Law permitting refugees to work in China. If a request for asylum fails for the first time after a favourable filing for asylum registration, the applicant can appeal (the appeal will be directed towards the US). If it fails a second time, the application can appeal (towards Geneva this time). If it fails a third time, the applicant will remain in China, pending other solutions, such as asylum in another country close to the applicant's country of origin. This often leads asylum seekers to become undocumented. Failed asylum seekers (those who failed the initial interview) will be jailed or deported by the Public Security Bureau – this stage is beyond the control of the UNHCR.

e. Findings from Research in Guangzhou

After the fieldwork in Beijing, I carried out additional research in the city of Guangzhou. As the epicentre of the African presence in China, Guangzhou opened critical aspects of the narratives of African migrants in China. In Guangzhou, I interviewed 19 undocumented migrants from the Nigerian community. My findings in Guangzhou provided a new dimension to my research that impacted its direction. My research, which was initially about the narratives of asylum seekers and undocumented migrations, grew to become about understanding the role that community plays in shaping the experience of migration, of the law, and of justice and human rights. Here are some of the observations I made:

(i) The migrants in Guangzhou are businessmen who came to China for business and overstayed for decades. They contribute massively to the local economy and the Chinese government turns a blind eye to undocumented migrants most of the time. Arrests are made only when there is a public outcry or a specific case of crime, like rape or fighting.

(ii) All the migrants I interviewed were male and married to Chinese women. This might be because in Guangzhou, most of the African migrants are male. The female migrants I met were not comfortable talking about their immigration status. All the men I interviewed intend to live in China for the rest of their lives.

(iii) The strongest community in Guangzhou is the Nigerian community, followed by the Malian community. The Nigerian community is the unofficial 'leader' of the African community in China.
(iv) The Nigerian community is very organised, with an elected government, a taskforce, a justice system and ties to the Chinese government.
(v) The Nigerian taskforce and justice system works in tandem with the Chinese Public Safety Bureau (PSB). For example, if a Nigerian or an African commits a serious crime, the taskforce will make an arrest and after a trial and a judgment in the community, the person will be handed over to the PSB. This largely depends on what crime was committed. Rape is one of the cases that has warranted the community to collaborate with the Chinese government.

I concluded my research in China on 12 March 2016. The following list gives the problems I encountered in China:

(1) *Mistrust of outsiders*: China is a very unsafe place for undocumented migrants and refugees; given this situation, many people were not comfortable talking about their status. Mistrust was particularly high in Beijing, unlike Guangzhou where the undocumented community has an established community support system. I found that people treated me like an insider when I was discussing the structure of the Nigerian community, undocumented narratives and experiences of Chinese law in the community. I was treated like an outsider when it came to the subject of asylum. People were largely uncomfortable sharing information about the fact that they were seeking asylum. I believe that the exclusion I faced was the result of the secrecy and the risks involved when migrants decide to travel to the UNHCR in Beijing to seek asylum. In Beijing, the atmosphere was less open than in Guangzhou. In Beijing, people were more open to sharing when I interacted in a less formal manner, listening instead of asking questions and observing instead of acting. However, in Guangzhou, people were more comfortable with face-to-face interviews. Many people in Beijing preferred using platforms like Skype and email, including the Chinese and non-Chinese support groups.
(2) *Hindrances created by gatekeepers*: in China, there are a number of researchers trying to monitor and understand the African community for different reasons. A few of them have gained the trust of people within the community and have in turn become gatekeepers of sorts who have access to the members of the community (this is especially true in Beijing). In my experience, these gatekeepers, most of them from the Global North, did not allow newcomers to interact with members of the community in an organic way; they tended to make themselves the go-between and 'voice' of the asylum seekers in Beijing. This was one of the reasons why it was important to adapt my research method to include volunteer work, observation and listening, because it allowed me to be less of a threat.

My identity as a woman led to challenges in Guangzhou, where most of the migrants in the community are male. To ensure my safety, I conducted my research in public spaces with more than one participant at any given time. In Beijing, I found that my gender had little impact on my research methods or my access to the community. Furthermore, my identity as a Nigerian enabled me to reach out to networks in both Beijing and Guangzhou; however, it was only beneficial to me in Guangzhou, where there is a large community of Nigerians. In Beijing, people were less willing to share their experiences with me as an outsider to their social or cultural circles. As a foreign student, I had access to places that most undocumented and asylum-seeking African migrants did not. For example, I had a level of access to the UNHCR and IOM, although when I originally approached the UNHCR, I was thought to be an asylum seeker, which made it difficult to find someone to talk to directly, until I told a security guard that I had an appointment to meet a specific UNHCR member of staff.

II. A BRIEF CONTEXT FOR THE NIGERIAN CASE STUDY

Nigeria as a state is a colonial creation; its colonial encounter began with the arrival of Portuguese and Spanish explorers in the sixteenth century in Lagos and Calabar. This trade-related interaction gave way to the practice of the slave trade, with the ports of Calabar, Bight of Biafra and Lagos becoming slaving ports. It is estimated that many enslaved people came from what is now Nigeria to feed Europe's need for free labour in Europe, America and other colonies.

When the slave trade was abolished in 1807 in Britain, there was a drive for 'legitimate trade' as an alternative. Legitimate trade created the need for European traders to establish stations and depots, and gradually this metamorphosed into the need to have a consul in the region to protect European interests and investments from the 1840s. Trading companies began to grow in power – particularly the Royal Niger Company, whose trading activities controlled the areas around the Rivers Niger and Benue, an influence that grew in parallel with the activities of Christian missionaries in the area. In 1884, after the Berlin Conference, Britain announced an 'Oil Rivers Protectorate' consisting of Calabar and the Niger Delta, and aimed to regulate trade in the area, incorporating the Royal Niger Company. Britain signed treaties of protection with local chiefs and kings, including the King of Old Calabar. In 1894, the protectorate expanded to Lagos and as far as Lokoja in the north.[38] In the 1900s, Britain appointed Lord Lugard as a High Commissioner and the treaties of 'protection' that were signed between traditional rulers and the British crown transformed to

[38] See JR Bassey, 'Anglo-German Treaty of 1913 and its Influence on World Court Decision in the Nigeria v. Cameroon Case Concerning Bakassi' (2014) 6(11) *International Journal of Current Research* 9832.

indirect rule (through the Fulani Emirs of the Sokoto Caliphate in the north and chiefs in the south). The unification of the Southern and Northern Protectorates took place in 1914 and Nigeria came into existence. In 1920, parts of German Cameroon were handed to Britain and also became part of the colony.

Between 1914 and 1960, the British administered the amalgamated protectorates indirectly, through the traditional rulers in the different regions, a colonial civil service and middlemen like the Royal Niger Company. Even though Nigeria was unified, its regions were only loosely integrated and remained distinct regional administrations of the east, mid-west, west and north. Nationalism began to rise in the western, mid-western and eastern regions, inspired by pan-African activism and the Civil Rights Movement in America in response to the failures and destructiveness of colonialism. The western, mid-western and eastern push against colonialism was not based on a Nigerian national identity, but on regional and ethnic consciousness in those regions, as well as a desire to be self-governed. By 1957, these three regions were self-governed and by 1959, the northern region followed suit. This led to a push for independence that culminated in 1960. However, ethnic, and regional identity had already taken root and created obstacles to a strong national identity. As a result of the arbitrary nature of Nigeria's borders and national identity, as opposed to ethnic identity, there are tensions between borders and identity that continue to resonate today. Majority groups like the Igbo, Hausa and Yoruba have often been at odds (leading to the Civil War in the 1970s); these tensions have created hierarchies and exclusions within the Nigerian system that impact minorities. This is the background that frames the Bakassi Peninsula dispute and the experience of Bakassi migrants in Nigeria at the same time.

This colonial-induced fragmentation created a constant struggle between identity, nationality and borders. Nigeria is the most economically powerful country in the African continent, but like China, it has numerous internal inequalities that shape its laws and policies and its self-perception at an international level. These characteristics make it a valuable case study on TWAIL; the study of Nigeria provides insights into the impact of contemporary international legal decisions on indigenous peoples and raises questions about the space they occupy in international law. It is a special case of the understudied impact of international law on thousands of indigenous people and in my view it should be a part of international legal discourse. It is important to analyse the experiences of Bakassi migrants, how they encounter the law and the state, and what this signifies for the future.

A. Geographical Location, Background and Description of Subjects in Nigeria

Bakassi is a peninsula off the Gulf of Guinea, between Calabar and Rio Del Rey, with very fertile fishing grounds and large oil deposits. Bakassi refugees represent an emerging narrative in migration in the region shaped by international law and their study can be contrasted with that of the more established communities in China.

In pre-colonial times, Bakassi was part of the Kingdom of Old Calabar. It was a cultural melting pot of different peoples and after centuries of migration and settlement, it became an ancestral land for its inhabitants. According to EE Alobo et al, there are two origins of the word 'Bakassi'. One of these is from the Efiks of Calabar, which derives Bakassi from the name of the first settler in the Peninsula 'Akai Abasi Eke' who was from Obutong in Calabar.[39] This account suggests that the name was distorted/anglicised over time by foreign sailors who came to refer to the peninsula as 'Bakassi'. The second account comes from the Mbo tribe in Southern Nigeria, in which 'bakkasi' means to 'go early and arrive' in reference to the long distance between the Peninsula and Mbo that the Mbo people crossed in order to fish and trade.[40] In both definitions, the one constant is the importance linking migration to and from Nigerian communities. Cameroon had no pre-colonial cultural, religious, ethnic or linguistic ties to the inhabitants of the Peninsula. It is for this reason that Cameroon's claim to the territory was reliant on treaties between colonial powers designating and/or sharing control over the Peninsula when a territorial dispute arose after Nigerian and Cameroonian independence in the 1960s.[41] Bakassi as a colonial territory was shifted between Britain, Germany and later France through colonial agreements. Britain signed a treaty of protection with the Old Kingdom of Calabar in 1884 (during the Scramble and Partition of Africa). It was also a part of the Oil Rivers Protectorate. During this period, there were a series of Anglo-German treaties (in 1885, 1906 and 1913) as Germany (which had acquired neighbouring Cameroon) needed access to the area for shrimping and Britain needed access to the sea from Calabar. In addition, Britain and Germany needed to delimit the boundaries of their colonies in order to avoid disputes and to stop the territorial expansion of both parties.

The 1913 Treaty placed Bakassi under German control. When Germany lost its territories in West Africa to Britain and France following the Treaty of Versailles in 1919, the Anglo-French treaty changed the ownership of Bakassi again. In 1919, the Anglo-French Agreement delimited territories between the two states. In 1930, this changed with another agreement that placed Bakassi within the 'British Cameroons'. After the Second World War, this changed again when North and South Cameroon were placed under the trusteeship of the newly established UN. This shifted the Peninsula back to the 1913 agreement – in South Cameroon, which was now under French control. All these agreements were made without the consent of the King of Old Calabar (Obong) or the indigenous people.

[39] See EE Alobo et al, 'The ICJ's Decision on Bakassi Peninsula in Retrospect: A True Evaluation of the History, Issues and Critique of the Judgement' (2016) 6(10) *International Journal of Humanities and Social Sciences* 108.

[40] ibid.

[41] ibid.

These numerous changes created the ambiguous nature of the ownership of the Bakassi Peninsula following the decolonisation of Nigeria and Cameroon in 1960. There were territorial disputes for many decades between the two independent states due to this lack of clarity. This conflict led both countries to present a case before the International Court of Justice (ICJ) in 1994. Cameroon's main claims were that the sovereignty over the Peninsula of Bakassi was Cameroonian by virtue of international law, that the Peninsula was an integral part of the territory of Cameroon and that Nigeria was violating the principle of respect for frontiers inherited from colonisation (*uti possidetis juris*).[42] Nigeria, on the other hand, claimed that sovereignty over the Peninsula was vested in Nigeria based on the pre-colonial jurisdiction of the Kingdom of Old Calabar (which was now under Nigerian jurisdiction) over the Peninsula.[43] In 2002, a judgment was made by the ICJ giving the Bakassi territory to Cameroon and rejecting Nigeria's claims of historical and cultural ties, along with the historical jurisdiction of the Kingship of Old Calabar, with 13 judges in favour of the judgment and three judges against.[44] One of the dissenting opinions from Judge Abdul Koroma focused on the significance of the pre-colonial jurisdiction of the Kingdom of Old Calabar and the fact that the treaty of protection between Great Britain and the King of Old Calabar was what it was – a treaty to protect the citizens of the kingdom and not to steal their territory from them. Therefore, basing the judgment on the illegal transfer of the territory between Great Britain, Germany and France, without the consent of the kings and chiefs of Old Calabar was a breach of the principle of *pacta sunt servanda*.[45]

The impact of this decision saw Cameroon claim ownership of the Peninsula based on the 1913 Treaty with reference to the *uti posseditis* principle. Cameroon then gave an ultimatum to the inhabitants of the Peninsula to either naturalise as Cameroonians and pay for residence permits or face eviction; those who refused to nationalise or were unable to obtain residence permits for different reasons were forced to leave. This displacement led many Bakassi people to become either resident permit-holders or undocumented migrants in Cameroon, or to migrate to Nigeria and settle in a refugee camp in Cross River State, where they have been since 2012.

A coalition of the UN, Cameroon, Nigeria and other stakeholders established the Cameroon-Nigeria Mixed Commission in 2004, which in 2006 brokered the Greentree Agreement (GA), the formal treaty that settled the longstanding conflict between both nations as to the ownership of the Bakassi Peninsula, ceding the territory to Cameroon.[46] It also provided guidelines for

[42] *Land and Maritime Boundary between Cameroon and Nigeria, Cameroon, and Equatorial Guinea (Intervening) v Nigeria*, Judgment, Merits [2002] ICJ Rep 303, ICGJ 63 (ICJ 2002), para 25.

[43] ibid at paras 194 and 201.

[44] ibid at para 325 III(B).

[45] See ibid, Dissenting Opinion of Judge Koroma, Judgment of 10 October 2002 at para 15.

[46] See Centre for Treaties of the Federal Republic of Nigeria, 'Greentree Agreement between Nigeria and Cameroon', 12 June 2006, http://lawnigeria.com/TREATIES/BAKASSI-PENINSULAR-THE-GREENTREE-AGREEMENT-BETWEEN-CAMEROON-AND-NIGERIA.html.

how the Bakassi people and their lands should be treated under the administration of Cameroon. As a result, while the Agreement gives rights to Cameroon, it also creates obligations for Cameroon towards the Bakassi people.

Article 3 of the GA holds that Cameroon will not force the Bakassi people to change their nationality, culture, language or beliefs. It affirms that they have a right to continue fishing and to practise agriculture on the Peninsula, and that their properties and customary land rights are to be protected. It also stipulates that Cameroon should not levy taxes in a discriminatory manner on the inhabitants of the zone, and that the Cameroonian government is responsible for protecting the lives of the Bakassi people from harm and harassment.[47] However, due to the failure of Cameroon to adhere to the obligations of the agreement, the persecution of Bakassi Peninsula residents continued, leading to mass migration out of the Peninsula and into Nigeria between 2008 and 2013.[48] There are currently two refugee camps close to the Cameroonian border in Ikang and Akwa Ikot Edem in Cross River State, which have become refugee communities in those spaces. The number of Bakassi people who remained in Cameroon is unknown, although there are estimates of about 300,000.[49] The exact number of those who left the Peninsula is also unknown, with estimates of between 10,000 and 15,000 refugees originally in the camps in Ikang and Akwa Ikot Edem. My research aimed to study the experiences and narratives of the Bakassi refugee community and their encounters with the law and the state within Nigeria.

There is also a socio-economic dimension to the loss of the Peninsula, as the Bakassi people practised fishing as the dominant occupation for many centuries. With the loss of the Peninsula, they have not been able to continue their livelihood in Nigeria. This phenomenon is a major part of the impact of the post-ICJ decision on the Bakassi people. The effect of this case decision is largely perceived not as an issue of international magnitude in international law, but rather as one of internal proportions. Displaced persons from Bakassi fall out of the narrative, even though they are international law's own refugees. This is reflective of the trend in international law to relegate South-South migrations as outside of the discourse and recalls Annelise Riles' argument[50] about the impact of perspective and scale on the law: the Bakassi fall outside the narrative of international law because the perspective of the ICJ does not go beyond global (ie, international boundary disputes) and national (ie, disputes

[47] ibid at art 3.

[48] See WikiLeaks, 'New Wave of Nigerians Return from Bakassi', (2009) at https://wikileaks.org/plusd/cables/09LAGOS465_a.html. See also Hindatu Maigari Yerima and DS Ranjit Singh, 'The Bakassi Dispute: People's Dynamics and the Rise of Militancy' (2017) 22(1) *IOSR Journal of Humanities and Social Science* 67.

[49] See 'Bakassi Residents to Pay Tax under Cameroon Sovereignty', *BBC News Africa*, 15 August 2013, www.bbc.co.uk/news/world-africa-23710733.

[50] A Riles, 'A View from the International Plane: Perspective and Scale in the Architecture of Colonial International Law' (1995) VI(1) *Law and Critique* 39.

about territory between states).[51] There was therefore a gap in a perspective from below that would have considered or included Bakassi narratives in the decision of the ICJ.

The contemporary displacement and migrations of Bakassi people following the impact of the ICJ decision is a missing aspect in legal research. Beyond exposing the narrative of the Bakassi people, using TWAIL as a methodology draws on the negative impact that international law can have when it ignores historical and cultural contexts, and imposes colonial rules and norms on people in developing countries. Using international rules and regulations strictly created a situation that led to the injustices against Bakassi people in the first place. In other words, TWAIL as a methodology in my research provides a means of escaping the trap of the rules and finding evidence of the truth in the real experiences of marginalised people.

i. Research Execution

a. Summary of the Interviews Conducted

I interviewed refugees in two camps: Akwa Ikot Edem and Ikang in Cross River State. In 2016, the camp in Akwa Ikot Edem was said to be home to over 3,000 refugees, while the camp in Ikang was said to have over 6,000 inhabitants. The numbers of people in the camp had dwindled over time because people were either returning to Cameroon to fish in the Peninsula or migrating to other parts of Nigeria for better opportunities. According to the camp leader in Ikang, many people had also passed away due to insecurity, health challenges and hunger.

I interviewed a total of 12 refugees in Akwa Ikot Edem and the people I spoke to were the leaders in the camp as well as the elderly. Young people were not available because most of them were hired hands in farms where they worked all day. For the sake of my security, I was advised to visit the camp only during the day. In Ikang, I listened to the narratives of over 30 refugees. I also interviewed National Emergency Management Agency representatives, the state Emergency Management Agency representatives, state and local leaders, academics at the University of Calabar, NGOs, the National Human Rights Council, security operatives and government officials in the state.

b. Research Methods Used

I used group observation, interviews, listening, watching and social interaction as research methods. All my interviews were conducted face to face. I utilised observations and listening sessions in my research in the refugee settlements, particularly because of the size of the groups I encountered.

[51] ibid at 48–49.

On most occasions when I came into the camps, all the people present at that time would come out to meet me because visits from outsiders were very rare. The camp inhabitants felt I might be from the government or the UN. Initially, there was hostility towards me in Ikang when I was perceived to be a government official, but people let down their guard when I introduced myself as a student who wanted to learn about their experiences in Nigeria. They were very willing to talk to researchers as they felt that it was a way of spreading their message to the public and the international community. It was impossible to meet with people individually on Ikang due to the high level of insecurity there. As a result, I was only able to conduct group listening in Ikang. The Akwa Ikot Edem camp was smaller, so I was able to speak directly to individuals and listen to their unique narratives. All my interactions with participants were face to face and all the people I met were willing to talk to me and share their stories and experiences.

c. Field Report

I arrived in Nigeria on 16 March 2016. I travelled to the Akwa Ikot Edem refugee camp in April, where I had the opportunity to speak to the chief of the community of refugees, the camp coordinators and an NGO representative. I was given a tour of the camp as well. The people at the Akwa Ikot Edem camp were forced to flee from Cameroon in 2013 due to the persecution they faced there. The camp coordinator claimed that the camp originally had 5300 people, but the numbers had dwindled due to deaths and the dispersal of the youth. Most of the people I met at the camp were the elderly or children. Young people were nowhere in sight, as most of them had gone to the city to look for jobs or were working as hired hands in farms in the community. The conditions in the settlement were very poor; the camp was a block of classrooms that a school had donated to the refugees. The camp coordinator said that they might be forced out of the classrooms because the school needed the blocks back. The chief described the experiences in Cameroon leading to their migration to Nigeria. Here are some of the points he raised:

- The Bakassi were not part of the legal process leading to the ceding of the Peninsula and the legal team from Nigeria that represented them included no Bakassi person. They were not consulted before, during or after the process.
- The Cameroonian gendarmes had been abusing Bakassi people since 2002 when the ICJ decision was made. Their properties were seized and destroyed by gendarmes. They were forced to either change their nationality/language or leave Cameroon. Many Bakassi people died as a result of the brutality of the gendarmes.
- There were no preparations made for Bakassi returnees in Nigeria and this had led to the destitution of the Bakassi people.

- Before the dispute between Nigeria and Cameroon, the Bakassi people did not need to identify as either Cameroonian or Nigerian. They did not consider themselves as Cameroonian and originally, their nationality was of no importance to them, but after the treatment they received in Cameroon, they chose Nigeria.
- There had been a lot of political manipulation of Bakassi leaders and people by different interest groups – as a result, they had a high level of mistrust towards everyone.
- Nigeria had not protected the rights of members of the Bakassi community; instead, the UNHCR and other NGOs had filled the gap.
- Cameroon did not abide by the Greentree Agreement, which gave rights to Bakassi people who lived on the Peninsula.

I interviewed 12 refugees and two NGO workers at Akwa Ikot Edem. I also interviewed representatives from the National Emergency Management Agency (NEMA) and the State Emergency Management Agency (SEMA). I got a sense of the Nigerian response to Bakassi people on and after arrival from them. Below are some of the key discoveries I made following my interview with the NEMA and SEMA representatives:

- The first set of refugees who arrived in Nigeria received a lot of media coverage and the state government provided a 'permanent camp' for them, as well as feeding them. This support did not last because the population of refugees kept increasing.
- There was an intense ongoing conflict between the refugees and their host communities. The refugees had no land, so they were forced to rent land to farm in order to eat.
- The Bakassi people practised fishing for a living but in Nigeria, they had lost their livelihood as they migrated without their fishing tools into communities that practised farming.
- The Bakassi community did not have Nigerian identification documents and were therefore unable to vote, participate in governance, apply for driving licences, register businesses, receive government allocations etc. It was also difficult for children to go to school without documentation. This meant that in Nigeria, they were the same as undocumented migrants, even though the state was aware of their presence and accepted them into Nigeria.
- Because of their status in Nigeria, they were forced to rely on militants for justice, security and even financial support. The militants in the region offered them protection, but at the same time, their presence is was source of insecurity. There was a high rate of rape and teenage pregnancy, especially in Ikang.

In May 2016, I went to the second camp in Ikang. I listened to the narratives of over 30 refugees, observing without asking many questions. I chose this method because of the atmosphere in the camp; those there were more hostile to outsiders than the people I met in the first camp. The Bakassi at Ikang had been refugees in Nigeria since 2009, when about 6,000 of them fled from Cameroon to Nigeria. The effect of their status in Nigeria was more extreme. The camp was unsafe, even for the refugees who stayed there. I spoke to the leader and elders of the camp. They echoed the same things I heard in Akwa Ikot Edem, but in this case, there was an element of insecurity caused by years of exclusion and extreme poverty.

Akwa Ikot Edem, being a new camp, received support from NGOs, the UNHCR etc, which the camp in Ikang did not. In this camp there was a strong rejection of local identity and Nigerian nationalism. I believe that some of the refugees I spoke to had joined the militants. Their leader stated that the community would be taking extreme measures to get the attention of the international community in the coming months. After my visit, I discovered that several refugees returned to Cameroon and accepted the terms of the Cameroonian government due to the harsh conditions in Nigeria. I could not return to Ikang after this meeting – the security in the area collapsed a few days later and the local government area was overrun by militant activities.

In June 2016, I met with academics who had interacted at different levels with the refugees as well as with security operatives to discuss the dimension of insecurity in the refugee camps. I interviewed three academics and four security operatives. Lastly, I was able to interview the local government chairwoman and everyone on her team. This gave me an insight into what was going on at the local level in terms of law and policy directed towards Bakassi refugees. One of the discoveries I made during the local government interview was that the Peninsula was a source of petroleum to the Nigerian government and, at that time, the benefits accrued to Cross River State and none went to the inhabitants of the Peninsula. When Bakassi residents fled to Nigeria, they were also denied state benefits because they had lost their 'oil-production' status. They were exploited multiple times by the state and this has an impact on how they perceived themselves in Nigeria. In July and August, I interviewed a representative from the NEMA regional office and the headquarters in the capital, Abuja.

d. Left in the Dark by International Law: A Snapshot of Chief A

Chief A grew up in the Bakassi Peninsula, as did his ancestors. He knew he had ties to Nigeria because his ancestors had gone back and forth between Nigeria and the Peninsula for centuries to sell their fish and crayfish, and some of them had settled in Nigeria. After his father passed away, he became the leader of his clan. He said that his people were completely left in the dark when the territorial dispute began between Nigeria and Cameroon and, one day, they were told that their ancestral lands now belonged to Cameroon. According to him, when this happened, the Cameroonian gendarmes came into the region and started destroying property, making arrests and implementing fines to force people to obtain residence permits, change their nationality or stop fishing. There were a couple of skirmishes between the youth and the gendarmes which led to the death of many. Chief A decided to lead his community out of the Peninsula to Nigeria after he had heard of the initial support that Nigeria had offered to the refugees fleeing Cameroon. With the help of unnamed supporters, they were able to leave the Peninsula and arrived in Cross River State, where their supporters were able to convince the local school to offer a classroom block to them temporarily. He spent most of his days trying to get support from the UNHCR to enable the refugees to get jobs and improve their skills in their new environment. He believed that the solution to the problem is for the government to give the Bakassi community land they can call their own in Nigeria so that they can live as a community together and continue their customs and their way of life.

B. Problems Encountered in Nigeria

i) *Politics*: politics was a huge impediment to getting into the space to understand what was going on. National-level politicians refused to grant me access to the camps after they learned that I had gone there to conduct interviews. In addition, local-level politicians attempted to change the narratives of the refugees. They insisted I conduct interviews with them as well, but in their interviews, they attempted to negate many of the claims that the refugees made. In order to overcome the political challenges, I interviewed all parties so as to give them a sense that their voices were being heard.

ii) *Mistrust*: as stated earlier, the refugees had a high level of mistrust for outsiders, particularly government officials. Apparently, many researchers came every year, in addition to UN officials and other players, and they made promises to the refugees that were unfulfilled. I was an outsider in both Ikang and Akwa Ikot Edem. I noticed that the people spoke as a group through leaders and representatives in the camp; as a result, I had more group interactions than individual conversations. I attributed this to the nature of the camp: as a community, the refugees usually have spokespersons who represent their interests to government officials, international organisations and NGOs. I overcame this distrust by going through channels that the refugees recognised. For example, at Akwa Ikot Edem, I went as part of the team of the NGO that provided education-related support. At Ikang, I went through the local security team of the police force, after interviewing the Commissioner of Police and other officers about the security aspects of the case. The team put me in contact with the High Chief of the community who took me to the camp. I was also very explicit about my identity and the aims of my research from the beginning of every interaction in the camps. I was treated as an outsider in both camps and in all the interviews I conducted and all the interactions I had throughout the research. This was surprising at first, but I was made to understand that the Bakassi in the camps did not feel that they were part of Nigeria and, as a result, they guarded their spaces fiercely from outsiders. In addition, I was treated as an outsider when I encountered local government and federal government officials, security operatives etc, probably because of my role as a researcher who was looking to learn more about Bakassi people in Nigeria. This perception of my identity did not matter as in the end, I was able to reach my core participants – the members of the Bakassi community – without restrictions or problems.

iii) *Financial responsibilities*: during most of the interviews, several people I interacted with assumed that I had funds to share with the refugees. In Ikang, I was compelled to give some of the money I had with me to the leaders of the camp in order to show my support. This was one such instance where I had financial responsibilities as a result of entering their space.

The field research in Nigeria and China changed my understanding and perspective on the case studies; many of the things I thought I would focus on changed based on the facts and experiences I encountered. As a result, I documented recurring themes and findings I noticed, which ultimately shaped the direction taken by this book.

III. SOME KEY FINDINGS AND THEMES FROM THE RESEARCH IN CHINA AND NIGERIA

Identity (international, state, regional, local and individual) is a key factor in both case studies. The refugee or undocumented migrant is seen and sees herself or himself in different ways. For example, in Cameroon, the Bakassi people are seen as Nigerians who must buy resident permits to stay. In Nigeria, they are seen as Nigerians, but are not accorded citizenship privileges by the Nigerian government. The visibility and invisibility of migrants at different levels was a recurring theme in both case studies. The state simultaneously acknowledges and denies the existence of these groups in its approaches towards them at the international, regional and local levels.

In both cases, refugees and migrants encounter the law in fascinating ways, like the establishment of their own alternatives to formal justice and laws, the ways in which they perceive themselves in relation to the law of the state, their consciousness of the law and how they mobilise to protect their interests.

Alternative justice, health, education, employment and political systems were formed in both case studies as a way of dealing with the lack of engagement of the state in the running of these communities. Finally, certain figures are taking advantage of the undocumented status of refugees and using it for their benefit. In China, some Chinese people exploit the undocumented status of migrants to make gains in business while people smugglers take advantage of the need for mobility within China. In Nigeria, local-level, state-level and national-level politicians manipulate the narratives of the refugees and prevent them from receiving the assistance they need.

In terms of the limitations on the case studies, I was not able to gain access to some levels or types of information. For example, I was unable to interview members of the Bakassi community who never left Cameroon or those who left Nigeria and returned to the Peninsula. This was mainly due to security, time and funding limitations. This is a gap that future research can fill; there is room for more study on the experiences of Bakassi people and their encounters with law in Cameroon, which could be compared with their experiences in Nigeria. In China, I was unable to interview a larger number of asylum seekers in Beijing due to limited access to members of the community and the overall unsafe atmosphere for asylum seekers. My positionality as an African female researcher in China also limited how far I could push my interview questions, who I could access, how long I could spend in certain spaces and how often I could interact with certain people. For example, I did not ask research questions on the experiences of undocumented migrants in prisons because people were not comfortable sharing these details with me.[52] I allowed people to reveal what they were comfortable with and sometimes this meant that the conversation focused on the business, health and other aspects of migrant experiences which were linked to the law indirectly. It was difficult to obtain a Chinese visa with my Nigerian passport. The intricacy and duration of the visa process initially posed a threat to my research plan. In addition, international organisations, NGOs and academia are limited in the access they can provide for individual researchers, so I relied on the members of the community for all the interviews I conducted, which I perceive to have been an advantage – even though the trust-building and research process took longer, it was more organic. I had better access and spent more time in Guangzhou, and this is where I conducted a higher number of interviews. As a result, Beijing remains an area where research can further develop.

In China, all my interviews in Guangzhou and Beijing were conducted in English; however, my intermediate comprehension of Mandarin helped me

[52] In ch 4, I will discuss the context of racial profiling and the imprisonment of undocumented migrants in the migrant community in more detail as part of discussing intersectionality within the community. Imprisonment is a very sensitive issue and, as such, it was not ethical to document related narratives and experiences while I was in China. See Guangzhi Huang, 'Policing Blacks in Guangzhou: How Public Security Constructs Africans as Sanfei' (2018) 45(2) *Modern China* 171.

understand the use of certain terminologies (for example, *san fei*, which is a term used to describe migrants who enter, work or live in China without documents, but refers specifically to Africans) in my interaction with Chinese migration law scholars and Chinese community organisations that work with migrants. In Nigeria, all my interviews at the camp were conducted in Pidgin English, which I speak with proficiency. Being able to communicate in Pidgin enabled me to understand and interact with my respondents easily, as I have no comprehension of the local languages in Cross River State (eg, the Efik language).

In the following chapters, I will focus on the case studies and will provide an analysis based on the evidence from research on China and Nigeria. Chapter 3 focuses on discussions on rights and responsibilities towards non-nationals engaging in different forms of migration in the Global South. I will begin by looking at debates on the tension between sovereignty and human rights in order to understand the literature on rights and responsibilities. I will then analyse works that discuss the idea of certain rights as ideals or duties and what this means for my research. I will use my case studies to look at evidence of Third World approaches to international, regional and national responsibilities towards undocumented, asylum-seeking migrants and refugees in the Global South.

4

Where Migrants Stand in South-South Migrating Communities

A Look at China and Nigeria

HANNAH ARENDT BELIEVED that the main adversity of the rightless is a lack of belonging.[1] She refers here to nationality and its impact on access to the benefits of human rights globally. Refugee, asylum-seeking and undocumented migrants are excluded from the full range of benefits that come with citizenship because their migrant status is not favourable to the receiving country.[2] This chapter discusses the ways in which states disengage from human rights and moral obligations when dealing with undocumented, asylum-seeking and displaced migrants. What are those specific characteristics that are shaping how states view or implement their responsibilities towards selected communities in Nigeria and China due to their migrant status? How does this affect the way in which migrant communities experience international law at the local level? Using the case studies in Nigeria and China as contextual evidence, this chapter analyses how this attitude affects the experience these groups and individuals have with international law, including refugee and human rights laws, as well as international rules and norms.

As was discussed in Chapter 2, to centre the Global South and to test TWAIL beyond theory, Eslava and Pahuja argue that interrogations of international law must include the impact of the law in the daily lives of people in the Global South. Understanding the law of the everyday in this context means analysing how migrant communities are coming to terms with the impact of international law and norms.[3] This chapter uses empirical evidence in the case studies and legal ethnographies to draw both critique and meaning from South-South migrations about the law and the impact of the hierarchies between citizens and migrants (both documented and undocumented), in addition to between nationals and stateless persons or refugees. As a result, it is infused with narratives

[1] Hannah Arendt, *The Origins of Totalitarianism* (New York, Schocken Books, 2004) at 292.

[2] Citizenship determines whether an individual or community participates in a society and enjoys a wide range of rights.

[3] Luis Eslava and Sundhya Pahuja, 'Between Resistance and Reform: TWAIL and the Universality of International Law' (2011) 3 *Trade Law and Development* 103 at 126.

from below, as well as a juxtaposition of national, regional and international legal realities. In this chapter, I also reflect on the gap between obligations to non-citizens, when their home state fails to protect them because diplomatic protection is not possible.

I. SOVEREIGNTY AND HUMAN RIGHTS: SYMBIOSIS OR ANTINOMY?

There has been extensive discussion on the tension between sovereignty[4] and human rights,[5] and how this shapes the effective implementation of international human rights rules and norms.[6] 'Sovereignty' as employed in this chapter is drawn from Anne Peters, who defines it in terms of responsibilities and obligations. Peters defines sovereignty as 'a legal status from which certain legal consequences, in particular rights, but also obligations, are derived'.[7] Given this definition, what is the relationship between sovereignty, human rights and the responsibility to protect human rights? The obligations owed are increasingly acknowledged as being external (ie, towards other states, not other citizens) and internal (ie, towards citizens via human rights law and doctrines such as the Responsibility to Protect).

Thomas Nagel argues that in order for human rights to be protected, they need the structure, resources and the power of the state, and, simultaneously, the power of the state severely limits human rights.[8] Nagel states that justice is

[4] Anne Peters, 'Humanity as the A and Ω of Sovereignty' (2009) 20(3) *European Journal of International Law* 515.

[5] Allan Buchanan and David Golove defined human rights as moral entitlements that accrue to all persons, regardless of whether they are members of a particular polity or race. This definition is important because undocumented, refugee and asylum-seeking migrants are outside the comfort of citizenship and nationality, which is often the benchmark states use to judge the apportioning and protection of a full range of rights. Golove and Buchanan note that human rights are entitlements for all person, regardless of whether they belong to the state or not. This definition of human rights automatically attaches itself to refugee, asylum-seeking and undocumented migrations, bringing them into the discussion on the tension between sovereignty and human rights, rather than the traditional focus on issues like humanitarian non-intervention as the tension between sovereignty and human rights, which often shift the focus to the state rather than to the individuals whose rights are at stake. See Allan Buchanan, and David Golove, 'Philosophy of International Law' in Jules Coleman and Scott Shapiro (eds), *The Oxford Handbook of Jurisprudence and Philosophy of Law* (Oxford, Oxford University Press, 2002) at 888.

[6] For example, see Jack Donnelly, 'International Human Rights: A Regime Analysis' (1986) 40 *International Organization* 599; Alexander Volsky, 'Reconciling Human Rights and State Sovereignty, Justice and the Law in Humanitarian Interventions' (2007) 3(1) *International Public Policy Review* 44; Michael W Reisman, 'Sovereignty and Human Rights in Contemporary International Law' (1990) Faculty Scholarship Series, Paper 872. Reisman argues that international law still protects sovereignty; however, it is the sovereignty of the individual that the law protects, not the sovereignty of the state. For him, one cannot speak about state sovereignty without speaking about human rights within that state. In other words, human rights and sovereignty are inextricably linked.

[7] Peters (n 4).

[8] See Thomas Nagel, 'The Problem of Global Justice' (2005) 33 *Philosophy and Public Affairs* 113 at 116.

only possible if a sovereign state is an enabler because justice requires the collective coordinated conduct of people. There are tensions between sovereignty and human rights, given that sovereignty is based on borders and citizenship, while human rights are borderless and applies to all human beings regardless of their status. Yet states are entrusted with the responsibility of protecting the human rights of people within their borders. This argument holds that state sovereignty is both a tool for and an obstacle to the protection of human rights, supporting the idea of a co-dependent nature between sovereignty and human rights. In order for human rights to be protected and promoted, states need to implement and uphold them, whereas the state needs human rights to be viewed favourably in the international community.[9] Arendt's perspective is similar, holding that even though the notion of human rights are tied to sovereignty, states choose to control access to human rights by denying access to nationality and citizenship through determining the admission and expulsion of migrants.[10] Here, one of the tensions between sovereignty and human rights is tied to citizenship and the admission and/or expulsion of migrants in the state; it is not just a matter of non-intervention or humanitarian intervention.[11]

Tomasz Widlak makes a different argument that in the international system, both states and human rights are essential: states represent order, whereas human rights represent justice.[12] Widlak argues that in fact, sovereignty and human rights are symbiotic rather than in conflict; sovereignty is crucial in the realisation of justice and justice is fundamental in the pursuit of all other values in the international community. Widlak notes that contemporarily, human rights is making sovereignty conditional, causing a 'vegetation' of sovereignty because states are under constant scrutiny in terms of their human rights records.[13] He agrees that there is a co-dependent relationship between human rights and sovereignty, not an antinomy.[14] Non-citizenship and applicable human rights protections remain a grey area of law, doctrines such as the responsibility to

[9] Kiyoteru and Wotipka also argue that socialisation in the international community is what propelled states to ratify human rights instruments, even though they interfere in the internal affairs of states. See Tsustui Kiyoteru and Christine Min Wotipka, 'Global Human Rights and State Sovereignty: State Ratification of International Human Rights Treaties, 1965–2001' (2008) 23(4) *Sociological Forum* 724.

[10] Arendt (n 1) 370.

[11] See International Commission on Intervention and State Sovereignty (ICISS), *The Responsibility to Protect* (Ottawa, International Development Centre, 2001). This chapter focuses sovereignty on human rights as it affects migrations, rather than non-intervention or humanitarian intervention, which have been the themes associated with sovereignty and human rights discussions.

[12] Tomasz H Widlak, 'Sovereignty vs Human Rights: A Case of the Relation between Order and Justice in International Society' (2009) 3 *Journal of Philosophy of International Law* 7 at 18.

[13] ibid at 19.

[14] For example, Benvenesti and Harel posit that there is a persistent tension and conflict between human rights and sovereignty, and this tension is necessary for the protection of individual freedoms: Eyal Benvenisti and Alon Harel, 'Embracing the Tension between National and International Human Rights Law: The Case for Discordant Parity' (2017) 15(1) *International Journal of Constitutional Law* 36.

protect have supposedly solved the human rights versus sovereignty conflict and have re-imagined sovereignty in an era of established human rights obligations for states, my research shows that this comes at the expense of non-citizens.[15] Peters argues that state sovereignty only exists because of humanity. In her words, sovereignty is not only 'limited by human rights, but is from the outset determined and qualified by humanity, and has a legal value only to the extent that it respects human rights'.[16] For her, sovereignty is responsibility in itself, because both external and internal sovereignty require justification through its functions, one of which is the protection of human rights.[17] She does not agree that sovereignty and human rights are an antinomy because sovereignty has its ultimate objective in humanity; in order to be enjoyed, human rights require a guaranteeing force or power.[18]

This idea of symbiosis as opposed to tension gives power to the impact of human rights on states and on international law, and centres the law on the protection of the individual. However, while this idea sounds good in theory, the overall picture is not so rosy. Because state sovereignty is still intrinsically linked to exclusive borders, it follows that human rights protection is affected by this exclusivity. Peters holds that the responsibility flowing from sovereignty 'exists for something (the task to be performed) and towards somebody'.[19] Peters would argue that the 'something' is to protect rights and the 'someone' is humanity. However, we cannot ignore the role that citizenship plays in limiting the responsibility of states towards 'everyone' – citizens are often considered first before foreigners and especially before undocumented, refugee and asylum-seeking migrants.

Bhupinder Chimni takes a more realist point of view and speaks of how states (particularly those in the Global North) have created barriers to the enforcement of the refugee regime they themselves created. He holds that policies like the *non-entrée* in countries like the US have taken international refugee law many steps back, influencing states in the Global South to also disregard refugee law.[20] In other words, bad behaviour is contagious in the international system. Chimni also holds that even though burden sharing is an established principle in the 1951 Refugee Convention, the intentional insulation of the Global North from other regions has resulted in a dwindling commitment to it. He states that the decline in burden sharing has also changed the attitudes of

[15] ICISS (n 11). See also JL Holzgrefe and Robert Keohane (eds), *Humanitarian Intervention: Ethical, Legal and Political Dilemmas* (Cambridge, Cambridge University Press, 2003).

[16] Peters (n 4) 514.

[17] ibid at 518.

[18] ibid at 543.

[19] ibid at 524.

[20] Bhupinder Chimni, 'Reforming the International Refugee Regime: A Dialogic Model' (2001), 14 *Journal of Refugee Studies* 151 at 155. Chimni states that, for example, Tanzania closed its borders to Rwandan refugees because of similar practices by Western countries.

African states towards refugees.[21] According to him, the solution to the barriers of enforcement of refugee law is inter-regional and intra-regional dialogue between states and the UNHCR on burden sharing, as well as the establishment of an independent refugee rights committee that will hold states accountable.[22] In contrast, the case studies in my research reveal that even when there is a dialogue on burden sharing and there are regional and national bodies that keep states accountable, the state still has to be willing to carry out recommendations to the letter by incorporating best practices into their national laws and policies. These discussions raise questions about whether Nigeria and China accept responsibility towards non-citizens like undocumented migrants, asylum seekers or refugees deriving from international, regional and national laws or policies or not, and whether they are engaging in burden sharing and dialogue in order to protect refugee rights.

II. PUSH AND PULL: RIGHTS, RESPONSIBILITIES AND MIGRANT STATUS

The debate on sovereignty and human rights has often focused on politically charged topics like non-intervention versus humanitarian intervention; however, it stretches beyond these norms into refugee law and the responsibility of states towards non-citizens, including those without status. This is because refugee law is intrinsically connected to the human rights protection of some of the most vulnerable in society. As discussed above, when it comes to the rights of migrants without status, including undocumented migrants and asylum seekers, rights and responsibilities are a grey area because of the citizenship problem. They cannot ask their home state to act on their behalf, so their capacity to invoke human rights protections (which really occurs in conversations between states, even though they are protection for individuals) is limited. Diplomatic protection does not apply to refugees because the state is usually the abuser or the place of risk.

Catherine Phuong sees the tension between sovereignty and human rights in the confusion around state responsibilities towards refugees and asylum seekers.[23] She identifies the specific responsibilities that states have towards these classes of migrants, highlighting that while there is a right to asylum in the Universal Declaration of Human Rights,[24] there is no corresponding state duty to grant asylum.[25] As a result, the right to asylum, which is customary international law, is only stated in a non-binding instrument and there is no

[21] ibid at 156 and 157.
[22] ibid at 165.
[23] Catherine Phuong, 'Identifying States' Responsibilities towards Refugees and Asylum Seekers', ESIL (2005), https://esil-sedi.eu/wp-content/uploads/2018/04/Phuong.pdf.
[24] UN General Assembly, 'Universal Declaration of Human Rights', 10 December 1948, 217 A (III) at Article 14.
[25] Phuong (n 23) 1.

obligation on states to grant asylum to refugees in legally binding instruments.[26] This creates a scenario where the human rights of refugees and asylum seekers are left to the discretion of the state to which they migrate because state sovereignty includes the control of admission. Hierarchies inevitably emerge around citizenship, politics, national interests, race and other factors when this control is left to the discretion of the state.

Apart from the principle of *non-refoulement*, which creates an obligation to ascertain the true status of migrants before removal, there is no delineation of the specific responsibilities that states should have towards refugees and asylum seekers during asylum procedures. As Phuong points out, the Refugee Convention 'does not mention asylum procedures or which state is responsible for determining whether a person is a refugee or not'.[27] In her opinion, the fact that responsibility sharing in refugee and asylum migrant protection is left to the discretion of states is a fundamental problem with the Refugee Convention. With no clarification of state responsibility towards refugees and asylum seekers, states often do not take full responsibility for the well-being and the rights of asylum seekers and refugees within their borders and those going through the asylum procedures pending durable solutions.[28] Just like Chimni, Phuong suggests identifying the general principles of responsibility sharing, which can be applied in different cases.[29]

Responsibility sharing in refugee and asylum migration protection cannot be left to the discretion of states, because states will always use the protection of their citizens as an excuse to avoid responsibility towards non-citizens. For example, the War on Terror and associated security concerns have become a way to trump the human rights of refugees and undocumented migrants through racialised discourses and legal regimes. As Chimni notes, African states are increasingly employing this stance.[30] For example, in Nigeria, global pressure to respond to the threat of Islamic extremism is shaping and leading state responses. To clarify the responsibilities states have towards refugees and asylum seekers, specific responsibilities must be included in the burden sharing and inter-/intra-regional dialogues between states and organisations, as well as in international and regional legal instruments.[31] By doing so, states can be held accountable to specific obligations at the international and regional levels.

Outside of the Refugee Convention, other international human rights instruments attempt to attribute responsibility to states towards refugees and asylum seekers. An example is the International Covenant on Economic, Social and Cultural Rights (ICESCR). The Committee on the ICESCR released a statement

[26] See Guy S Goodwin-Gill, *The Refugee in International Law* (Toronto, Oxford University Press, 983) at 121.
[27] ibid at 4.
[28] ibid at 11.
[29] ibid at 12.
[30] Chimni (n 20).
[31] ibid at 65.

on the duties of states towards refugees and migrants under the Convention in 2017.[32] The statement notes that the Convention complements the Geneva Conventions and then goes on to say that:

> All people under the jurisdiction of the State concerned should enjoy the Covenant rights: this includes asylum-seekers and refugees, as well as other migrants, even when their situation in the country is irregular.[33]

According to the Committee, refugees, asylum seekers and undocumented migrants should enjoy the rights in the Convention, including access to minimum standards of education, healthcare, access to water and food without discrimination.[34] The statement goes as far as to include the right to self-employment as one of the guarantees for refugees.[35] Self-employment is particularly important to non-documented migrants and asylum seekers because they are often discriminated against in the job market based on their status. For example, in China, all my research respondents who were undocumented were self-employed. The same was true in Bakassi. This was often linked to how discrimination restricts access to jobs for these groups of migrants due to their lack of documentation. The ICESCR statement focuses on non-discrimination as being the central responsibility of the state towards asylum seekers and refugees.[36] The statement identifies these specific rights and core obligations that states are responsible for protecting even towards undocumented migrants and non-nationals.[37] The statement reiterates that a lack of documentation does not exclude asylum seekers and refugees from the protections of the ICESCR.[38] This means that the Committee can hold states accountable for specific obligations towards undocumented migrants and non-citizens under the ICESCR. Nevertheless, the Committee recalled Article 2(3) of the Convention, which sets the exception to the principle of non-discrimination as nationality.[39] Here, citizens come first in the enjoyment of human rights protections; security discourse is used to maintain this position and trump human rights. Also, in paragraph 4 of the statement, the Committee recognises that these rights 'can only be progressively realised, to the maximum available resources of each State party'.[40] This raises confusion on responsibility again due to its vagueness. If it is the state that determines what 'maximum available

[32] Committee on Economic, Social and Cultural Rights, 'The Duties of States towards Refugees and Migrants under the International Covenant on Economic, Social and Cultural Rights', E/C.12/2017/1 (2017).

[33] ibid at para 3.

[34] ibid at para 9.

[35] ibid at para 6.

[36] ibid at para 7.

[37] ibid.

[38] ibid at paras 6 and 11.

[39] UN General Assembly, International Covenant on Economic, Social and Cultural Rights, 16 December 1966, United Nations, Treaty Series, vol 993, p 3, at art 2(3).

[40] Committee on Economic, Social and Cultural Rights (n 32) para 4.

resources' are, then responsibility remains a matter of discretion, not a duty.[41] At the same time, the statement recalled that when there are failures to meet core obligations – education, food, water and healthcare – states must prove that they used their best efforts and all the resources available to meet them. It is not clear what qualifies as proof of best efforts and maximum resources available. Unfortunately, this is again left to the discretion of the state, although the Committee can play a role in guiding standards.

Meher Talib disagrees with Phuong on the topic of state responsibilities towards asylum seekers being enshrined in the law. Instead, he argues that because the interpretation of these responsibilities is left to states, it creates an incoherence in the international refugee regime because states do not understand and implement their responsibilities uniformly.[42] This enables states to disengage from their responsibilities towards asylum seekers and refugees, and to shift the burden to others. Both the Refugee Convention and the ICESCR are clear examples of Talib's analysis in practice. Talib argues that the original intention of policy has shifted from protecting refugees to one of containment, attributing this to something he calls 'the myth of difference' in reference to Chimni's discussion on the geopolitics of refugee studies.[43] The myth of difference refers to the perceived change in the type of refugees and asylum seekers involved in contemporary migration in the late twentieth and into the twenty-first centuries, as can be observed in the switch in the number of European migrants to migrants from developing countries in the Global South who are seeking asylum in the West.[44] Talib and Chimni agree that states, particularly those in the West, have used the myth of difference to contain rather than protect forced migrants. This point of view highlights another dimension as to why the human rights of refugees and asylum seekers remain a source of tension to the internal sovereignty of states. Simply put, it is easier for states to accept and protect asylum seekers who have a shared history, culture and other characteristics with the receiving state; forced migrants from different regions are too 'other' to benefit from the largesse of the state.[45] Talib, like Phuong, traces the problem back to the failure of international legal instruments to prioritise a right to be granted asylum in favour of concerns of state sovereignty.[46] As a result, states can legitimately limit

[41] The Committee refers specifically to developing countries, which due to their economic limitations have the discretion to determine the extent to which they can guarantee the economic rights enshrined in the Convention to non-nationals: ibid at para 8.

[42] Meher Talib, 'Numbers versus Rights: State Responsibility towards Asylum Seekers and the Implications for the International Refugee Regime' (2013) 27 *Georgetown Immigration Law Journal* 405 at 405.

[43] ibid at 408.

[44] See BS Chimni, 'The Geopolitics of Refugee Studies: A View from the South' (1998) 11 *Journal of Refugee Studies* 350.

[45] I have discussed earlier how this approach shaped China's perspective on non-Chinese asylum seekers and refugees and below I will discuss how this is impacting China's attitude towards them.

[46] Talib (n 42) 410.

the rights and protections afforded to asylum seekers, when and how asylum is granted, the duration of asylum, restrictions on whether asylum seekers and refugees can work, and where they can live.

Kathleen Hossack also discusses the ambiguity of the responsibilities of states towards refugees. In her opinion, humanitarian principles are an imperfect duty, making them almost impossible to enforce, which results in them being left to the discretion of the state.[47] This opinion holds that responsibility is unenforceable because states see protection of the rights of asylum seekers and refugees as a voluntary duty of virtue rather than a necessary duty of justice. This is particularly true for countries like China and many developing countries where rights are perceived as an aspiration as opposed to a concrete and enforceable judicial duty[48] Hossack uses Immanuel Kant's philosophy of distinguishing between the perfect duty of justice and the imperfect duty of virtue[49] to understand the problem of responsibility towards refugees, asylum seekers and undocumented migrants.[50]

As discussed above, international law is ambiguous about state responsibility for protecting refugees, asylum seekers and undocumented migrants. This is because the protection of refugees is seen as secondary to the protection of citizens. Looking through the lens of Kant, the protection of non-nationals is an imperfect duty of virtue. This limits the enforceability of refugee law and creates circumstances where certain obligations are ideals rather than duties rooted in customary international law. If the protection of refugees, asylum seekers and undocumented migrants is a duty of virtue, this means that these groups of migrants will be protected only if the state is 'virtuous' enough to do so. It excuses the irresponsibility of states with regard to human rights norms (whatever those norms are) and enables states to prioritise certain obligations over others and to discriminate against certain categories or types of migrants.

Hossack believes that the problem of assigning responsibility for refugees is a result of the conflict between the moral claims of refugees and the moral claims of citizens; the state has to satisfy its citizens before satisfying non-citizens. Hossack holds that the problem with assigning responsibility also comes from the approach towards the human rights principles in the Refugee Convention. The rights in the Convention include *non-refoulement*, non-discrimination, non-penalisation and responsibility/burden sharing or refugee protection.

[47] Kathleen Hossack, 'Duties of Virtue and Justice: Rethinking Responsibility in the Global Refugee Regime' (PhD thesis, Brandeis University, 2016).

[48] See Sonya Sceats and Shaun Breslin. 'China and the International Human Rights System', Royal Institute of International Affairs, Chatham House, 2012, https://www.chathamhouse.org/sites/default/files/public/Research/International%20Law/r1012_sceatsbreslin.pdf.

[49] Imperfect duties do not have specific acts that the actor must perform to achieve a certain goal. Perfect duties, on the other hand, are obligatory and enforceable; see Hossack (n 47) 17.

[50] ibid.

Referring to Kant's method of distinguishing between perfect and imperfect duties, Hossack believes that the solution to the problem lies in establishing positive and negative duties for states towards refugees and asylum seekers.[51] Negative duties here refer to duties that protect others from the harm emanating from one's own actions, ie, a duty not to harm or create further harm. In more concrete terms, this translates to a reformation of those institutions, regulations and policies that cause harm or lead to human rights violations. Hossack concludes that after the adoption of policies that hold states responsible for the protection of refugees and asylum seekers as an enforceable duty of justice, the next step would be to create enforcement mechanisms.[52]

According to Jacqueline Bhabha, in the current system of international law, asylum seekers need to prove that they are real refugees before gaining specific rights in a state.[53] Without this proof, the state will treat them in a discriminatory manner. This is complicated more by the fact that most asylum seekers rely on false documentation to gain access into a state or are undocumented when they claim asylum, which automatically puts them into conflict with the state. Bhabha discusses the challenge of establishing the responsibility of a state to protect the rights of asylum seekers and refugees, given the issue of identity and the exclusionary nature of states.

Taking into consideration the arguments of Chimni, Talib and Phuong, there is a disconnection between human rights and state responsibility when it involves the protection of non-members (non-citizens) of a state, particularly migrants from developing countries who are undocumented or seeking asylum. This is one of the areas in which the chain of 'symbiosis' between sovereignty and human rights is strained; states still refuse to accept the protection of the human rights of migrants who are not citizens or proven refugees. This is because according to the full range of rights available to non-citizens, especially undocumented or asylum-seeking migrants is often framed as contrary to the national interests of the state, which is the exclusivity of its borders, the privilege of citizenship and protecting domestic welfare provisions from illegitimate claimants. Bhabha also agrees with the aforementioned argument and contends that asylum bridges the gap between morality and law, 'entrenching a regime of international sovereignty and solidarity within an increasingly harsh and discriminatory state-based system'.[54] She holds that it is asylum that enables states to justify and defend migration exclusion and the exclusivity of borders, under the guise of combing through the mass of undocumented migrants who may pose a threat to security and cohesion to find the real refugees.[55] In other

[51] ibid at 16.

[52] ibid at 52.

[53] Jacqueline Bhabha, 'International Gatekeepers: The Tension between Asylum Advocacy and Human Rights' (2002) 23 *Immigration and Nationality Law Review* 159, at 173.

[54] ibid at 161.

[55] ibid.

words, migration exclusion as an act of state sovereignty is in conflict with the protection of human rights.[56]

The refugee regime is purposely exclusionary and restrictive because it is, as Bhabha states, a 'compromise between unfettered state sovereignty over the admission of aliens, and an open door for non-citizen victims of serious human rights violations'.[57] Bhabha refutes the idea that citizenship is still an important criterion for eligibility for domestic protections like social welfare. Non-citizens may access domestic protections only by converting from asylum seekers to refugees in order to access permanent residence, social welfare, and perhaps citizenship and other protections against removal and deportation.[58] However, it not easy or accessible for migrants to convert from the status of undocumented asylum seeker to refugees so as to access these protections. Third World migrants are particularly affected by discrimination based on their countries of origin and the myth of difference. The study of refugee and migration law evolves through the prioritisation of Western understandings of citizenship rights and law, as well as borders and sovereignty. The study of South-South migrations demonstrates how the application of this model permits similar behaviour among powerful states in the Global South, like China and Nigeria. Regional solutions and histories of migration flows (such as peaceful cross-border movements in Africa or Chinese responses on internal migration) are overlooked as holding potential solutions to vulnerable communities. For this reason, it is necessary to centre the Global South in the study of refugee and migration law from a different angle; the impact of the law at the local level reveals the continuities and discontinuities between international and regional approaches versus local realities, as a TWAIL methodology suggests.

Sonya Sceats and Shaun Breslin argue that developing countries see human rights as an ideal and a virtue, in Kantian terminology, as opposed to a duty of justice that is fully enforceable.[59] This shapes responsibility and the interpretation of the implementation of human rights, as well as the approach towards burden sharing. In relation to the Global South and South-South migrations, the question arises as to whether there is a willingness and capacity to be responsible towards undocumented or asylum-seeking migrants from other developing countries based on historical and socio-political contexts. This capacity will be based on the different ways that states in the Global South perceive their role

[56] Scholars like David Miller note that it is well within the rights of a state excluding migrants and other outsiders to be able to have self-determination. This opinion holds that states should be able to have control over their territory, as well as authority over who can become a member of that territory. See David Miller, 'National Responsibility and Global Justice' (2008) 11(4) *Critical Review of International Social and Political Philosophy* 230.

[57] Bhabha (n 53) 167.

[58] ibid at 164.

[59] Sceats and Breslin (n 48).

in the protection of the rights of non-citizens in comparison to their internal responsibilities and realities.

Responsibility (or the lack thereof) affects how states interact with refugees, asylum seekers, the undocumented and the displaced. It also impacts how these communities or individuals experience justice and how they respond to injustices in the host state. In other words, lack of enforceability is tied to injustice, and experiences of injustice shape undocumented and asylum-seeking migrants' experiences. It is the reaction of the state towards these migrants that creates the need to establish alternative mechanisms to fight injustices, like the informal justice mechanisms at the community level. Migrant communities need to form these mechanisms because the host state will not guarantee justice or protect their rights.

III. LACK OF AWARENESS, MISCONCEPTIONS AND MULTIPLE VULNERABILITIES: STATE RESPONSIBILITY AND MIGRANT STATUS IN CHINA

A. The Role of the UNHCR in the Asylum-Seeking Process

In China, the protection of asylum seekers and refugees is the sole responsibility of the UNHCR (albeit with some funding from the Chinese government).[60] The Chinese government does not engage with asylum seekers and refugees until there is a failure of the asylum claim and the UNHCR is bound to hand over the asylum seeker to the Chinese PSB for detention and deportation. This complete lack of responsibility of the state in the entire process of asylum has an impact on the overall experience of asylum in China.

According to Mr H, a high-level staff member at the UNHCR in Beijing, Beijing is the only place in China where asylum seekers can seek refuge. As a result, the UNHCR cannot engage with asylum seekers anywhere else. The UNHCR building is also the only place where people can claim asylum – the UNHCR does not have access to airports, borders or other access points because China limits its sphere of influence within the state. Refugees are limited as a result; they must travel to the UNHCR office in Beijing to seek asylum. Abdul Knowles notes that China does not allow the UNHCR to access areas where 'persons of concern' are located and this impedes refugee protection in China.[61] Elim Chan and Andreas Schloenhardt note that refugees have also resorted to forced entry into embassies and diplomatic compounds and foreign buildings

[60] In 2016, funding for the UNHCR from the Chinese government stood at US$2,808,971. In February 2018, it stood at US$889,118. See UNHCR, 'Donor Profiles', http://reporting.unhcr.org/donor-profiles. China has donated more money to the EU for the refugee crises in Europe than to the UNHCR for the refugee influx in China.

[61] See Abdul Knowles, 'Implementing International Refugee Law in the People's Republic of China' (2018) 9 *Beijing Law Review* 67.

in order to seek asylum.[62] According to Mr H, the UNHCR is under threat of ejection from China if they overstep their boundaries in their engagement with asylum seekers; as a result, the organisation abides by the limits placed on it by the government in order to be able to function at all.

This puts the onus on migrants to find ways to reach the UNHCR building in Beijing from their port of entry. Two female asylum seekers from Liberia revealed in interviews that they had relied on smugglers and fake Nigerian passports to get from Dongguan to Beijing.[63] They also alluded to the high cost of obtaining false documentation and the risk of human trafficking and labour exploitation in the process. This shows that the disengagement of the state from the asylum process is creating other human rights abuses. Reliance on false documentation to enter Beijing forces undocumented migrants to rely on smugglers, thereby exposing them to other risks and further human rights abuses. China only acceded to the Palermo Protocol on Human Trafficking in 2010, but has not acceded the Protocol on migrant smuggling.[64]

Mr H also stated that the UNHCR does not receive funding for the influx of refugees into China. What this means is that there is generally no capacity in Beijing to meet the basic needs of asylum seekers and refugees.[65] In addition, it is prohibited for the UNHCR to collaborate with other UN bodies, local and international organisations or with churches to work with refugees as China is suspicious of foreign interference in internal matters. Mr H states that this creates a situation where human rights protection is incapacitated and the basic needs of refugees in China are unmet.[66]

The Chinese government provides no stipends for refugees and refugees have no permission to work in China. Access to education, healthcare and housing is also severely limited, and responsibility to provide these services falls on 'friendly associations' (a term used in China as NGOs are prohibited).[67] Lack of financial support and lack of employment and a source of livelihood increase the vulnerability of asylum seekers and refugees in China. Often, they either must rely on their families outside of China to survive or take on clandestine work, which is often fraught with risks of abuse, human trafficking, crime or further friction with the Chinese authorities.

[62] See Elim Chan and Andreas Schloenhardt, 'North Korean Refugees and International Refugee Law' (2007) 19 *International Journal of Refugee Law* 215 at 237.

[63] Personal interview with A and B in Yanjiao, December 2015, on file with the author.

[64] See Protocol to Prevent, Suppress and Punish Trafficking in Persons, Especially Women and Children, Supplementing the United Nations Convention against Transnational Organized Crime, 15 November 2000. See also UN General Assembly, United Nations Convention against Transnational Organized Crime: Resolution/Adopted by the General Assembly, 8 January 2001, UN Doc A/33/383 at 25 (2000), UN Doc A/RES/55/25 at 4 (2001), 40 ILM 335 (2001).

[65] Personal interview with Mr H at the UNHCR headquarters in Beijing, China, January 2016, on file with the author.

[66] ibid.

[67] I interviewed members of two religious groups, one community group and one 'friendly' association ('friendly association' here is used instead of 'NGO' because NGOs are banned in China).

According to the UNHCR, when an asylum seeker arrives at the UNHCR building in Beijing, she or he must then get an interview date to be screened for asylum registration. It takes two weeks to get an appointment. It then takes between 14 to 16 months to be registered as an asylum seeker in China and to get identification documents.[68] Failed asylum seekers (meaning those who do not pass the initial interview for asylum registration) are immediately jailed or deported by the PSB; at this stage, protection is beyond the control of the UNHCR. If a case succeeds, the asylum seeker will be assigned refugee status, but if it fails after this initial success, during the refugee status determination interview, the applicant may appeal a first time. This first appeal is to the US and if the US is accepting refugees, the asylum seeker will begin the process again for resettlement there. If this first appeal fails, the applicant can appeal a second time to Geneva and if Switzerland is accepting refugees, the asylum seeker will appeal to resettle there. If it fails a third time, the applicant will remain in China, pending other solutions, which may include seeking asylum in another country that is closer to the country of origin. It is clear here that China does not perceive itself as a destination for refugees who are non-Chinese. In China, the global refugee crisis is viewed mainly as a European or American-created problem and responsibility, and not as a Chinese problem. Likewise, refugee protection is a virtue rather than a responsibility with legal implications.[69] As a result, asylum applications are targeted at other countries where asylum is more favourable. Going by China's current policy towards the UNHCR, where the body is solely responsible for the status determination and welfare of refugees, we can see that China does not intend to create a state-led refugee regime. According to Knowles, the Chinese authorities will not participate in refugee status determination until China adopts a national refugee law and refugee status determination policies.[70]

Officials of the PSB communicate in the Chinese language only and so cannot engage with non-Chinese migrants and asylum seekers.[71] This leads to unique challenges. Under Article 46,[72] China's Entry and Exit Law provides

[68] Personal interview with Mr H (n 65).

[69] See Jiangtao Shi, 'China Willing to Open Pockets Not Borders to Middle East Refugees', *South China Morning Post*, 26 June 2017, https://www.scmp.com/news/china/diplomacy-defence/article/2099908/china-willing-open-its-pockets-not-borders-middle-east.

[70] Knowles (n 61) 67–74.

[71] Refugees cannot speak Chinese and those who can (refugees with PhDs, for example) still have no opportunities for work and advancement in China, according to UNHCR staff. Mr H suggests that China can hire some of the very fluent refugees to assist them in their work with refugees and other migrants, but this will not be possible because of China's approach towards foreigners on such matters (working with the PSB). It is impossible for foreigners to work in any capacity in areas that are deemed to be of domestic or national interest.

[72] See China: Law of 2012, Exit and Entry Administration Law of the People's Republic of China, Order No 57, 1 July 2013. Article 46 can provide identification that can enable refugees and their children to access education and potentially work. Because of a lack of engagement with the implementation and the full meaning of art 46, we do not know the extent of the benefits that can come through this article.

identification certificates for refugees; however, lack of communication on the part of the Chinese government along with lack of knowledge of the aforementioned article and what it means on the part of refugees often leads to the non-implementation of Article 46. Perhaps non-implementation is rooted in China's rejection of a state-led refugee regime. If refugees are not invoking Article 46 at the PSB, the Chinese government has no responsibility to implement it. A possible combination of lack of knowledge, fear of risking arrest by the PSB due to lack of status, or lack of an ability to communicate fluently in Chinese language might prevent asylum-seeking migrants from invoking Article 46 at the PSB. Most of the African undocumented migrants interviewed were unaware that they had any rights if they were refugees, such as the right to seek asylum, a right to be screened by the UNHCR and a right to appeal the decision. For example, A, B and S (who were seeking asylum in Beijing in 2016) had no knowledge about asylum rights; they attributed the permission for them to stay in China pending the refugee determination process as the benevolence or goodwill of the UNHCR and China. Mr H indicated that the African community that is the most knowledgeable about these rights is the Somali community. This can be attributed to the size of the Somali refugee community in China. Somali networks share information with Somalis in Kenya's refugee camps about the process in China and, as a result, they are often better prepared for the process than other Africans are. Mr H stated that Somali refugees often know that China does not allow refugees to have a means of livelihood or offer stipends to refugees, so they come prepared and receive funds from their families in Kenya or the Diaspora. The Nigerian community is known to have the best access to finances within China, as well as the most networks for the provision of documents and other resources to African asylum seekers trying to reach Beijing for asylum.

China's responsibility towards refugees can be said to be dependent on whether political or national interests are involved or not.[73] In addition, China reports refugees to their embassies due to diplomatic agreements, even more so if the country in question is an ally of the Chinese government. This ultimately endangers refugees with political issues. China puts more weight on national interests, politics and diplomatic ties than on international refugee law norms and practices like *non-refoulement* and refugee status determination, which it still sees as a Western ideal rather than a norm that must be enforceable domestically.[74] An example of this can be seen in the case of North

[73] In the case of Myanmar and North Korea, China sees accepting refugees from those places as interfering in the domestic affairs of their political allies. Non-interference is still a core principle in China's foreign policy and interpretation of international law.

[74] See Lili Song, 'China and the International Refugee Protection Regime: Past, Present, and Potentials' (2018) 37(2) *Refugee Survey Quarterly* 139. See also Miwa Hirono, 'Exploring the Links between Chinese Foreign Policy and Humanitarian Action: Multiple Interests, Processes and Actors', Humanitarian Policy Group Working Paper (2018).

Korean asylum seekers, where China's policy has been to deport refugees to North Korea in favour of the bilateral agreements between both countries, including a Sino-Korean Treaty that allows for the removal of undocumented North Korean citizens from China.[75] These conceptions have shaped China's outlook on international refugee law and refugee rights; however, this outlook is evolving.[76]

B. The Myth of 'False' Asylum Seekers

While the UNHCR did not reveal a breakdown of all the nationalities involved in the asylum process at the time of my research, Mr H disclosed that there were about 43 different nationalities seeking asylum in China. According to him, there were 160 recognised refugees in China at that time, all located in Yanjiao. In January 2016, he stated that there were about 800 asylum cases before the UNHCR in Beijing, out of which 200 were Somali asylum seekers; that number has since increased to 1,160 in 2022, according to the UNHRC China website. According to Mr H, there were also as many Nigeria asylum seekers. This means that a sizeable number of Africans have sought or are seeking asylum in China.

Mr H believed Africans abused the asylum application system. According to him, many African applicants did not come to China originally to seek asylum, but they applies for asylum to achieve another end – usually to extend their stay in China after their visas expired. H. described overstaying Africans who did not want to be arrested or deported as using asylum as a 'get out of jail free card'. He maintained that the high number of applications from 'false' asylum seekers was a disadvantage to 'real' refugees. This opinion of African asylum seekers and migrants was widespread. Interviews with the UNHCR, Chinese scholars and local organisations revealed a perception that many Africans who sought asylum in China did so to escape the harsh penalties for breaches of Chinese migration law. There may be some truth to this, as some Africans come into China with other intentions (like business or education) initially and then use asylum as an opportunity to avoid arrest or deportation after overstaying. However, this generalisation is dangerous. It stereotypes asylum seekers even before they seek asylum, which goes against the principles of refugee law. Whether or not some Africans are being untruthful about their reasons for applying for asylum should be decided by the refugee status determination process. All the people I interviewed in Beijing had different reasons for seeking asylum (or not). To give only a few examples, A and B were seeking asylum because they had experienced labour and sexual exploitation while looking for

[75] Chan and Schloenhardt (n 62) 223–24; Knowles (n 61).

[76] See Xiaodong Wang, 'China Raises Humanitarian Profile Globally', *China Daily*, 19 March 2019, www.chinadaily.com.cn/a/201903/19/WS5c904f77a3106c65c34ef630.html.

work opportunities abroad,[77] S sought asylum during the outbreak of Ebola in Liberia,[78] there were Nigerians seeking asylum to escape conflict in Northern Nigeria, and Sudanese and Somali migrants were fleeing conflict. The undocumented migrants in Guangzhou did not appear interested in seeking asylum, whether they had legitimate claims or not. Most of the migrants I interviewed in Guangzhou were interested in conducting their businesses and prospering in China regardless of their status or documentation.

The idea that Africans abuse the system does not consider the level of discrimination in the Chinese immigration system and its impact on the daily lives of Africans in China. North Americans and Europeans whose visas are nearly expired are often able to extend or renew their visas within China or, at most, in Hong Kong as Chinese immigration policy towards Americans and Europeans is favourable. In fact, Westerners can change their visas from visitor to work visas if they find jobs. It is common to see job advertisements looking specifically for Westerners and promising a change of visa status as part of the package. Even when Westerners overstay, there is room to manoeuvre the system, whereas for non-Westerners, penalties are strict and immediate. Immigration rules are very harsh on Africans specifically, as there is no room for visa status changes and no one is willing or even capable of offering such visa status changes to Africans. Guobin Zhu and Rohan Price note that even though the Chinese Constitution does not discriminate between different types of foreign migrants, the ways in which foreigners experience immigration law and policy differ. Zhu and Price argue that migrants from the West have the advantage of 'determinate legal protection', while Africans and Southeast Asians are 'indeterminate' and enjoy fewer rights and protections.[79]

The UNHCR organises capacity-building events to disseminate knowledge to the government and other stakeholders in China, but there is a general lack of understanding of who refugees and asylum seekers are and why China should be responsible for and welcoming to them. Most of the Chinese people I interviewed seemed confused as to what asylum and refugee status meant, and why foreigners who were undocumented expected support and permission to stay in China. They are also unaware that most refugees and asylum seekers stay in neighbouring countries or even in their country of origin. My interviews with Chinese academics and students at the only university that offers courses on international migration revealed that many Chinese citizens have no concept of what asylum or refugee status means, or about the laws behind these terms.[80] The misconceptions of undocumented or illegal migration overshadow all other forms of immigration and, as a result, there is very little public awareness and/or support for asylum seekers and refugees, particularly if it involves non-Chinese

[77] Personal conversation with A and B in Yanjiao, China, November 2015, on file with the author.

[78] Email correspondence with S in December 2015.

[79] Guobin Zhu and Rohan Price, 'Chinese Immigration Law and Policy: A Case of Change Your Direction, or End up Where You are Heading' (2013) 26 *Columbia Journal of Asian Law* 1 at 6.

[80] Interview with Chinese migration law scholars at the Beijing Institute of Technology, January 2016.

migrants. Mr H from the UNHCR stated that this stems from a misconception of statuses; there is either no understanding or no acceptance of international refugee norms domestically. China's complex history of internal migration and population control has shaped public opinion[81] and the development of policies and laws on refugees and refugee protection.[82] The weight of decades of extensive migration and population control has created an unfavourable atmosphere for foreigners in China, particularly those who are refugees, asylum seekers and undocumented migrants, particularly if they are African.

C. The Unique Challenges Women Face

The African experience of the asylum and refugee processes in China is unique. In addition to being characterised as illegal, there is another layer of vulnerability rooted in racism or prejudice. African asylum seekers interviewed in Beijing recounted numerous experiences of racism they experienced at the hands of Chinese people, particularly in the labour market. For example, A and B (both Liberian asylum seekers) recounted instances of harassment and hostility in public spaces and dehumanising working conditions in the underground economy.[83]

Furthermore, the African asylum-seeking and refugee community faces other dangers like forced prostitution and drug trafficking due to the challenges of finding employment in China.[84] According to Mr H, it is more difficult for African asylum seekers to find a source of income in China, due to racial discrimination in both the informal and formal job markets. Women specifically face the risk of prostitution and trafficking in the community. In addition, Mr H claimed that there has been an increase in the number of single women in the (non-Chinese) community in Beijing leading to concerns about issues like pregnancy and access to healthcare, which means that there are new layers of vulnerabilities arising for members of the community.[85] Most African asylum seekers are male and, overall, they seem to have more access to information and support systems than female asylum seekers. Male asylum seekers also appear to have more financial resources and are more prepared before and upon arrival in China than female asylum seekers, leaving women at higher risk in the community compared to men.

[81] See Manya Koestse, 'Chinese Netizens on World Refugee Day: "Don't Come to China"', *WhatsonWeibo*, 23 June 2017, https://www.whatsonweibo.com/chinese-netizens-world-refugee-day-dont-come-china.

[82] See Kam Wing Chan, 'Is China Abolishing the Hukou System?' (2008) 195 *China Quarterly* 582; Amy Hampton, 'Population Control in China: Sacrificing Human Rights for the Greater Good' (2003) 11 *Tulsa Journal of Comparative and International Law* 321.

[83] Personal interview with A and B (n 76).

[84] Personal interview with Mr H (n 65).

[85] Both Mr H and A and B mentioned that lack of employment was a problem for African asylum seekers in China and the risk of forced labour or trafficking.

What the above indicates is that within the racial hierarchies and exclusions in China, African asylum seekers and refugees are one of the most vulnerable, and within those spaces, women face a deeper level of vulnerability and exclusions. This is due to the limits on the kinds of jobs available for women in the underground economy and fewer opportunities for them to access financial support in the community. I will return to this issue in Chapter 5, where I study discrimination, and in Chapter 6, which covers informal legal structures.

IV. BROKEN PROMISES, EXPLOITATION AND COMPLICATED SOCIO-ECONOMIC DYNAMICS: NIGERIA'S APPROACH TOWARDS BAKASSI REFUGEES

A. In Pursuit of Legal Identity

Nigeria accepted Bakassi refugees fleeing from Cameroon at the height of the conflict in the 1990s and 2000s with promises to protect and resettle those who chose to migrate. This assurance of protection and resettlement motivated many Bakassi residents to flee to Nigeria.[86] During the dispute with Cameroon over ownership of the Peninsula, Nigeria laid claim to the territory because its inhabitants shared historical and cultural ties with Nigeria.[87] When Nigeria lost the case at the ICJ, part of the Greentree Agreement (GA) to resolve the hostilities between Nigeria and Cameroon stated that Cameroon had a responsibility to protect members of the Bakassi community who chose to remain in the Peninsula.[88] However, nothing in the agreement obliged Nigeria to protect Bakassi people who chose to leave Cameroon. When the agreement was drafted, the Cameroon-Nigeria Mixed Commission in charge of it did not foresee Bakassi inhabitants of the Peninsula being compelled to migrate in order to flee from the oppression of Cameroonian gendarmes to Nigeria. In my interviews with Bakassi refugees and leaders, there were narratives of persecution, discrimination and exploitation of and violence against Bakassi people by the Cameroonian government. There were allegations of forced payment of exorbitant fees to own boats, houses and land, to fish on the Peninsula, to go to school etc. The Cameroonian government demanded a fee of 100,000 Naira for the issuance of residence permits, which most of the members of the fishing community could not afford. As a result, they could not obtain residence permits and faced punitive measures of the Cameroonian government for being undocumented.

[86] Listening session at Ikang Resettlement Camp in Cross River State, Nigeria, June 2016.

[87] ibid.

[88] See the Greentree Agreement between Cameroon and Nigeria, Agreement between the Republic of Cameroon and the Federal Republic of Nigeria Concerning the Modalities of Withdrawal and Transfer of Authority in the Bakassi Peninsula, 12 June 2006, www.peaceau.org/uploads/cn-agreement-12-06-2006.pdf, art 3.

According to the Head Chief of the Bakassi refugee camp in Ikang, the promise of resettlement and reintegration was made to the Bakassi people as part of the conflict resolution process during the height of the conflict. In 2009, when a large wave of refugees fled from the Peninsula to Nigeria, both the federal and state governments promised to provide permanent resettlement to the refugees, along with gainful employment, education and land where they could settle as a community in Nigeria. The Nigerian government established the resettlement camp in Ikang under Law No 7 of 2007: Akpabuyo/Bakassi Boundary Adjustment and offered about 200 housing units for nearly 10,000 people, which was clearly insufficient. Law No 7 indicates that the government accepted responsibility to resettle Bakassi refugees in Nigeria with the rights and privileges of Nigerian citizens. The law carved out three wards of Ikang from the Local Government of Akpabuyo and designated it to the Bakassi people.

However, in the listening session I attended at the resettlement camp in Ikang, refugees stated that resettlement and reintegration had not been fulfilled. They pointed out the Nigerian government's disengagement from their responsibility since the establishment of the camp. It is difficult to identify who is truly from Bakassi and poor identification measures have excluded members of the community from political participation and voting, education, healthcare, government allocations etc.[89] On both the Cameroonian and Nigerian sides of the border, Bakassi refugees have no means of legal identification. In Cameroon, Bakassi people are forced to become undocumented migrants on the Peninsula, lacking legal documents permitting them to stay. This has made them susceptible to discrimination and harassment by the Cameroonian authorities. On the Nigerian side, members of the refugee community face difficulties participating fully in Nigerian life due to the lack of documentation. They do not have access to the benefits that come with residency or citizenship. In other words, in Nigeria, Bakassi refugees remain undocumented migrants.

Like the Chinese case study, local NHOs and international organisations like the UNHCR carry the weight of the responsibility for Bakassi refugees due to a lack of engagement from the Nigerian government. For example, the federal and state governments initially accepted responsibility for the gainful employment of Bakassi people, but did not provide actual or sufficient resources or infrastructure. A female refugee leader in Ikang stated that she took up a job as a hired hand in a farm after she fled to Nigeria, and she earned 150 Naira a day and had been unable to feed or educate her children with her earnings. The Bakassi have historically lived by the sea and practised fishing as their source of livelihood. However, the location of the camp does not allow them to practise fishing and therefore the community had lost their chief

[89] Personal interview with the Bakassi Local Government Chairwoman and the Bakassi Local Government Officials in Calabar, August 2016.

source of income. Responsibility had fallen on the UNHCR to carry out skill and cash transfer programmes for the refugees. In addition, the government had disengaged from a promised stipend programme, provision of education for children, healthcare etc.

Bakassi refugees indicated that there was large-scale and continuous fraud in the government whenever funds were released at both the federal and state levels to the refugees. Mr Joseph, the 'national coordinator' of the camp, alleged that in the resettlement camps, state government officials had leased out some of the 200 housing units that were constructed for Bakassi refugees, putting further strain on the already insufficient housing supply for members of the community. According to him, the Nigerian government implemented a stipend of 5,000 Naira per month to facilitate the resettlement of the refugees, but this cash transfer programme had not been implemented since 2013. However, the State Emergency Management Agency reported that the programme is still being implemented by the Federal Government. In addition, the leaders of the refugee community claimed that about 3 billion Naira in funds released for the refugees from the Nigerian and Cameroonian Boundary Commission in 2009 never reached them, despite media reports alleging that the funds were received by the refugees.

Because the camp in Ikang is the only camp created by law, refugees there believe that the establishment of other 'fake' refugee camps is a ploy by state officials and politicians to divert funding and support meant for true Bakassi refugees. The allegations of fake refugee camps came up several times at Ikang, showing the distrust among refugees due to the corruption of government officials. Both the State and National Emergency Management Agencies have reported that the refugees in Ikang have been resettled and reintegrated, whereas members of the refugee community in Ikang continue to be severely marginalised.

B. Differing Opinions on the Status of Bakassi Refugees

At the federal level, refugees fleeing Boko Haram in the northeast are the priority of the government due to the massive scale of displacement and the impact of insecurity. On the other hand, the passage of time between the loss of the Bakassi Peninsula, the arrival of Bakassi refugees in Nigeria and the length of their residence have deprioritised their level of protection. This is reflected in interviews with officials in the SEMA and the NEMA, as well as with former state government officials, some of whom believed that the Bakassi people are no longer 'at risk' in comparison to the situation before and immediately after the ICJ ruling and the GA.

According to Mr J, a former state-level representative in the House of Representatives, the GA gave three options to the Bakassi people: to become Cameroonian, to obtain residence permits as foreigners in Cameroon or to leave Cameroon, whereas the provision of Nigerian citizenship is not explicit.[90] He stated that every person on the Peninsula faced that dilemma in that period and made a choice. The political elite opted to leave Cameroon and migrate to Nigeria, whereas a greater number of the poor remained on the Peninsula to either become Cameroonian or obtain foreign permits to remain there without changing nationality. According to Mr J, the Bakassi elite have always seen themselves as Nigerian; as most of them were educated in Nigeria, resettlement and reintegration was no issue. He noted that economic factors influence resettlement opportunities, but the temporal dimension of resettlement was limited to immediately after the ruling and the GA reduced state perceptions of responsibility.

Nonetheless, there are people who neither chose to become Cameroonian and were too poor to afford residence permits and pay taxes in Cameroon. These are the groups who faced persecution in Cameroon and who fled to Nigeria and formed the refugee community in places like Ikang. In other words, there are different responses to the ceding of the territory and the refugees are a part of a larger community that has resettled in both Nigeria and Cameroon. According to Mr J, the fact that other members of the community (in this case the elite) have been able to resettle means that the Bakassi people are no longer at risk, ignoring economic and other vulnerabilities (such as gender) within the community. This oversight is a key reason Makau Mutua states that intersectionality is crucial as a method in TWAIL in studying the Global South. Without an understanding of how different vulnerabilities are created due to the position that Bakassi people occupy in Nigeria, there is a high probability of assuming that the experiences of the elite represent everyone.

Chief H, a former Bakassi Local Government Chairman, went on to say that the Bakassi people both in Cameroon and Nigeria had already dealt with the involuntary change in citizenship and/or location and that there was no longer any resettlement or refugee question.[91] These accounts underscore the disparity in the barriers to resettlement faced by the elite and underprivileged members of the Bakassi community in Nigeria or Cameroon. The elites have not only resettled but are also now active in Nigerian state-level politics. The impact of the ceding of the Peninsula is mostly felt by poorer Bakassi people who did not have the privilege of being socialised, educated or settled in Nigeria before fleeing from the Peninsula. What this means is that Bakassi refugees in Nigeria are marginalised both in Cameroon and in Nigeria due to their socio-economic status. Far from reducing the narrative of the refugees, the differing opinions about their status reveal the impact of privilege or the lack of it on experiences of justice, asylum, the freedom to migrate and ease of resettlement and reintegration.

[90] Personal Conversation with Mr J, June 2016, University of Calabar, Cross River State, Nigeria.

[91] Personal conversation with Chief H, a former Local Government Chairman of Bakassi, University of Calabar, August 2016. In addition to this role, Chief H had a high-level role in the state government.

This also exposes the understanding of the responsibility of a state towards refugees as being a short-term support, rather than a long-term obligation. Many other government officials, including those interviewed at the NEMA and the SEMA, did not believe the government had any further responsibilities towards the refugees in Ikang because of the passage of time and the resulting resettlement that must have occurred. Mr J held that the only problem left for the government to solve was the issue of identification, which limits the ability of Bakassi people to fully exert their rights in Nigeria. However, from their arrival in the resettlement camp, Bakassi refugees in Ikang have not had access to basic amenities that would at least enable them to survive in Nigeria.

V. RIGHTS AND RESPONSIBILITIES IN THE CHINESE CASE STUDY

A. Domestic Law is Silent about Responsibilities

China has no domestic refugee policy or state-led mechanism for refugee status determination. This is revealed in the narratives of non-Chinese refugees and asylum seekers in China. Jennifer Yip studies the resettlement applications of Pakistani refugees in China and argues that China's main focus in terms of responsibility towards non-Chinese refugees is *non-refoulement*, which is the minimum standard of protection that the state is willing to offer asylum seekers and refugees.[92] While this may be true as China permits and does not interfere in the refugee status determination process and funds the UNHCR, it is cannot be said to be the centre of China's refugee policy. In the past, China has supported the *refoulement* of refugees from Myanmar and North Korea in favour of protecting diplomatic interests over human rights.[93]

Chinese law does not provide any definition for the term 'refugee'.[94] In interviews with Chinese legal scholars at the Beijing Institute of Technology, I noticed that there was no clear distinction between undocumented migration, asylum migration and refugee rights. These interviews indicated that China is just beginning to understand, analyse and discuss international refugees and asylum seekers in China. While these discussions have begun, there have been no further legal or policy developments domestically on the protection of refugees

[92] Jennifer Yip, 'Stranded Amidst Resettlement Applications: A Case Study of Pakistani Refugees in China' (2011), Central European University, Department of Political Science, Budapest at 18.

[93] See United Nations General Assembly, 'Report of the Commission of Inquiry on Human Rights in the Democratic People's Republic of Korea' (2014) A/HRC/25/63.

[94] The only mention of refugees is in art 32 of the Chinese Constitution and Article 46 of the Exit and Entry Law of 2012. Article 32 of the Constitution states that China may grant asylum to foreigners who request it for political reasons, whereas Article 46 of the Entry and Exit Law notes that recognised refugees can be given identity certificates from the PSB and those seeking refugee status temporarily can also be given temporary IDs during the process of status determination. See Constitution of the People's Republic of China of 1982: Zhonghua Renmin Gongheguo Xianfa, 1982.

and the status determination of asylum seekers because of the scale and impact of internal migration. China also privileges Chinese identity in its refugee/asylum policy and, by so doing, excludes those of non-Chinese descent.

The Chinese Entry and Exit Law clearly states that its primary purpose is to regulate exit and entry administration, with a goal of safeguarding national sovereignty and promoting national development.[95] These two goals indicate that the only migration-focused law in China has two inward-looking goals: sovereignty and development. Hence, it can be said that by extension, China's approach towards foreign asylum seekers, refugees and other classes of migrants is driven by these two goals. An important feature of the law is to emphasise the need for the management and control of 'illegal' or 'irregular' migration, including on-the-spot inspection, investigation, immigration detention and deportation of foreigners who have committed one or more of the 'three illegals' or 'san fei' (entry, stay and employment) or have violated Chinese law.[96] As a result, the Chinese Entry and Exit Law focuses on irregular migrations, even though Article 46 mentions that refugees may enter or stay illegally before filing for asylum and may be forced to work illegally because they have no legal permission to work.

China also did not have specialised institutions that focus on immigration, particularly refugees or asylum seekers, for many decades. It was in 2018 that the National Immigration Administration was established to tackle immigration issues specifically. Before then, the Ministry of Foreign Affairs, the Ministry of Public Security through the PSB and Border Control shared the responsibility for immigration administration. The PSB carried the weight of this by overseeing not only internal and external migration, but also policing, law and order, and public security. This explains why China has a criminal justice approach towards immigration – the institution that oversees policing also administers many aspects of immigration law and policy. Guofu Liu discusses the impact on the refugee and asylum determination process: there are no rules or regulations for Refugee Status Determination (RSD), nor are there rules for the application of humanitarian status.[97] In addition, Zhu and Price note that immigration administration faces problems because the officials within these aforementioned institutions are unwilling to engage with foreigners and foreign-related cases due to 'poor language skills, low level of experience, and cumbersome procedures and rules'.[98] Zhu and Price's research indicated high levels of hostility and discrimination towards migrants of African descent. These disconnections between the administration and African migrants affect how the undocumented migrants, asylum seekers and refugees experience immigration laws and policies.

[95] Personal interview with Mr P from the International Organisation of Migration, Beijing, December 2015.

[96] China: Law of 2012, Exit and Entry Administration Law.

[97] Guofu Liu, *Chinese Immigration Law*' (Farnham, Ashgate, 2011) at 89.

[98] Zhu and Price (n 78) 12.

B. International Refugee Law Has Not Been Incorporated into Domestic Law

Even though China acceded the Refugee Convention and its protocol, it does not intend to become a destination where refugees can work or settle in because this does not suit its national interests.[99] China's policy of internal rural to urban migration control through the household registration (*hukou*) system placed severe restrictions on Chinese citizens migrating within China. Even though this system is currently being reformed, internal migrants continue to be restricted. The household registration regulations require Chinese citizens to register as permanent residents where they reside and sets rules for birth registration, rules for moving from one's registration jurisdiction and even rules for temporary residence in places like hotels.[100] Hayden Windrow and Anik Guha discuss how the *hukou* system created a divide between rural and urban citizens by linking social services like access to education and urban employment to ownership of residence permits, as well as creating internal 'undocumented' or unregistered migrations and labour on a massive scale.[101] The scale of internal migrations frustrates the government's attempts to regulate internal migration, and foreign migrants like refugees have no place in the already complicated internal immigration regime, even though the Chinese government is gradually adapting its internal migration policy.

China does the bare minimum, allowing the UNHCR to bear the responsibility of refugees in China. However, China is obligated to adhere to the provisions in the Refugee Convention and its protocol in good faith.[102] If the Refugee Convention has not been subsumed by domestic law or if China has not allowed for the direct implementation of the Convention domestically, then it remains unenforceable in China.[103] Article 46 of the Chinese Entry and Exit Law indicates the only responsibility that China has acknowledged and incorporated from the Convention, which is that the state is responsible for providing refugees and asylum seekers in the process of refugee status determination with identification certificates. Article 46 states that:

> Foreigners applying for refugee status may, during the screening process, stay in China on the strength of temporary identity certificates issued by public security organs; foreigners who are recognised as refugees may stay or reside in China on the strength of refugee identity certificates issued by public security organs.[104]

[99] China has been particularly strict about population control in the past and, as a result, public support is low for the migration and settlement of foreigners in China.

[100] See Zhonghua Renmin Gongheguo Hukou Dengji Tiaoli [The Household Registration Regulations of the People's Republic of China] § 1 (Nongcun Fagui Quanshu 1958), arts 6, 7, 10, 15 and 16.

[101] See Hayden Windrow and Anik Guha, 'The Hukou System, Migrant Workers and State Power in the People's Republic of China' (2005) 3 *Northwestern Journal of International Human Rights* 1.

[102] Vienna Convention on the Law of Treaties, 1155 UNTS 331, 23 May 1969 (entered into force 27 January 1980), art 26.

[103] The Chinese Constitution does not have any provisions on the implementation or interpretation of international treaties in domestic law.

[104] China: Law of 2012, Exit and Entry Administration Law, art 46.

Article 46 provides for both asylum seekers and refugees. It can be deduced that 'foreigners applying for refugee status during the screening process' refers to asylum seekers, meaning that asylum seekers can be issued temporary identity certificates by public security organs. However, the inclusion of Article 46 in the Entry and Exit Law in 2012 has not led to any changes in the status quo as it has not yet been implemented. As a result of China's continued lack of involvement in the refugee status determination process, there are no grounds for the PSB to issue identity certificates to either asylum seekers or refugees. The only facet of the Refugee Convention that has made it into domestic law is still ineffective.

As was discussed in Chapter 3, China has ratified numerous international legal instruments relating to the rights of refugees. China has adopted domestic laws to implement the obligations of these and other treaties. In 1980, China ratified the CEDAW and in 1992 adopted a Women's Act, which aimed to offer domestic protections to Chinese women, reflecting the obligations and norms in the CEDAW.[105] It then established a working committee to harmonise the work of government departments in protecting the rights and interests of women and children. In addition, beyond the national level, provinces, autonomous regions and municipalities have implemented the Women's Act.[106] Of course, there are limitations and problems with its implementation in China, but the fact that the Women's Act has been incorporated into national, provincial, regional, and municipal levels of law and policy indicates a purposeful acceptance of international legal standards and norms.

Obligations in the Women's Act are not targeted at non-Chinese migrants. Recalling Guo's argument, Chinese courts require citizens to bear obligations in order to enjoy rights; if rights are restricted for citizens, there is a gap in the domestic legal regime concerning non-citizens.[107] For example, concerning the trafficking and forced prostitution of A and B from Liberia, both women could not be said to be protected by Chinese domestic law, even though it has specific protections for women against trafficking and forced prostitution in Articles 39, 40 and 41.[108] Without the identification certificates from the PSB or identification from the UNHCR, A and B were considered to be undocumented migrants. In China, only people with 'green cards' authorising permanent

[105] China: Law on the Protection of Women's Rights and Interests of the People's Republic of China, promulgated by the Standing Committee of the National People's Congress, 28 August 2005, effective 1 December 2005, CLI.1.59781(EN) (Law on the Protection of Women's Rights and Interests of the People's Republic of China).

[106] Committee on the Elimination of Discrimination against Women, Consideration of Reports Submitted by States under Article 18 of the Convention on the Elimination of Discrimination against Women (1997), CEDAW/C/CHN/3-4.

[107] See Sanzhuan Guo, 'Implementation of Human Rights Treaties by Chinese Courts: Problems and Prospects' (2009) 8 *Chinese Journal of International Law* 161.

[108] Law on the Protection of Women's Rights and Interests of the People's Republic of China, arts 38, 39 and 40.

residence can claim similar rights as Chinese citizens in very specific areas like education, employment and investment.[109] In this manner, China can incorporate international human rights laws at the national and provincial levels, but again these domestic responsibilities are owed to Chinese citizens, not foreigners and especially not to undocumented migrants, asylum seekers or refugees.

Lili Song notes that China now shows greater interest in refugee affairs through increased funding for refugee protections.[110] At the 2016 UN Summit for Refugees and Migrants and the 2017 Belt and Road Forum for International Cooperation, China pledged significant funding. It also showed an increased funding track record in Pakistan, Bangladesh and Ethiopia, among others, through the UNHCR and UNICEF. Song interprets the increase in Chinese funding from 2016 onwards as a change from China's hands-off approach to a leadership role in global refugee governance. The question remains whether this change in approach will affect domestic laws and refugees in China or only those in other territories.[111]

C. Regional Frameworks are Lacking

Regionally, there are no comprehensive frameworks through which refugees and asylum seekers can be protected; there are no regional binding human rights instruments from which obligations can be invoked concerning responsibilities towards refugees or internally displaced people. This is because many Asian countries have not signed the Refugee Convention and, generally, regional cooperation is weak, save for a few bilateral agreements and protocols which are not particularly focused on the treatment of refugees or asylum seekers.

The Asian-African Legal Consultative Organisation (AALCO) attempted to create a framework for the protection of refugees adopting the Bangkok Principles on the status and treatment of refugees in the region.[112] China was active in the process of drafting and discussions concerning the Principles.[113] However, the Bangkok Principles have yet to become a framework for refugee protection in the region or have an impact on state practice. The delay in implementing the Principles in Chinese domestic law is attributable to a few factors – for example, the non-binding nature of the Principles is more of a blueprint on the treatment of refugees than a set of rules or obligations.

[109] See Administrative Measures on Entitlements of Foreigners with Chinese Permanent Residency (PR) in China (Ren She Bu Fa [2012] No 53 (Circular No 53)).

[110] Lili Song, 'Strengthening Responsibility Sharing with South-South Cooperation: China's Role in the Global Compact on Refugees' (2018), 30 *International Journal of Refugee Law* 687.

[111] ibid.

[112] The Asian-African Legal Consultative Organisation 1966 Bangkok Principles on Status and Treatment of Refugees, as adopted on 24 June 2001 at the AALCO's 40th Session (hereinafter 'Bangkok Principles').

[113] Song (n 72).

Nonetheless, the implementation of the Principles expands the definition of who a 'refugee' is beyond the definition in the Refugee Convention to include people fleeing from ethnic, gender and race-based persecution, foreign domination or occupation etc.[114] This broad definition provides a wider range of protections for different kinds of migrants. The Principles further delineate rights that are not in the Refugee Convention, like a right to return (Article 6)[115] and a right to receive compensation from a refugee's state of origin if the state or state officials cause bodily injury, deprivation of freedom or death to the refugee or a person of whom the refugee is a dependant (Article 9).[116] In the implementation of refugee rights, the Principles create responsibilities for the country of origin through Article 9, which is a big departure from the Refugee Convention, where only receiving states bear responsibilities. Article 10 focuses on burden sharing and delineates that it should be applied progressively to refugees in other regions and to all aspects of the refugee situation, and that it should be implemented with concrete measures of which a majority should be borne by developed countries.[117] This is ahead of the Refugee Convention, in which cooperation is mentioned only in reference to the UNHCR in Article 35 of the Convention.[118] However, the very expansive nature of the Principles makes implementing it a challenge. The restrictive Refugee Convention is the substantive law and as a result, there is no incentive for states to choose the sweeping obligations in the Principles over the Convention.

The Bali Process on People Smuggling, Trafficking in Persons and Related Trafficking in Persons is another forum aimed at raising awareness of the impact of transnational organised crime, trafficking and smuggling of people in the region. It is made up of over 48 members from Asia-Pacific, the Middle East, North America and three international organisations, and focuses on the Asia-Pacific region. The forum drafted the Bali Declaration in 2016, a set of ideals which are non-binding on member states rather than obligatory, on the prevention of transnational crime and the protection of victims of trafficking.[119] The Declaration calls for a regional approach to and collective responsibility for irregular migration. This is significant because refugees and asylum seekers may have irregular status, which indicates that member states now see the value in a regional approach towards migrants without status. As the declaration is aspirational, it does not have an immediate or tangible impact. China has signed the UN Convention on Transnational Organised Crime and its protocols, and

[114] Bangkok Principles, art 1, paras 1 and 2.
[115] ibid at art 6.
[116] ibid at art 9.
[117] ibid at art 10.
[118] Convention Relating to the Status of Refugees (adopted 28 July 1951, entered into force 22 April 1954) 189 UNTS 137 (Refugee Convention), art 35.
[119] Bali Declaration on People Smuggling, Trafficking in Persons, and Related Transnational Crime, 23 March 2016, www.refworld.org/docid/5799ef3c4.html.

acceded its protocol on human trafficking, so there is substantive law that can be implemented in place of the Declaration.[120]

VI. RIGHTS AND RESPONSIBILITIES IN THE NIGERIAN CASE STUDY

A. Domestic Law Protects Refugees – Except Bakassi Refugees

Nigeria's concept of responsibility towards Bakassi refugees slightly differs from the situation in China. Nigeria has legal and institutional frameworks to protect refugees and IDPs domestically, as well as important regional obligations and human rights structures. Unlike Article 32 of the Chinese Constitution, the Nigerian Constitution does not have any provisions for asylum seekers and refugees.[121] Nevertheless, the National Commission for Refugees, etc Act, 1989 (hereinafter the 'NCFR Act') established the National Commission for Refugees with the aim of protection of refugees in Nigeria.[122] The Secretary to the Federal Government is responsible for the supervision of the commission under Article 2 and consists of a chairman, a commissioner and other officials appointed by the federal government.[123] The UNHCR also has observer status at the Commission. Furthermore, the NCFR Act sets out the definition of 'refugees',[124] details the procedures for refugee status determination and the appeal process,[125] and outlines the rights and duties of refugees in Nigeria.[126]

Nigeria has welcomed and protected refugees from Liberia, Sierra Leone[127] and other parts of West Africa, and has provided identification, stipends, housing and food for them as part of its Pan-African foreign policy.[128] This is an indication that Nigeria accepts responsibility for refugees on its territory and offers a level of protection to them. Even though domestic law has a sturdy framework for the protection of refugees in Nigeria, the narratives of Bakassi

[120] ibid.

[121] See Constitution of the Federal Republic of Nigeria, Act No 24, 5 May 1999.

[122] Nigeria: National Commission for Refugees Act, Cap N21 LFN 2004, 29 December 1989.

[123] ibid at ss 2 and 3.

[124] ibid at s 20(1). The definition of refugee in the Act is from the UN Refugee Convention and its Protocol, as well as in the Organisation of African Unity Convention on Refugees.

[125] ibid at s 8.

[126] ibid at s 15.

[127] For example, UNHCR, 'Multipartite Agreement for the Local Integration of Liberian and Sierra Leonean Refugees in Nigeria' (2007), www.unhcr.org/49e479ca22.pdf. See also Gbenga Adeniji, 'Nigeria Tried for Us But We Need Help to Return Home – Oru-Ijebu Ex-refugees from Sierra Leone, Liberia', *Punch*, 28 January 2018, http://punchng.com/nigeria-tried-for-us-but-we-need-help-to-return-home-oru-ijebu-ex-refugees-from-sierra-leone-liberia.

[128] See Juna Mohammed Juma, 'The Role of Nigeria in Peace Building, Conflict Resolution, and Peacekeeping since 1960' (Conference Paper, Ahmadu Bello University, Zaria, 2005). See also Charles B Azgaku, 'The Role of Nigeria in Peace-Keeping Operation in West Africa: 1960–2010' (2015) 5(22) *IISTE Research on Humanities and Social Sciences* 88; Charles Dokubo and Oluwadare Abiodun, 'Nigeria's Role in Conflict Resolution: A New Paradigm' (2011) 3(3) *Journal of Alternative Perspectives in the Social Sciences* 551.

refugees reveal gaps in implementation. The root of the problem lies in the international nature of the circumstances that led to the forced migration of Bakassi people out of the Peninsula. As was discussed in Chapter 2, the GA only created obligations for Cameroon in relation to the treatment of Bakassi people on their territory; there were no international obligations on the treatment of Bakassi people if they migrated to Nigeria because the breaches of Article 3 of the GA by Cameroon were not foreseen. The obligations in Article 3 also did not include the provision of legal documentation such as residence permits in Cameroon or Nigeria. Furthermore, during the dispute, Nigeria claimed both the territory and inhabitants of Bakassi due to centuries of historical and cultural ties to the Calabar Kingdom, which is in Nigeria. The Nigerian government thus believed the Bakassi people to be Nigerian citizens on Nigerian territory. However, ceding the territory to Cameroon and the resulting GA muddled the nationality of the Bakassi people. As mentioned above, some chose to remain in Cameroon by either gaining residence permits or remaining undocumented, while others fled to Nigeria. Because Nigeria originally claimed Bakassi people as Nigerian citizens, there was a resulting perception that those who fled political, religious and economic oppression in Cameroon were 'returning' citizens. In interviews with government officials in the NEMA, the SEMA, the Local Government and security operatives, interviewees referred to Bakassi people in Ikang as citizens returning to Nigeria, even though they have no legal documentation linking them to Nigeria.[129] This is problematic because it infers that Bakassi people are returning to something or somewhere in Nigeria (rather than a refugee camp) and reduces the protections available to them under Nigerian law. In particular, if we see the Bakassi as returning citizens, they are not covered by the NCFR Act, which, for example, entitles them to identification certificates.[130] The Bakassi people currently do not have identification or communal land in Nigeria. As a result, they are in an identity limbo where they are neither citizens nor foreigners. They do not benefit from the privilege of citizenship, but are considered to be citizens of Nigeria. This is the reason why Nigeria has been unable to take responsibility for the treatment of Bakassi refugees, as opposed to other refugees and IDPs in Nigeria.

The Nigerian Constitution makes provisions for both civil and political rights, as well as economic, social, and cultural rights that apply to Bakassi refugees. According to Chapter 2, section 15(3)(a) and (b) of the Nigerian Constitution, the government has an obligation to promote integration by providing adequate facilities for free mobility of people and to secure the full residency rights of every citizen. If Bakassi people are Nigerian citizens, Nigeria is responsible for resolving their residency, documentation and identity problems.[131]

[129] Personal interview with SEMA officials, Calabar, June 2016; phone interview with NEMA official, June 2016; personal interview with the Nigerian Police Commissioner of Cross River State, August 2016.

[130] National Commission for Refugees Act, s 11.

[131] Constitution of the Federal Republic of Nigeria, ch 2, s 15(1).

Section 17 obliges the government to provide all citizens with access to a means of livelihood, humane and healthy working conditions, access to health facilities, protection from exploitation and access to public assistance.[132] Notwithstanding all these provisions and frameworks domestically, Bakassi refugees are not protected in Nigeria due to a lack of political will to protect the people without access to the oil-rich territory of the Peninsula. In 2016, the UNHCR stated that Bakassi refugees are in danger of becoming stateless in Nigeria and Cameroon because they lack proof and documentation in both countries and, as a result, they are excluded from legal remedies to injustices they face on both sides of the border; moreover, they also lack the capacity to represent their interests locally, regionally, and nationally.[133]

Nigeria has ratified the 1951 UN Convention Relating to the Status of Refugees and its 1967 Protocol Relating to the Status of Refugees. The NCFR Act incorporated the norms, procedures, definitions and standards from the Convention and the protocol.[134] The definition in Article 1 of the Convention applies to refugees in Nigeria and refugees with a well-founded fear of persecution because of race, religion or nationality, and those without nationality have a right to be protected in Nigeria. In addition, the refugee rights created by the Convention are applicable under the NCFR Act, including the principle of *non-refoulement*, which is implemented via Article 33 of the Act. It has been proven that Cameroon targeted Bakassi inhabitants during the conflict and after the ceding of the Peninsula based on their lack of legal documentation in Cameroon and affiliation with Nigeria.[135] However, the Bakassi people who fled to Nigeria have not been accorded the treatment and procedures laid down in the Refugee Convention. From the narratives of Bakassi refugees, the rights stipulated in the Convention, including but not limited to employment, education, identity papers and travel documents, have not been made available to them by the Nigerian government. This is not the same treatment accorded to refugees from other African countries who have been accepted and resettled in Nigeria in the past.[136]

As mentioned above, Nigeria has also ratified a number of international human rights conventions, which create responsibilities towards refugees. These conventions have not yet been incorporated into domestic law or tested in the

[132] ibid at ch 2, s 17(3).

[133] See Omeiza Ajayi, 'Bakassi People on Verge of Becoming Stateless, UNHCR warns', *The Vanguard*, 6 October 2016, https://www.vanguardngr.com/2016/10/bakassi-people-on-verge-of-becoming-stateless-unhcr-warns.

[134] The NCFR Act uses the definition of 'refugee' in art 1 of the 1951 UN Convention Relating to the Status of Refugees and art 1 of the 1967 UN Protocol Relating to the Status of Refugees in s 20 of the Act.

[135] See 'Bakassi Residents to Pay Tax under Cameroon Sovereignty', *BBC News*, 15 August 2013, www.bbc.com/news/world-africa-23710733.

[136] Sierra Leonean and Liberian refugees resettled in Nigeria in 2007 and 2008. See 'Liberian, S Leonean Refugees to Settle in Nigeria', *Reuters*, 7 August 2007, https://www.reuters.com/article/us-nigeria-refugees/liberian-s-leonean-refugees-to-settle-in-nigeria-idUSL0759686620070807.

Nigerian courts of law. Nevertheless, the amendment of the 1999 Constitution in 2011 included international human rights obligations in Chapter 4, including the right to life (Article 33), prohibition of inhumane and degrading treatment, slavery and forced labour (Article 34), personal liberty (Article 35), entitlement to a fair hearing (Article 36), privacy (Article 37), freedom of religion, thought and expression (Articles 38 and 39), freedom of assembly (Article 40), freedom of movement (Article 41) and non-discrimination (Article 42).[137]

B. Regional Frameworks are Expansive but have Gaps

Regionally, there are comprehensive frameworks that create a responsibility for Nigeria to protect Bakassi refugees. First, section 20(1) of the NCFR Act incorporates the definitions of 'refugee' from Article I of the African Union Convention Governing the Specific Aspects of Refugee Problems in Africa, acting as a complement to the 1951 Refugee Convention and its Protocol. The AU Refugee Convention does not supersede but complements the 1951 UN Refugee Convention and its 1967 Protocol. The African Union Convention on Refugee Problems extends the definition beyond persecution for reasons of race, religion, nationality, membership of a particular social group or political opinion to include refugees who:

> [O]wing to external aggression, occupation, foreign domination, or events seriously disturbing public order in either part or the whole of his country of origin or nationality, is compelled to leave his place of habitual residence in order to seek refuge in another place outside his country of origin or nationality.[138]

This expansion significantly includes refugees fleeing from foreign domination, occupation or aggression. Aggression from the Cameroonian gendarmes on the Peninsula towards the Bakassi people was the motivating factor for their migration to Nigeria. Bakassi refugees were forced to seek refuge outside their ancestral lands and so it can be argued that they are refugees under the AU definition. The Convention also created obligations for states parties on non-discrimination (Article 4) and the issuance of travel documents to promote freedom of movement (Article 6). However, it does not create obligations relating to housing, employment, education or resettlement, which are key issues faced by the Bakassi refugee community in Nigeria. The Bakassi people are considered citizens, as evidenced by Nigeria's claims over the Peninsula during the dispute with Cameroon.[139] However, they are stateless because they do not

[137] Constitution of the Federal Republic of Nigeria, ch 4.

[138] OAU, Convention Governing the Specific Aspects of Refugee Problems in Africa, 10 September 1969, 1001 UNTS 45, art 1(2).

[139] *Land and Maritime Boundary between Cameroon and Nigeria, Cameroon and Equatorial Guinea (Intervening) v Nigeria*, Judgment, Merits [2002] ICJ Rep 303, ICGJ 63 (ICJ 2002), 10 October 2002, UN; ICJ, para 218.

have ancestral lands in Nigeria and do not have access to identification like birth certificates or passports. As a result, they do not have access to social services like national health insurance and cannot fully participate in or benefit from civic duties/rights like the right to vote.

Nigeria has ratified and incorporated the African Charter on Human and Peoples' Rights hereinafter the 'Banjul Charter') into domestic law under the African Charter on Human and Peoples' Rights (Ratification and Enforcement) Act.[140] The Banjul Charter creates rights for Bakassi refugees and obligations for the Nigerian government towards them. Article 13(1) provides the right to participate freely in the government of one's country directly or via a chosen representative. The Bakassi people are unable to participate in the government (at the local, state or federal level) in Nigeria due to the identification problem. According to Article 13(1), Nigeria has an obligation to ensure that they can participate directly in government.[141] Article 17 of the Charter protects the right to education and the right to freely take part in the cultural life of one's community. For Bakassi refugees, access to education and freedom of expression of Bakassi cultural life has been hindered by living for a protracted period in the resettlement camps. Over 90% of Bakassi children in Nigeria are said to not attend school.[142] Life in the camp has prevented Bakassi people from having a normal communal life, as well as proper integration in Cross River State, where they are located. Article 22 states that individuals have a right to economic, social and cultural development with respect to their freedom and identity, whereas Article 24 contains the right to an environment favourable to their development. The environment of the resettlement camp is not conducive to the development of Bakassi people because they do not have access to employment, education, healthcare, electricity, clean water or other basic necessities, even though Nigeria has an obligation under Articles 22 and 24 to ensure that the living conditions of Bakassi people favour their development.

Nigeria has ratified the Protocol to the Banjul Charter on the Rights of Women in Africa in 2003. Article 4 on the right to life (specifically paragraphs E and F) notes that states parties have a responsibility to punish perpetrators of violence against women, to implement rehabilitation programmes for victims and to make reparations available.[143] From the narratives of women in the camp, rape, insecurity and unwanted pregnancies are the greatest problems

[140] See African Union (AU), 'African Charter on Human and Peoples' Rights', 27 June 1981, CAB/LEG/67/3 rev 5, 21 ILM 58 (1982) (hereinafter the 'Banjul Charter'); and the African Charter on Human and Peoples' Rights' (Ratification and Enforcement) Act, Cap A9, Laws of the Federation of Nigeria, 2004.

[141] Banjul Charter, art 13(1).

[142] Personal interview with the Bakassi Local Government Chairwoman and the Bakassi Local Government Officials, Calabar, August 2016.

[143] African Union, Protocol to the African Charter on Human and People's Rights on the Rights of Women in Africa, 11 July 2003 (hereinafter the 'Maputo Protocol'), http://wwwwww.refworld.org/docid/3f4b139d4.html.

faced by Bakassi women; however, the Nigerian government has not taken action to punish perpetrators or to protect women.[144] Other rights enshrined in the Protocol are the right to education (Article 12), economic and welfare rights (Article 13), reproductive rights (Article 14), the right to food security (Article 15), the right to adequate housing (Article 16) and the right to a healthy environment (Article 17). According to Nneka Chukwuma, the Banjul Charter is a union of universal human rights norms with an African perspective of human rights based on the real-life situation in Africa.[145] The provisions in the Protocol effectively show compliance with international human rights law, as it reflects both economic and social rights, as well as humanitarian obligations. The Protocol goes a step further to create responsibilities for states to punish perpetrators of violence against women in Article 4. The Protocol defines violence against women as:

> [A]ll acts perpetrated against women which cause or could cause them physical, sexual, psychological, and economic harm, including the threat to take such acts; or to undertake the imposition of arbitrary restrictions on or deprivation of fundamental freedoms in private or public life in peace time and during situations of armed conflicts or of war.[146]

This is a very broad definition that covers peacetime and conflict and a range of causes of harm. Article 4 creates responsibilities to punish individuals who commit crimes of violence against women and Nigeria has responsibilities towards Bakassi people under these provisions, regardless of their status in Nigeria because Article 2 of the Banjul Charter states that the rights guaranteed in the Charter apply to every individual regardless of their national or social origin, ethnicity etc.[147] A case might be brought to the African Court of Human Rights by states parties, an African intergovernmental organisation, NGOs or individuals and submitted to the seat of the court according to Articles 24 and 25 of the Protocol to the Charter.[148]

Nigeria has also ratified the African Charter on the Rights and Welfare of the Child (ACRWC). Under the Charter, Nigeria has a very wide range of responsibilities towards children regardless of their status due to the non-discrimination provision in Article 3. Article 6 states that children have the right to be registered immediately after birth. Children in the resettlement camp do not have legal identification because members of the community do not have identification documents in Nigeria, so Article 6 is applicable in the protection of the Bakassi

[144] Listening session at the Ikang resettlement camp, Cross River State, Nigeria, June 2016.

[145] Nneka Chukwumah, 'The Banjul Charter and Universal Human Rights: A Comparative Analysis' (2016), https://www.legal-tools.org/doc/04810f, at 13.

[146] Maputo Protocol, art 1.

[147] Banjul Charter, art 2.

[148] AU, 'Banjul Protocol on the Establishment of the African Court on Human and Peoples' Rights' (1998), OAU/LEG/EXP/AFCHPRIPROT(III) (hereinafter the 'Banjul Protocol') at arts 5, 24 and 25.

children. Article 11 obliges Nigeria to provide education to Bakassi children; however, Nigeria has abandoned the education of Bakassi children, leaving it to the UNHCR and NGOs. Article 14 guarantees the right to health, whereas the health conditions in the resettlement camp are very poor. The Charter focuses on the rights of refugee children in Article 23 and creates state responsibility to provide adequate protection and humanitarian assistance to them. Finally, Article 27 obliges states to protect children from sexual exploitation in all its forms, which means that the safety of children in the resettlement camp is a right under the ACRWC.

Subregionally, Nigeria is a member of the Economic Community of West African States (ECOWAS). The ECOWAS Commission provides another institution through which refugees in the region can be protected. The ECOWAS Common Approach[149] to migration is a political framework dealing with migration challenges in the region and one of its priority areas is the protection of the rights of migrants, asylum seekers and refugees through the ECOWAS Treaty of 1975[150] with the 1979 Protocol Relating to the Free Movement of Persons, Residence and Establishment,[151] which provide rights of entry, residence, work and establishment to refugees and asylum seekers in the region (Articles 59(1) and Article 2, respectively). The Common Approach aims to establish mechanisms for granting rights of residence and establishment to refugees from ECOWAS countries.

Generally, Nigeria is not lacking in frameworks for refugee protection. As we have seen, international, regional, subregional and domestic laws and frameworks create responsibilities and obligations for Nigeria regarding the treatment of refugees, including Bakassi refugees. On the other hand, these laws and frameworks create rights for refugees that are applicable to the Bakassi refugees. However, the challenge with international and regional laws and norms lies not only in the harmonisation with domestic laws, but also in their implementation, especially the political will to do so. Even with all these international, regional, and domestic frameworks in place, Nigeria is still unwilling to be fully responsible for the resettlement of Bakassi refugees.

[149] ECOWAS, 'ECOWAS Common Approach to Migration', 33rd Ordinary Session of the Head of State and Government Ouagadougou, 18 January 2008, www.unhcr.org/49e47c8f11.pdf

[150] ECOWAS, Revised Treaty of the Economic Community of West African States (ECOWAS), 24 July 1993.

[151] ECOWAS, Protocol Relating to Free Movement of Persons, Residence and Establishment, 29 May 1979, A/P 1/5/79.

5

Identity, Intersectionality and South-South Migrations

> I don't care that I am illegal, I chose this to live this life of no papers. I am proud of myself, and I believe in my resourcefulness. I am rich because of my hard work in China. Here, people treat us poorly because we are Africans, but they cannot deny the huge profits we are making in business.[1]

> Nigeria has never been a problem because the truth remains that almost all the elites who are educated received their education in Nigeria and essentially grew up here. You are essentially looking at the illiterate people that are still in the village, they are the ones who would have problems, those who never migrated for better opportunities in Nigeria.[2]

THIS CHAPTER EXAMINES the impact of migration status on the identity of the migrant communities in my case studies. It looks at the intersection of migrant status with other factors, including economic status, gender and ethnicity, and examines whether identity positions such migrants within constraints that enhance hierarchies within the Global South and increase invisibility and marginalisation, as well as impact how resistance or empowerment occurs. I define identity as encompassing multiple intersecting social categories either imposed by oneself or others that define those that arise out of different historical, political, cultural and social phenomena over time. Identity is also the site of power struggles between those who are at the periphery and those at the core for access, recognition and equity. Identity is more than category and context; it is also about access, justice and acceptance. All these issues come to play in South-South migrations, in communities within and outside borders and citizenship. Identity is significant in shaping how migrant communities in their path to justice experience law.

I do not frame identity on the questions of identity politics and race (which are often central in the discourse on identity in the Global North), one-dimensional questions of identity or the romanticisation of marginality.

[1] Personal interview with Mr T in Baiyun District, Guangzhou, March 2016, on file with the author.

[2] Personal conversation with Mr J, at University of Calabar, Cross River State, Nigeria, June 2016, on file with the author.

Instead, I discuss identity and intersectionality solely for the purpose of showing the complexity behind how different people within migrant communities experience marginality and structural/systemic discrimination in the Global South. Identity is central in discussing South-South migrations and as a part of TWAIL discourse because of the history of colonialism, borders, and how it has shaped who we are and how we see ourselves within national, regional and international stratifications.[3] Identity affects perceptions of visibility and invisibility of these undocumented or displaced communities at the international, regional and domestic levels, and how this impacts resilience or victimhood in South-South migration narratives and experience of the law.

Intersectionality is important here because identity shapes the way in which undocumented or displaced communities experience or create the law from below and how marginalisation, resistance or empowerment occurs. Beyond influencing how the law is experienced, unpacking identity also helps me to see the different experiences of law within communities based on the intersection of varied factors. There is no monolithic experience of marginality in the Global South; within communities that are marginalised, there are still privileges that make certain members of the community better off than others. Without an understanding of the intersections of identity in my case studies, I will not be able to paint an accurate picture of the realities at the lowest levels of society. In my case studies, I draw ideas from feminism and CRT that identities are central to both how the social environment within temporal and spatial confines shapes the perception of oneself and the other. These schools of thought also explain how identity delimits the 'ins' and the 'outs' with the labelling of citizens and non-citizens, legal and illegal, refugees and asylum seekers, what the state does with these labels, and how undocumented or displaced people or groups respond. Both case studies reveal that groups that are othered or excluded cannot become fully formed or fully part of the larger society due to the marginalisation resulting from power struggles. The alterity of these communities limits the space they occupy and the influence they can exert within the states in which they find themselves. Their identities are formed and forced on them, based on exclusions from the dominant groups in the Global South, and, as a result, they are 'peripheralised' within the periphery. At the same time, laws and policies are formed around the continued subordination and exclusion of these communities.

Reiterating the discussion in Chapter 4, even though human rights are intrinsic to human beings, non-citizens as outsiders do not belong to the state and therefore cannot receive the same treatment as citizens and have no power in defining their status. The international system as well as the implementation of human rights are still limited by 'hegemonic ideal' of citizenship, as it

[3] Colonialism has many different contexts. There are different colonial forms in China (where China has colonised/occupied neighbouring territories, but has also been impacted by British colonialism and imperial trade routes).

defines what the boundaries of community are, as well as who is a valid political actor.[4] In this chapter, I will discuss how migration status and the intersection of factors ranging from economic status to gender and ethnicity impact the migrant communities in my case studies and create the context of oppression and marginalisation on the one hand and sites of resistance and the reconstitution of identities on the other. This chapter frames the discussions in Chapter 6, which will cover how migrants resist systems of justice and laws that institutionalise structural violence and discrimination, and create their own paths to justice.

I. UNDERSTANDING IDENTITY

There have been numerous attempts to determine what identity means and its significance in the distribution of power in society, as well as its role in creating stratifications and hierarchies in social, cultural and political spaces. Osamudia James defines identity as a person's 'internal sense of self ... an association of that self with a particular group or groups ... shaped by multiple social categories including gender, religion'.[5] She recognises that identity is shaped by the individual's perception of themselves, as well as the relationship of that 'self' with others. It is made of both what she terms as 'internal navigation' of the self and 'external imposition' by others and marked by multiple layers or categories created by both internal and external factors, which, according to her, are race,[6] gender, religion, ethnicity and religion among others.[7]

This definition centres identity on the social environment and its impact on the interaction and perception of the self in relation to others. Migrants lose the stability of the social environment that informs their sense of identity on two levels: when factors like persecution or insecurity cause them to migrate and when they arrive in a new state. Take, for instance, the Bakassi fishing communities whose localised understanding of shared history and codes of belonging derived from fishing were lost when they were persecuted on the Peninsula and again when they arrived in refugee camps in Nigeria – where they have no access to fishing as a source of livelihood and a central part of their culture. In new spaces, identities are reconfigured and shaped by the context, and realities in that space and migrants are forced to either conform to new identities or resist them.

[4] Trevor Purvis and Alan Hunt, 'Identity versus Citizenship: Transformations in the Discourses and Practices of Citizenship' (1999) 8 *Social & Legal Studies* 457 at 460–61.

[5] Osamudia R James, 'Valuing Identity' (2017) 102 *Minnesota Law Review* 127 at 130.

[6] Specifically, on racial identity, James argues that racial identity is a social construct that feeds on both physical and social attributes; in other words, while race can manifest itself through physical features, it can also convey other attributes like class, geography and political affiliation. See James (n 5) 149.

[7] ibid.

According to James, identity is fundamental to dignity, which 'encompasses the idea that every human being possesses an intrinsic worth by virtue of being human'.[8] She states that in the rejection of identity (or identities), the dominant group withholds dignity from others and in so doing denies their humanity.[9] In other words, by rejecting otherness, dominant groups deny the rights of minority groups. James adds that human rights and equality demands dignity for all, regardless of whether they belong or not 'and the parts of their identity which differ from ours are nevertheless dignified, worthy and valuable'.[10] In Eileen Pittaway and Emma Pittaway's discussion on the negative impact of labels on female refugees, they define identity as a process that occurs due to the engagement with social phenomenon at a given time and in a given space. According to them, identity is not fixed or static, but 'temporary, fragmented, unstable and at times contradictory' because the relationship people have with those around them is in a constant state of flux.[11] This definition highlights the mercurial and contradictory nature of identity which is drawn from the social environment at a particular time and in a particular space. Due to its temporal and spatial characteristics, identity is constantly shifting. What this indicates is that identity occurs or is created through a series of experiences, encounters or actions over time and space. Pittaway and Pittaway hold that the identity of an individual is tied to their inclusion or exclusion from another socio-cultural groups and give examples: a woman is a woman and is also not a man, and this simultaneous inclusion and exclusion has implications for women.[12]

Another very important observation in Pittaway and Pittaway's analysis is that identity is the site of power struggles because of the boundaries between self and others. As a result, it has been used as a tool of oppression. Identities or labels can be forced on a marginalised group (eg, refugees) by a dominant group (eg, citizens). Pittaway and Pittaway hold that forcing one identity label on multiple identities is an oppressive tool that shrinks the labelled individual or group to one primary identifier. This eventually becomes the defining characteristic of that group or individual in their encounters with others and also eventually changes the perception of self in relation to the perception of the other.[13]

Stuart Hall conceptualises two models of identity.[14] The first model sees that in identity, there is an intrinsic attribute that is the essence of a person or group. This could be a shared history – for instance, this intrinsic value gives

[8] ibid at 161.

[9] ibid.

[10] ibid.

[11] Eileen Pittaway and Emma Pittaway, 'Refugee Woman: A Dangerous Label' (2004) 10(1) *Australian Journal of Human Rights* 119 at 123.

[12] ibid at 124.

[13] ibid.

[14] See Stuart Hall, 'Cultural Identity and Diaspora' in Jonathan Rutherford (ed), *Identity: Community, Culture, Difference* (London, Lawrence & Wishart, 1990) at 222–37.

the individual or group a 'stable frame of reference'. Conversely, in the second model, identity is not stable because it is constantly transforming itself due to the continuous impact of culture, history and power.[15] As a result, identity is never complete. This perspective marries the idea that identity is as much about attributes as it is about the processes that shape, institutionalise, challenge and change them. Yussef Al Tamimi defines identity based on attributes that help us to 'recognise an individual or collective from others'.[16] He holds that identities work as points of reference solely because they function by excluding others. Here, he sees that others who are excluded are an excess to whatever identity is at the core. In other words, dominant groups perceive those who do not belong or 'fit in' to be an excess to their identity – he encapsulates this as 'internal unity' of the powerful and external excess of those at the periphery.[17] He highlights the contradictions inherent in exclusion: the insiders exclude outsiders because of their identity, but need those identities to exist in order to exclude them in the first place. In my understanding, this means that oppression uses exclusion and hierarchies to maintain the power status quo, but without those who can be excluded or 'othered', the oppressor cannot exist. Tamimi states that we cannot understand the narratives of any identity without first understanding the power mechanisms that created that identity.[18] He analyses identity and human rights in the EU, and holds that in addition to being a 'reference point' for people's identities and influencing public attitudes towards identity, human rights regulate how states and institutions 'engage' with identity and influence public attitudes.[19] He goes further and discusses how national identity has been given legal priority in human rights law and discourse because the law 'gives normative priority to national identity over other forms of identification' to the point that those who are 'othered' are made so within the constraints of national identity.[20] In this way, identity is linked to how undocumented, displaced or asylum-seeking migrants experience the law. It is also why I discuss South-South migrations with TWAIL, which challenges the power mechanisms that created the hierarchies between the Global North, the Global South and the peripheries in those areas.[21]

Furthering the analysis of the relationship between identity and power, Clarissa Hayward defines identity as mechanisms of power to people who

[15] ibid.

[16] Yussef Al Tamimi, 'Human Rights and the Excess of Identity: A Legal and Theoretical Inquiry into the Notion of Identity in Strasbourg Case Law' (2018) 27(3) *Social & Legal Studies* 283 at 284.

[17] ibid at 285. See also Ernesto Laclau, *New Reflections on the Revolution of Our Time* (London, Verso, 1991).

[18] Tamimi (n 16) 286. See also Jacques Derrida, 'Differance' in Peggy Kamuf (ed), *A Derrida Reader: Between the Blinds* (New York, Columbia University Press, 1991) at 59–79.

[19] Tamimi (n 16) 284.

[20] ibid at 286.

[21] Makau Mutua, 'Critical Race Theory and International Law: The View of an Insider-Outsider' (2000) 45 *Villanova Law Review* 841.

'belong' and that 'legitimise violence and coercion' to people who do not belong.[22] Hayward focuses on the state as the sculptor of national identities via citizenship laws, for example, and how the state shapes racial and ethnic identities, institutionalising them in laws and policies by 'distributing resources and opportunities along group lines'.[23] This in turn creates hierarchies between those who belong and those who do not, and shapes how people mobilise themselves along these lines. Within any given state, there are dominant groups (based on race, gender, religion and other markers) who benefit more from the laws and policies of the state. These dominant groups have first access to the distribution of resources and opportunities, while other groups face exclusion and oppression – the further away one is from the centre, the further one is from power and resources.

Paul Horwitz takes a different approach to identity, describing it not as a perception, process or possession, but a thing all human beings 'utilise' and 'perform'.[24] In this definition, both marginalised and dominant groups use identity to define themselves; for marginalised groups, identity is used to resist oppression or domination, whereas for dominant groups, it is used to maintain or legitimise the status quo. Horwitz sees identity as a tool both in the hands of the oppressed and the oppressor; one uses it as resistance, and the other as a claim to power and entitlements. Similarly, Trevor Purvis and Alan Hunt see identity as a tool used to achieve certain ends. They discuss citizenship as a distinct identity with conditions of membership and exclusion institutionalised in law and policy.[25] The conditions of membership are identification and recognition by the state, conditions which Purvis and Hunt describe as 'policing the dividing practices that have hardened the gap between the "responsible" and the "irresponsible"'.[26] Here, the responsible (citizens) are given differential treatment in governance and the irresponsible (the marginalised) are excluded, but are policed in both public and private arenas of life.[27] Purvis and Hunt see identity as a tool which hegemonic powers use to force harmful and disadvantageous identities on marginalised groups in order to exert power over them and rob them of their ability to define their own identities. This materialised in both the China and Nigeria case studies; in both countries, the migrant communities experienced different forms of state-backed policing due to their otherness within the state. Nigerians experienced higher forms of policing in cities like Guangzhou and Bakassi people face the same forms of harassment in Cameroon and Nigeria as well. This will be discussed further below in the analysis of the case studies.

[22] Clarissa Rile Hayward and Ron Watson, 'Identity and Political Theory' (2010) 33 *Washington University Journal of Law & Policy* 9 at 21–22.

[23] ibid at 32.

[24] Paul Horwitz, 'Uncovering Identity' (2007) 105 *Michigan Law Review* 1283 at 1292. See also Pittaway and Pittaway (n 11) 124.

[25] Purvis and Hunt (n 4) 462.

[26] ibid at 470.

[27] ibid at 470 and 475.

A. From Nationality to Ethnicity: Making Sense of African Identity

African identity is complex; it is a broad racial categorisation, but within it, there are many much narrower categories. Blackness is often used as an identifier when people of African descent are in a space with white and other racial categories, but the experience of Blackness is dependent on the context of the location. For example, Black identity is the US has a different context from Blackness in South Africa or China. Africans have national identities shaped by the context of colonialism, the resulting creation of borders, and the amalgamation of different cultural and ethnic groups within a state, among other things. Africans also have ethnic identities, which are shaped primarily by shared pre-colonial cultural, linguistic, historical, religious and other factors. African people or people of African descent experience these different identities in a wide variety of ways, shaped by a multiplicity of contexts. As a result of this diversity, there is always a tendency that the category 'African' or 'Black' will become a primary identifier while nationality, ethnicity and other individual or communal identities take a back seat. Nationality and ethnicity are not as obvious as Blackness; therefore, in some spaces that people of African descent share with other racial identities, Blackness becomes the primary identifier. Many Africans are still coming to terms with what African-ness and Blackness mean in spaces where Africans or people of African descent are minorities.

In China, I noticed that Africans are called hēirén (黑人), meaning 'Black people', or fēizhōu rén (非洲人), meaning 'African people'. African people were not often referred to by their national or ethnic identities. To Chinese locals, African-ness and Blackness are clearer identifiers than 'Nigerian' or 'Yoruba'. On the other hand, Africans in China see themselves as being African, in addition to their national and ethnic identities. All the people I interviewed referred to national communities (like the Nigerian community), but also referred to themselves and others as Africans. In Nigeria, Bakassi identity is shaped by ethnicity, as well as the colonial context of the Nigerian and Cameroonian borders and the Bakassi Peninsula. One of the challenges and limitations of my research deals with the problem of the collapsing of diverse African lives/identities/communities into the umbrella term 'African'; some Africans may see themselves as African, but some identify more with ethnicity or nationality, and it is very difficult to capture the real nuances between every single individual in research of this magnitude. Therefore both 'African' and national identities are categories of analysis in China, whereas in Nigeria, 'Bakassi' identity remains the relevant category not only in this chapter but also throughout the book, because it is how people in the community identify themselves and it is the unit of identity that shapes their experiences in Nigeria.

During my field research in China, I found that by virtue of my Africanness, people assumed that I was an undocumented migrant, and this identity shaped their interaction with me. As was mentioned in Chapter 2, I was unable to easily access the UNHCR building in Beijing to conduct an interview because the staff thought I was seeking asylum; I was allowed into the building only after it was proven that I was a researcher with an appointment with a staff member. This spoke volumes on the general perception of Africans and on the difficulty asylum seekers face in order to access support and protection in Beijing. Even though Africans engage in diverse types of migration, there was a conflation of anyone from the continent with a certain type of migration, and this impacts how Africans experience everyday life in China and other parts of the world.

II. THE TENSION BETWEEN MIGRANT IDENTITIES AND CITIZENSHIP

Tayyab Mahmud discusses the colonial encounter and how it shaped migration and migrant identities. Using the encounters in India with British colonisation, he describes the position and identity of migrants of the Global South within the spaces they migrate to as:

> [A]n outsider, an alien body, to be normalized, homogenized, and assimilated. As a non-citizen, she is to be marginalized in distribution of legal rights and political protections. As a cultural signifier, she is to be erased. As a violator of borders, she provides the rationale to ever strengthen the territorial divides. The threat perception triggered by the immigrant traverses two fields: that of the state, and that of the nation. The immigrant puts at issue the inviolability of borders, territoriality of sovereignty, particularity of jurisdiction, and uniformity of citizenship fundamental characteristics of the modern state. The immigrant calls into question cultural homogeneity, linguistic commonality, shared history, a sense of belonging, and security of identity – the key ideologies of the nation.[28]

Here, Mahmud identifies three different consequences of non-citizenship. He points out the fact that migrants in the Global South challenge the ideas and notions of state and nation due to their foreign-ness and otherness. They challenge the cohesiveness of citizenship, the sacrosanctity of borders, the territorial sovereignty and jurisdiction of the state by virtue of being outsiders. Migrants also challenge the general ideal of homogeneity and cohesion. They call to question all the special or unique privileges that citizenship in its 'traditional' form bestows, like belonging, a shared history, cultural homogeneity (whether real or imagined), uniformity of language and security of identity. This was evident in the local perceptions in China about Africans; people felt threatened by the presence of people who did not look or sound like them in Guangzhou, and this has led to discrimination and hostilities.[29] For example, Mr T, a businessman

[28] Tayyab Mahmud, 'Migration, Identity & the Colonial Encounter' (1997) 76 *Oregon Law Review* 633 at 643.

[29] These responses to African-ness were confirmed in interviews with Ms Y, a member of staff of a Chinese community organisation working with African migrants, Ms M, a Chinese migration researcher, and during the listening session with Chinese immigration law scholars at Beijing Institute of Technology in 2016. All my interviewees stated that locals perceived the presence of Africans to be a disruption of the cohesion in China.

with undocumented status, shared that people refuse to sit beside him in the bus or in the subway. Finding a job was so taxing for Mr T that he was forced to become self-employed.[30] In Nigeria, communities to which Bakassi people migrated also felt uneasy as a result of the influx of new people who occupied space and resources. This led to some manifestations of exclusion and oppression, as I will discuss later on in this chapter.

Purvis and Hunt analyse how citizenship stems from Western political thought and point to the West as the root of the 'tensions between citizenship, identity and inclusion and exclusion … citizens as pre-eminent political identity with the practical effect of displacing, occluding or supplanting alternative identities, banishing them to the realm of extra- or pre-political'.[31] This conception of citizenship is not disrupted in China or Nigeria due to the absorption and normalisation of the exclusivity of borders and citizenship in both states. The international system is set up, from statehood to borders, to citizenship to race and ethnicity, to benefit the Global North and the elite in the Global South, and to enable them to exert power over others. The history of international law is a series of processes that shaped and institutionalised the domination of a majority by a few; for some (particularly the global elite and citizens in the Global North), immigration is trouble-free and a means for self-empowerment. Immigration regimes are one of the ways in which hegemonic systems re-enact old methods in new terms. It is another means through which hierarchies and exclusions are enforced and normalised.

TWAIL challenges the power mechanisms that created the hierarchies between the Global North, the Global South and the peripheries. Resistance, defined by Sujith Xavier as the struggle for access, justice and redistribution, is central to the analysis of the Global South both within itself and in relation to the West.[32] Ibironke Odumosu holds that in order for TWAIL to meet its challenges and limitations, there is a need to consider the role of ideas and power, as well as questions of identity.[33] According to her, the law is an incarnation of dominant ideas and norms; because of its hegemonic nature, it has the capacity to give justice to people in the Third World, but this is only possible if the identities that 'reflect domination are addressed, resisted and reconstituted, for the identity of the actor forms a crucial factor in the establishment of its ideas'.[34] What this means is that justice is only possible when identities or labels resulting from oppression are resisted and reconstructed. Odumosu believes that the reconstruction of identity is justice itself. In my

[30] Personal interview with Mr T (n 1).

[31] Purvis and Hunt (n 4) 462.

[32] See Sujith Xavier, 'Learning from below: Theorising Global Governance through Ethnographies and Critical Reflections from the Global South' (2016) 33 *Windsor Yearbook of Access to Justice* 229.

[33] Ibironke T Odumosu, 'Challenges for the (Present/)Future of Third World Approaches to International Law' (2008) 10 *International Community Law Review* 467.

[34] ibid at 472.

understanding, this means that the freedom to challenge and change harmful identities is a path to justice. In relation to my case studies, the ways in which migrant communities resist and change identities foisted upon them by the state is a path to justice. How these communities reconstruct and challenge identities becomes their form of power with which they can 'facilitate the reconstitution of identities of domination'.[35]

TWAIL scholars such as Eslava, Pahuja and Xavier have conceptualised resistance and empowerment as affirmations of the realities of the Global South – not as far-flung places or people from which anthropological, historical and other observations can be made, but as sites of real and ongoing struggles of communities and individuals against different forms of hegemony and marginality.[36] Going by these ideas, international law can be changed when resistance and empowerment happen as a result of encountering hegemonic laws, policies and norms in the everyday experiences of people in the Global South and in its study. Resistance and empowerment are not abstractions; they are tangible, material responses to exclusions and power struggles. In relation to South-South migrations, resistance means the ways in which the migrant communities in my case studies encounter and resist marginalisation because of their migrant status, as it intersects with their other identities.

Looking at identity and resistance through the eyes of Odumosu, resistance is a form of power which is the tool to reconstruct identities of domination. In pointing out that labels and identities can be resisted, reconstructed and changed, Odumosu highlights the agency of people in the Global South. Marginalised people and communities are not powerless even in the face of simultaneously occurring oppressions, violence, coercion and control. This is significant because it means that even though these communities are limited by the hegemonic ideals and norms like citizenship, nationality, race and borders, they also have the agency to resist these ideals and create new ones over time. Agency is a very important part of the discussion on identity because it also critiques the stereotypes of victimhood and powerlessness of the marginalised in the face of injustice. The agency of undocumented migrant communities in the Global South is their power to fight against hegemony. I believe that the way that accumulations of hegemonic ideals can lead to oppression is the same way that the accumulation of resistance over time can gradually reconstitute identities and change the power dynamics in the Global South.

III. IDENTITY AND INTERSECTIONALITY

Identity is not singular or binary in nature. It is multidimensional, complex and overlapping. Multiple categories of identities can intersect or accumulate to

[35] ibid.

[36] Luis Eslava and Sundhya Pahuja, 'Between Resistance and Reform: TWAIL and the Universality of International Law' (2011) 3 *Trade Law and Development* 103 at 129; Xavier (n 32) 245.

create 'social inequality that define an individual's identity in a unique way'.[37] This idea of the 'intersectionality' of identities was birthed by Black feminist writing and pioneered by Kimberlé Crenshaw in the US in the 1980s and other scholars, including Patricia Collins, Leslie McCall, Davies, Francisco Valdes and Evelyn Glenn.[38] Crenshaw conceptualised intersectionality as structures that focus on only one dimension of Black women's identities and, in so doing, erase others and entrench discrimination and oppression.[39] One of the structures that Crenshaw discusses is the legal system: courts in the US adopt a one-dimensional approach in discrimination cases due to the influence dominant groups have over the establishment and implementation of the law.[40]

In this system where either race or gender is centred, Black women who face both race and gender-related oppression cannot achieve justice due to the distinct prejudices that arise when race and gender intersect. Crenshaw states that more than being just about the multiple identities a person or group can have, intersectionality is about structures that make certain identities the 'consequence of and the vehicle of vulnerability'.[41] Here, it is about how structures created or influenced by dominant groups make others vulnerable by erasing the complexity and multidimensional nature of their narratives and simplifying their experiences. According to Crenshaw, one cannot discuss intersectionality without looking at the context, the types of discriminations happening, and the policies and institutional structures that contribute to the exclusion and oppression of some people over others.[42] Also, identity cannot be discussed as a self-contained unit because it is a relationship between people and history (or histories), people and communities, and people and institutions.[43]

Intersectionality is not without its limitations. Jennifer Nash identifies problems with intersectionality, including a lack of a clear intersectional methodology, the centrality of Black women as the subjects of intersectional discourse, the ambiguity of the definition of intersectionality and the lack of

[37] Bolatito Kolawole, 'African Immigrants, Intersectionality, and the Increasing Need for Visibility in the Current Immigration Debate' (2017) 7 *Columbia Journal of Race and Law* 373 at 386.

[38] See Patricia Hill Collins, *Black Feminist Thought: Knowledge, Consciousness, and the Politics of Empowerment* (Boston, Unwin Hyman, 1990); Francisco Valdes, 'Sex and Race in Queer Legal Culture: Ruminations on Identities and Inter-connectivities' (1995) 5 *Southern California Review of Law and Women's Studies* 25; Evelyn N Glenn, 'The Social Construction and Institutionalization of Gender and Race: An Integrative Framework' in Myra Ferree (ed), *Revisioning Gender* (Thousand Oaks, CA, Sage Publications, 1999); Leslie McCall, 'The Complexity of Intersectionality' (2005) 30(3) *Signs* 1771.

[39] Kimberlé Williams Crenshaw, 'Demarginalizing the Intersection of Race and Sex: A Black Feminist Critique of Antidiscrimination Doctrine, Feminist Theory and Antiracist Politics' (1989) 1 *University of Chicago Legal Forum* 139 at 140.

[40] ibid.

[41] Kimberlé Williams Crenshaw, 'Intersectionality NOT Identity', keynote speech at Women of the World Festival at the Southbank Centre, London, 13 March 2016, https://www.youtube.com/watch?v=-DW4HLgYPlA.

[42] ibid.

[43] ibid.

consistency between intersectionality and lived experiences.[44] She argues that Crenshaw and others limit intersectionality by focusing on race and gender, when other factors like class, language, ethnicity, sexuality and nationality also complicate the experiences of Black women and other minorities. She also states that this leads to the representation of Black women as a monolithic group, in which every Black woman experiences everything in the same way.[45] Similarly, Nira Yuval-Davis critiques intersectional analysis that does not make distinctions between social locations, identities and political values, which homogenises notions like Blackness and womanhood.[46] Because intersectionality focuses on race and gender, another question is whether it is a theory for understanding multiply marginalised people or whether it should be broadened to be a general theory of identity. Nash opines that it should be broadened for the reasons given above. In real life, experiences of marginality are on a spectrum; individuals within a group may be marginalised because of one factor but privileged because of another, and intersectional analysis must show these nuances.

Nevertheless, in line with Makau Mutua's reasoning, beyond the context of race and identity politics in the US, intersectionality is a useful tool to unpack oppression and understand the experiences of minority groups who are erased or excluded due to the generalisations of majority groups. It is a tool for critiquing the distribution of justice and power in society and, as a result, it is useful for legal and policy reform in so many different areas of life. Mutua sees intersectionality as a comprehensive tool that can be applied in the context of the Global South because it analyses multiple facets of hierarchies and powerlessness, and disaggregates complex social and legal phenomena.[47] TWAIL-focused work, in tandem with intersectionality, is a surveillance and dissection of power disparities. It questions the 'expanding multi-dimensional forms of informal imperialism' and 'global asymmetries of power', and thinks of how to change those asymmetries.[48] Intersectionality has broadened beyond the study of Black women to include other marginalised groups that face problems arising from an intersection of multiple categories within queer identities,[49] disabilities,[50]

[44] Jennifer C Nash, 'Rethinking Intersectionality' (2008) 89(1) *Feminist Review* 1 at 4.

[45] ibid at 7.

[46] Nira Yuval-Davis, 'Intersectionality, Citizenship and Contemporary Politics of Belonging' (2007) 10(4) *Critical Review of International Social and Political Philosophy* 561 at 565–66.

[47] Mutua (n 21) 841 and 849.

[48] Luis Eslava, 'TWAIL Coordinates', *Legal Critical Thinking*, 2 April 2019, http://criticallegalthinking.com/2019/04/02/twail-coordinates.

[49] See Henry H Ng, 'Intersectionality and Shared Decision Making in LGBTQ Health' (2016) 3(5) *LGBT Health* 325; Lynda Johnston, 'Intersectional Feminist and Queer Geographies: A View from "Down-Under"' (2018) 25(4) *Gender, Place & Culture* 554.

[50] See Anastasia Liasidou, 'Intersectional Understandings of Disability and Implications for a Social Justice Reform Agenda in Education Policy and Practice' (2013) 28(3) *Disability & Society* 299; Jacqueline Moodley and Lauren Graham, 'The Importance of Intersectionality in Disability and Gender Studies' (2015) 29(2) *Agenda* 24.

HIV/AIDS,[51] mental illness,[52] age[53] and migrations.[54] In my mind, the intersections of identities are multiple sets of overlapping concentric circles, each circle representing an identity (the primary identifier, according to Pittaway and Pittaway).[55] Within migrations, race, gender, undocumented status and class intersect and overlap, so using the framework of intersectionality to discuss migrations (and particularly South-South migrations) is very useful.[56] A Nigerian asylum seeker in China experiences exclusion in a unique combination of factors: their race, the specific immigration policies towards their nationality in China, their class, their nationality in relation to other African and non-African nationalities, their immigration status, as well as the history of China's attitude towards non-Chinese refugees, as was discussed in Chapter 4. Through examining identity in terms of migrations, another social category emerges: the identity of that which is undocumented or documented, 'illegal' or legal, settled or displaced, and citizen or non-citizen, so in addition to Blackness, foreign-ness becomes another label that colours the experiences of African migrants. Undocumented status is not a social category per se; however, it is a factual situation that leads to social categorisation. Undocumented migrants may be categorised within the state in which they reside as 'poor' or 'unemployable', but within an undocumented community, there exist varying levels of poverty and access to employment, for example, and these categorisations and realities impact daily lives. Using intersectionality to understand other social categories broadens its applicability and nuances to a more generalised theory of identity, and shows a greater range of experience, varying from marginality to some level of privilege.

Hope Lewis focuses on race in the discussion on human rights and identity because race is indicative of numerous identity categories, including culture, class and ethnicity, but is also distinct from them.[57] Race is very important in

[51] See Larry M Gant, 'Intersectional Contexts of HIV/AIDS: Global Examples' (2017) 16(1) *Journal of HIV/AIDS & Social Services* 1; Ashley Lacombe-Duncan, 'An Intersectional Perspective on Access to HIV-Related Healthcare for Transgender Women' (2016) 1(1) *Transgender Health* 137.

[52] See Kira H Banks and Laura P Kohn-Wood, 'Gender, Ethnicity and Depression: Intersectionality in Mental Health Research with African American Women' (2002) 8 *African American Research Perspectives* 174; Kristina Hallett, 'Intersectionality and Serious Mental Illness: A Case Study and Recommendations for Practice' (2015) 38(1–2) *Women & Therapy* 156.

[53] See Catherine E Harnois, 'Age and Gender Discrimination: Intersecting Inequalities across the Lifecourse' in Vasilikie Demos and Marcia Texler Segal (eds), *At the Center: Feminism, Social Science and Knowledge* (Bingley, Emerald Group Publishing, 2015) at 85–109; Michelle Gander, 'The Intersection of Gender and Age: An Exploration' (2014) 18(1) *Perspectives: Policy and Practice in Higher Education* 9.

[54] Hans-Joachim Bürkner, 'Intersectionality: How Gender Studies Might Inspire the Analysis of Social Inequality among Migrants' (2012) 18(2) *Population, Space and Place* 181; Mastoureh Fathi, *Intersectionality, Class and Migration: Narratives of Iranian Women Migrants in the UK* (New York, Palgrave Macmillan, 2017).

[55] Pittaway and Pittaway (n 11) 124.

[56] Kolawole (n 37) 392.

[57] Hope Lewis, 'Transnational Dimensions of Racial Identity: Reflecting on Race, the Global Economy, and the Human Rights Movement at 60' (2009) 24 *Maryland Journal of International Law* 296.

human rights discourse; racism is the cause of large-scale civil and political rights violations, as well as economic, social and cultural exclusions globally.[58] Lewis critiques international human rights instruments that are only able to focus on single issues, whereas the people they intend to protect face multiple exclusions due to the complex interplay of their identities.

Lewis uses the example of the experience of human trafficking which might be different for an Eastern European woman in comparison to a South Asian woman because of the interplay of class, ethnicity, religion etc. The human rights instrument that deals with trafficking is ignorant of the disparity and does nothing to address these differences.[59] Lewis holds that this approach 'essentialises' people who should be protected.[60] I agree that while categories by themselves are neutral, identity markers become imagined into the application of the law. Lewis focuses specifically on Black transnational migrants with complex and multidimensional identities facing racism, sexism and exploitation at the same time. Yet analyses of the rights of these migrants often do not see the multiple dimensions of violations, but rather usually address just one dimension of the problem; intersectionality helps here.[61] Basically, Lewis argues that human rights law ignores the intersection of race, gender, migration status and other identities in human rights protection of Black migrants in particular, and that all these dimensions must be taken into consideration in order for human rights to be achievable.[62] Another example from Lewis shows that Black men in the US experience violence and abuse because of racial profiling and stereotypes, but that there is another layer of oppression when the Black man is also an immigrant who will also be profiled for his migration status.[63] There is never a full discussion of all the different dimensions that come into play in the oppression of marginalised groups. Intersectionality projects attempt to precisely do this.

In addition, Lewis critiques the prioritisation of civil and political rights violations over economic, social, and cultural rights violations in the refugee law regime. She states that:

> Black transnational and internal migrations also challenge the political-economic distinction in asylum status and in the protection of human rights. Many Black transnational migrants are attempting to escape extreme economic privation rather than explicit political persecution, or they seek to escape a combination of the two. Yet the prioritization of civil and political violations … marginalizes Black migrants, or excludes them entirely, from important protections.[64]

[58] ibid at 298.
[59] UN General Assembly, Protocol to Prevent, Suppress and Punish Trafficking in Persons, Especially Women and Children, Supplementing the United Nations Convention against Transnational Organized Crime, 40 ILM 335 (2001); UN Doc A/55/383 at 25 (2000), 15 November 2000.
[60] Lewis (n 57) 300.
[61] ibid at 303.
[62] ibid.
[63] ibid at 304.
[64] ibid at 305.

I witnessed this in the UNHCR's approach towards African asylum seekers in China (see Chapter 3), where asylum seekers from African countries are disbelieved and discredited because some of them are not fleeing civil and political persecution; as such, they are not 'real' refugees because they came to China and overstayed their visas. The UNHCR centres refugee status on civil and political rights, and is incapable of offering protections and refugee status to those who are fleeing poverty and the oppression that comes with it. As a result, migrants who may need protection are disadvantaged by virtue of their migration status, and numerous aspects of the experiences that forced them to migrate are overlooked. In order to discuss identity and human rights, it is crucial to see the multidimensional and intersectional nature of marginalised experiences.[65] Bolatito Kolawole's work on intersectionality and African migrants takes a similar slant. According to Kolawole, intersectionality is an empirical research paradigm that asks new questions, seeks new answers and strategies for political and legal reform; here, intersectionality is broadened and used as a tool to identify areas of intervention and call for the reformation of law and policy.[66] She uses intersectionality in ways that give it the kind of specificity that Nash envisioned beyond race and gender alone, broadening its explanatory power.

Race and nationality combine to make African migrants both invisible and hyper-visible in the countries they migrate to and according to Kolawole, this makes them vulnerable to the policies that affect them.[67] On the one hand, African migrants are invisible by virtue of being foreign – they are not part of the political processes shaping legal and policy reforms and, as a result, laws and policies do not develop in ways that include them. On the other hand, African migrants are hyper-visible because of Blackness and what this signifies in the context of the receiving state. In the words of Ramon Grosfuguel, Laura Oso and Anastasia Christon, no neutral space exists for migrants; migrants come into metropolitan spaces that have been tainted by long histories of coloniality, racial and ethnic hierarchies and hegemony, and this has a direct impact on their experiences.[68] According to Kolawole, intersectionality can be a resource in understanding how African migrants experience their racial and national identities.[69] This is the reason why intersectionality is linked not only to identity and migrations but also specifically to the migrations of Black people and the challenges they face in their day-to-day experiences of the law and policies.[70] Kolawole explains that race and nationality work together to create

[65] Mutua (n 21) 848–49.
[66] Kolawole (n 37) 386.
[67] ibid at 373.
[68] Ramon Grosfoguel, Laura Oso and Anastasia Christou, '"Racism", Intersectionality and Migration Studies: Framing Some Theoretical Reflections' (2015) 22(6) *Identities* 635 at 641–42.
[69] Kolawole (n 37) 393.
[70] ibid at 397.

discrimination and, as a result, the line where racial discrimination ends and nationality discrimination starts is thin.[71] To my understanding, Kolawole means that African migrants are often oppressed on two levels: discriminated against because of race and also because of nationality when they are in spaces where they are minorities, ie, outside Africa. In China, this manifested in how all Africans are treated to the same stringent visa application, renewal or extension rules at the local level, regardless of the diverse range of diplomatic relationships that China has with different African states. Beyond these two categories of race and nationality, there are other hidden or ignored identities of African migrants, as my case studies will show. When these hidden layers in the experiences of South-South migrants are unpacked and discussed, one can then think of ways in which discrimination might cease. The case studies demonstrate the impact of multiple oppressions on the experience of the law in the everyday, as well as how these multiple and simultaneous oppressions lead to invisibility and vulnerability, but also create an environment for resistance.

In the Chinese context, the Nigerian community faces various types of exclusions from Chinese communities and institutions by virtue of their foreign-ness, African-ness, migrant status, gender and class, as well as the history of China's relationship with African peoples in China. In the Nigerian context, Bakassi people face multiple exclusions because of their undocumented statuses, ethnicity, class, sex and lack of ancestral lands due to the decision of the ICJ that rendered them 'landless' in a space where land is an indication of ancestry, identity and culture. Without unpacking these exclusions, it will be impossible to understand and represent the lived experiences of these communities in their path to justice. In discussing intersectionality, it is evident that we cannot truly understand the power dynamics in the Global South without looking into the impact of overlapping identities on the manifestation of multiple and simultaneous experiences of oppression. Because of its multidimensional approach, intersectionality moves beyond the rigidity of identity politics. Intersectionality as well as TWAIL allow the hidden layers and identities that shape the complex communities I have discussed in the preceding chapters to be rendered visible.

IV. SITUATING INTERSECTIONALITY IN SOUTH-SOUTH MIGRATIONS

A. China's Approach towards Nigerian Migrations

There has been a long history of migrations from non-Chinese peoples to ports like Guangzhou for trade.[72] Migrations from other Global South locales are

[71] ibid at 398.

[72] See Teobaldo Filesi, *China and Africa in the Middle Ages*, David L Morison (trans) (London, Frank Cass in association with the Central Asian Research Centre, 1972).

also not new and have been occurring for centuries. However, none of these migrations was large-scale and at that time, there were no strict definitions of borders, nationality, citizenship or a refugee regime. Before the opening-up of China's economy to the international community, there were no refugees or undocumented migrants from African countries. Due to this history of accepting returning Chinese and the low level of migrations from Africa, China did not develop a clear legal or policy approach towards non-Chinese undocumented migrants or asylum seekers until the 2000s. Internationally since Deng Xiaoping, the government has had a policy of an open and collaborating China. After China 'opened', the government now faced the challenge of accepting foreigners in a country where homogeneity was central to its laws and policies. Opening meant that China was switching from a communist to a capitalist system of operation; China now welcomed foreign business, but a long history of introspection resulted in constant tension between the two opposing systems, resulting in a very hierarchical and oppressive system. Therefore, this openness does not match local realities shaped by great internal migration restrictions and population pressures which shaped internal laws and policies. China's Sino-African diplomacy has not matched how Africans are perceived or treated in China for this reason.

An open economy is linked to increased immigration and as more foreigners, including many Africans, migrated to China, Chinese immigration law began to evolve, and visa laws and policies tightened from the 2000s as more foreigners settled in China.[73] The visa-on-arrival policy came to an end, and longer-term and non-tourist visas became difficult for Africans to obtain or extend.[74] Some of my Nigerian respondents migrated to China in the late 1980s and have lived in China for over 30 years, experiencing the evolution of Chinese immigration laws for a long period of time. Nigerians get short-term visas – often a week to 30 days in length with single entries – whereas Canadians, for example, can apply for 10-year visas with multiple entries and have opportunities for visa extensions.[75] Other nationalities (particularly Western nationalities) can extend their visas through visa agents or by leaving China and re-entering because of multiple-entry, longer-length visas.[76] I observed that visa agents do not offer services to Africans because of visa discrimination; most Africans have visas that do not allow them the same freedom of movement as other foreigners. Visa agents that I reached out to refused to engage in a conversation about visa renewal procedures when they heard that I was Nigerian by

[73] See Adams Bodomo, 'The African Trading Community in Guangzhou: An Emerging Bridge for Africa–China Relations'(2010) 203 *China Quarterly* 693.

[74] Daouda Cisse, 'South-South Migration and Trade: African Traders in China', policy briefing, Centre for Chinese Studies at Stellenbosch University, 2013.

[75] See Heidi Ostbo Haugen, ''Nigerians in China: A Second State of Immobility' (2012) 50(2) *International Migration* 65.

[76] I contacted different visa agencies to make enquiries about visa extension and status changes for Africans in Beijing in December 2015 and in Guangzhou in March 2016.

nationality, a common response was that Africans cannot renew visas because it is too complex, with no reasoning or explanations being given for this.

Coupled with compulsory police registration, immigration raids, random documentation checks carried out by the PSB and other measures, Chinese immigration law and policy has evolved to target Africans more than other foreigners.

B. The Heavy Burden of *Sanfei*: Intersectionality and the Nigerian Community in China

Looking at the narratives of members of the African community in China, it is possible to pinpoint intersectionalities. Most of my respondents belonged to the Nigerian community and this informed my focus on its members' narratives. As previously discussed, in China, African identity – ie, being of African origin or nationality – greatly impacts the experience of immigration and other domestic laws. China's visa laws and policies discriminate against Africans by making the application process difficult and only granting short-term visas. Many of the interviewees faced difficulties in obtaining or extending visas[77] Africans are more likely to be stopped and questioned about their documentation, experiencing door-to-door inspections, raids, and police intimidation in cities like Guangzhou.[78] Mr T, a Nigerian who migrated to China in 2012, stated that Africans were denied visa renewals if they did not register at the police station when they arrived; other foreigners could rely on visa agents to renew their visas with or without police registration. He also claimed that immigration raids in Guangzhou focused on Africans and felt that these raids and checks coincided with whenever the government wanted to demonstrate to the citizenry that immigration was under control.[79]

This is the reason Africans seem to commit more immigration offences than others. The *sanfei* label (which describes people who enter, work or stay in China illegally) has become attached to Africans by China's public security apparatus. The *sanfei* tag has been used for racial profiling by security bodies, further entrenching the image of Africans as criminals or law breakers and institutionalising racism against African migrants.[80] Africans also face discrimination in the job market because of work visa restrictions, as well as other negative stereotypes, even though many Africans in China are well educated. According to Min Zhou, Tao Xu and Shabnam Shenasi, African entrepreneurs are often more educated than their Chinese counterparts and

[77] Personal interview with Mr B, Baiyun District, Guangzhou, 15 March 2016.

[78] See Guangzhi Huang, 'Policing Blacks in Guangzhou: How Public Security Constructs Africans as *Sanfei*' (2018) 45(2) *Modern China* 171.

[79] Personal interview with Mr T (n 1).

[80] Huang (n 78).

are more likely to have undergraduate degrees (60% versus 20%).[81] According to Mr B, one of the first Nigerians to migrate to Guangzhou in the 1990s, because there are no legal jobs or opportunities for Africans, many are forced to do business illegally, sell drugs or fall into prostitution in order to survive.[82] This is a cycle that begins with stringent immigration laws and ends, in the most extreme cases, with the incarceration or deaths of Africans, revealing how the state can perpetuate and institutionalise stereotypes. For example, Article 29 of the Entry and Exit Law states that:

> Where the duration of stay needs to be extended, the visa holder shall file an application with the exit/entry administration of public security organ under the local people's government at or above the county level in the place of his stay seven days prior to the expiry of the duration specified in the visa and shall submit information of specific application matters in accordance with relevant requirements. If upon examination, the reasons for extension are appropriate and sufficient, such extension shall be granted; if an extension is denied, the foreigner shall leave China on the expiry of the duration.[83]

However, according to all the respondents, this does not apply to them on account of their African-ness, as well as their Nigerian nationality. When they tried to follow due process at the PSB in 2016, they were told that visa renewal at the PSB was not possible for Africans, disregarding the provision in the Entry and Exit Law. This intersection of nationality and race inhibits Africans from enjoying some of the provisions in the Entry and Exit Law. It is important to note that this experience is not the same across the board – migrants who moved to China earlier (in the 1990s) were more likely to have obtained residence permits when the number of Africans in China was small and immigration laws were still taking shape. As a result, people like Mr B do not face visa extension or renewal issues, although they must travel outside China annually to renew their residence permits. This means that at one end, people like Mr B have some privileges, while more recent and undocumented migrants like Mr T face extra limitations due to their race and nationality.

According to Guangzhi Huang, the *sanfei* label has become synonymous with African migrants in China and, as a result, Africans have become the main targets in the PSB's campaign against *sanfei*, even though other nationalities overstay their visas.[84] According to Huang, these campaigns include garnering public support through the media, visa raids, stop-and-search inspections, heavy fines and prolonged detention. Furthermore, Chinese immigration rules are

[81] See Min Zhou, Tao Xu and Shabnam Shenasi, 'Entrepreneurship and Interracial Dynamics: A Case Study of Self-Employed Africans and Chinese in Guangzhou, China' (2016) 39(9) *Journal of Ethnic and Racial Studies: Ethnic Entrepreneurship in Intersectional Perspectives* 1573.

[82] Personal interview with Mr B (n 77).

[83] China: Law of 2012, Exit and Entry Administration Law of the People's Republic of China, Order No 57, 1 July 2013 at art 29.

[84] Huang (n 78).

very unpredictable; the rules are constantly changing at a fast pace, so Africans face the ever-present risk of breaking rules that are implemented without prior notice or information at the municipal level.[85] Huang gives an example of the random quota implemented on the number and duration of registration certificates issued by the PSB in Xiaobei, a place where a lot of African immigrants have settled in Guangzhou.[86] The quota was implemented entirely at the discretion of the police and civilian personnel, and had nothing to do with the Entry and Exit Law itself.

Ms M, a Chinese migration researcher who has carried out research on the relationships between locals and the African immigrant communities in Guangzhou, stated that these changes reflect a disconnection between the top and bottom levels of the Chinese government. According to her, these changes happen at the municipal level and not at the national level because the pressure of the African presence is more strongly felt at the municipal level in public administration and public service.[87] In cities like Guangzhou, Africans often face the random curtailment of their temporary residence registration certificates, which is a compulsory document issued by the PSB within 24 hours of arrival to all foreigners. Curtailing these certificates without prior notice is a tool used to force Africans to leave China, but, in the end, it only reinforces the *sanfei* label – it drives documented visitors or migrants to become undocumented as the fear of arrest leads many to go into hiding.[88] Huang also states that African communities in places like Xiaobei in Guangzhou are heavily policed and excessively fined in comparison to other migrant communities. He notes that Africans make easy targets as *sanfei* because:

> First, unlike white foreigners, who are scattered around the city, Africans are concentrated in a few areas, with Xiaobei being the most prominent. Also, the police know that Africans are more likely to rent from private landlords and not have the RCTR since the RCTR is issued by the police themselves. Because white foreigners are usually formally employed or stay in hotels, the RCTR is less of an issue for them.[12] Finally, African sanfei are much easier to catch. The term 'sanfei' includes those without valid immigration documents and those working in China without authorization. However, the way the law is enforced is heavily biased against the former group. Since many Africans violate the sanfei law by overstaying their visas, instead of working without authorization, they are very easy to catch and convict as all the police need to do is check their passports. Illegal workers, on the other hand, are much harder to convict, despite their large numbers.[89]

Heavy fines leveraged on African migrant communities incentivise high-handed policing. Local low-ranking officers give surcharges from fines to the police, a practice which has become a lucrative business. Here, the labelling of Africans

[85] ibid.
[86] ibid at 2–3.
[87] Skype conversation with Ms M, 16 December 2015, on file with the author.
[88] Haugen (n 75).
[89] Huang (n 78) 17.

is used to legitimise extortion or, according to Hayward, 'violence and coercion'.[90] This is similar to Purvis and Hunt's argument that identity within a state is tied to recognition from the state and when the state does not recognise a person or a group of people, it excludes them by policing their public and private lives.[91] In this case, we see that Africans are excluded and policed in both the private and public arenas based on their national and racial identities, as well as perceptions of their economic statuses, education and employability in China.

As Nigerians make up the largest number of documented and undocumented Africans in China, the Nigerian community bears the weight of this discrimination and negative labelling more than other African communities.[92] The Nigerian community has the largest population of Africans in Chinese prisons and activists within the community have spoken against the stereotyping of Africans as drug dealers, which fuels not only the attitude of the locals, but also the approach of the PSB and the Chinese criminal law system towards them.[93] Leaders in the community like Mr B initiate different intra-community initiatives (eg, commemorating Africa Day in Guangzhou) to change the perceptions of Nigerians in cities and to positively impact the way in which Africans are treated in China. Community leaders are also involved in advocating for the release of the estimated 2,000-plus Nigerians in Chinese prisons.[94] In all cases in which migrants were killed during immigration raids, the migrants were Nigerian nationals. The Nigerian community rioted against police brutality carried out during these raids.[95] The Nigerian migrant-led riots in 2009, 2011 and 2012 made things difficult for Africans generally and Nigerians in particular, according to Mr T.[96] The size of the Nigerian

[90] Hayward and Watson (n 22) 21–22.

[91] Purvis and Hunt (n 4) 470, 475.

[92] Generally, there is no exact record of the real number of Africans in China or Nigerians in China. Estimates from different people have ranged from 1,500 to 20,000, 100,000 and 200,000 Africans in China, with the majority of them in city of Guangzhou, but there is no official confirmation of these numbers. Focusing on Nigerians, it is impossible to estimate the size of the undocumented population because they are undocumented. However, the Nigerian government gave an estimate of 10,000 documented Nigerians in China by 2014. See Africa Independent Online, 'Nigeria-China Relations Deepen as Senator David Mark Visits Chinese Parliament', 15 May 2014 www.aitonline.tv/post-nigeria_china_relations_deepen_as_senator_david_mark_visits_chinese_parliament. The number of Nigerians with long-term residence permits is between 700 and 800; see Roberto Castillo, 'Feeling at Home in the "Chocolate City": An Exploration of Place Making Practices and Structures of Belonging amongst Africans in Guangzhou' (2014) 15(2) *Inter-Asia Cultural Studies* 235.

[93] Haugen (n 75).

[94] Chiemelie Ezeobi. 'Nigerians Languish in Chinese Jails', *Thisday*, 17 March 2016, https://www.pressreader.com/nigeria/thisday/20160317/281646779253050.

[95] See Ivan Zhai, 'Africans Protests in Guangzhou after Nigerian Feared Killed Fleeing Visa Check', *South China Morning Post*, 16 July 2009, https://www.scmp.com/article/686919/africans-protest-guangzhou-after-nigerian-feared-killed-fleeing-visa-check; see also Hannah Beech, 'A Nigerian Dies in China – and Racial Tensions Heat up', *TIME*, 20 June 2012, http://world.time.com/2012/06/20/a-nigerian-dies-in-china-and-racial-tensions-heat-up.

[96] Personal interview with Mr T (n 1).

community in relation to other African communities has also led to resulting stereotypes. Overstaying and drug and criminal offences are often seen to be committed mainly by Nigerians. The community is subject to tougher scrutiny, higher incarceration rates and less leniency during immigration raids and other procedures as a result.[97] Because of these negative labels placed on the community, Nigerian businesspeople face discrimination based on their race and nationality at the same time.[98]

From my interviews, the time of migration also determines how individuals and members of the community experience the law. Older migrants are better adapted to Chinese laws because they migrated before Chinese laws became stringent towards African, and specifically Nigerians. Thus, within the Nigerian community, time creates hierarchies and exclusions that are hard to see. Most of those who migrated in the early 1980s faced fewer legal hindrances and were able to attain respect both within the local Chinese community and the Nigerian community – in the case of the latter, this respect resulted in them securing leadership positions and other privileges. The majority of the older members of the community were also richer because they had built businesses over three decades. Those who migrated after the early 2000s arrived when the law had changed; they had to confront a shifting social environment and have faced greater challenges. Economic and social class within the community also shape how Nigerians in China engage with the law. Mr B is an educated man who migrated in the late 1990s and married a highly educated Chinese national. He occupies a higher economic and social class and can conduct business in accordance with Chinese laws.[99] In comparison, Mr T, who was poor and uneducated when he arrived in China in 2011, experienced more discrimination, police brutality and instances of business fraud. Even though he had become wealthy by 2016, his experience of life in China greatly differed from that of Mr B.[100] Mr T stated that many people like him were in jail for breaking Chinese immigration laws. Conversely, Mr B's peers have not engaged with Chinese immigration law in the same manner; recent migrants often rely on the clout and support of more established members of the community in order to access justice and legal support in China. Mr C, who is a student and a businessman, is also privileged within the community as he possesses a more stable and long-term student visa. As such, he can carry out his business without the same burdens as Mr T.[101]

[97] According to the Nigerian Consulate in Guangzhou, in 2018, the number of Nigerians in Chinese prisons was 600, but other estimates suggested that it could be higher than this. See 'Why Many Nigerians are in Chinese Prisons', *The Vanguard*, 26 February 2018, https://www.vanguardngr.com/2018/02/many-nigerians-chinese-prisons-envoy.

[98] Prisca Sam Duru and Vera Anyagafu, 'Nigerians in China Cry out, Drug Traffickers Robbing Us of Privileges', *The Vanguard*, 7 January 2017, https://www.vanguardngr.com/2017/01/nigerians-china-cry-drug-traffickers-robbing-us-privileges.

[99] Personal interview with Mr B (n 77); personal interview with Mr T (n 1).

[100] Personal interview with Mr T (n 1).

[101] Personal interview with Mr C, Xiaobei, March 2016, on file with the author.

Because of his privilege in the community, Mr B has become a person who people rely on for support whenever there are arrests, deaths and other problems in the community. He is one of the few people who has a rapport with the PSB and other important local figures in Guangzhou. This example illustrates how within the community, economic and social standing shape the way in which members experience the law and immigration policies. Economic standing consolidates the hierarchies within the community and determines who has the capacity to gain justice, access or recognition. Nevertheless, from interviews I conducted with Chinese locals in 2015 and 2016, there was a pervasive labelling of Africans as poor, regardless of people like Mr B who were wealthy or people like Mr T who had built wealth in China.[102] This reveals that the hierarchies in the community do not apply on the outside, where Blackness and Africanness come with designations that cut across every member of the community regardless of their real-life situation. Migrants like M T know that they are undocumented by law and live with the consequences of this identity in their daily lives; however, Mr T and others I interviewed saw themselves as more than the identities that the state had foisted upon them. Mr T was a businessman responsible for his siblings and parents in Nigeria and had chosen to live undocumented in order to be able to meet the demands of daily life and the structural problems in Nigeria. Mr T and others are changing the power dynamics in China by becoming successful, even though they are undocumented or are faced with discriminatory laws and policies.

Gender and citizenship also intersect to impact the experience of Chinese laws. Chinese women have the privilege of citizenship and the legal right to open and run businesses in China, which is a right that members of the Nigerian community – especially those with undocumented status – do not have. Most of the members of the Nigerian community and all the businesspeople I encountered were male. All the men I interviewed in Guangzhou had married Chinese women and many of them were involved in marriages of convenience in order to ease the harsh impact of immigration laws and policies on their lives and businesses.[103] Female asylum seekers faced unique challenges in China due to the intersection of gender, race, economic status and immigration status. They experienced forced prostitution, rape and employment discrimination and harassment, which men did not experience.[104] Liberian asylum seekers A and B faced sexual and labour exploitation in Dongguan because they were women.[105] According to them, employment opportunities for female African migrants in Dongguan and Beijing are fewer than those available to men. Moreover, men

[102] Personal interview with Ms Y, Baiyun District, Guangzhou, February 2016, on file with the author; Skype interview with Ms M, 13 January 2016, on file with the author.

[103] Personal interview with Mr B (n 77); personal interview with Mr T (n 1); personal interview with Mr N, Yuexiu District, March 2016, on file with the author.

[104] Personal interview with A and B, Yanjiao, December 2015.

[105] ibid.

within both the African and Chinese communities often demanded sex from A and B when they searched for jobs.[106] None of the male participants interviewed revealed such experiences. The male respondents appear to have had easier access to information and support systems than female respondents. Male asylum seekers also had more financial resources and were more prepared before and upon their arrival in China. This is an indication that sex class impacts female members of the migrant community in addition to other identities like race and economic status. Even within the community, there are varying experiences of marginality shaped by the intersection of identities, as well as the social, cultural and political environment. These overlapping identities greatly impact the manifestations of multiple and simultaneous experiences of oppression experienced by the Nigerian community, as well as Africans in general in China.

C. Nigeria and the Question of Bakassi Identity

Before colonialism, Bakassi identity was flexible: there were no borders or citizenship norms guiding migrations to and from the Peninsula in pre-colonial times. Earlier in history, Bakassi was under the jurisdiction of the Kingdom of Akwa Akpa (also known as Old Calabar), which later became part of Nigeria. In addition to these historical ties, Bakassi people share the same ethnicity, language, culture and religion as the Efik people who inhabit the Cross River and Akwa Ibom States in Nigeria. Because there were no strict borders historically, the Efik people, as well as other ethnicities like the Ibibio, Oron, Ijaw and Mbo, migrated freely between the Peninsula and what is now considered to be Nigeria for many centuries to fish and/or settle.[107] The freedom of movement that existed in pre-colonial times became restricted as colonial powers divided the continent during the Scramble for Africa after the Berlin Conference. Western powers established arbitrary borders to mark territories as theirs and these borders circumscribed the Bakassi people – preventing them from migrating freely – and divided the ethnic group on both sides of the border.[108] Germany initially took possession of Kamerun on one side, while on the other side, the British held sway. The British signed a 'treaty of protection' with the King of Akwa Akpa in 1884, which gave the British Empire control of Calabar, including Bakassi, which subsequently became a part of Nigeria. Germany lost Kamerun

[106] ibid.

[107] See Eni Eja Alobo et al, 'The ICJ's Decision on Bakassi Peninsula in Retrospect: A True Evaluation of the History, Issues and Critique of the Judgement' (2016) 6(10) *International Journal of Humanities and Social Sciences* 108.

[108] Over 177 African ethnic groups were divided by arbitrary borders during colonialism. See AI Asiwaju, 'Partitioned Culture Areas: A Checklist Africans' in AI Asiwaju (ed), *Ethnic Relations across International Boundaries 1884–1984* (London, C Hurst & Co, 1985) 256–58.

after the First World War and France took over the administration of Cameroon. These changes in administration, as well as the different treaties between colonial powers at different times, created the legal and identity conundrum that led to the territorial dispute between Nigeria and Cameroon after decolonisation, as was discussed in Chapter 3, as well as the questions about Bakassi identity contemporarily. The colonial creations of Nigeria and Cameroon, the arbitrary boundaries between them, and the treaties between these colonial powers legitimising these creations and boundaries were upheld by the ICJ in its 2002 decision. The Court imposed the rigidity of Western-centric rules and norms about the law and migration in the region, dramatically impacting the approach towards the Bakassi people in both Nigeria and Cameroon.[109]

After the territory was transferred to Cameroon, Bakassi inhabitants were treated as undocumented migrants on the Peninsula. As has already been discussed in Chapter 3, Cameroon's legal approach towards its Bakassi inhabitants is in contravention of the bilateral GA stemming from the ICJ judgment, which allowed for the pre-colonial fluidity of movement and identity to continue under Article 3.[110] Having based a judgment on the rigidity of the colonial rules and Western norms and agreements, it has been impossible to maintain the African and pre-colonial migration patterns and systems of the Bakassi people. International law was a tool that states employed to force identities tied to specific nationalities and boundaries on the Bakassi people who have lived free of those identities for centuries.

Nigeria claimed the Peninsula as its territory and the inhabitants as its citizens before and during the dispute, but has been unwilling to afford Bakassi migrants the protections and benefits of citizenship in Nigeria and has been indifferent to their plight. The GA does not specify Nigeria's obligations towards Bakassi migrants who choose to leave the Peninsula and does not address their citizenship in either Cameroon or Nigeria either. According to Odinkalu, the agreement does not:

> [P]rovide adequate safeguards for access to residency or identity documents for the Nigerians in Bakassi, or for those who would wish to acquire Cameroonian nationality, nor does it provide mechanisms to prove entitlement to either nationality. Third, there is no obligation on either Cameroon or Nigeria to ensure adequate access to the contents of the Greentree Agreement for all persons among the affected populations in English, French or the local languages. Finally, there are no provisions for independent monitoring of the obligations assumed by the parties.[111]

[109] The findings in the case were discussed in ch 2.

[110] See the Greentree Agreement between Cameroon and Nigeria. Agreement between the Republic of Cameroon and the Federal Republic of Nigeria concerning the Modalities of Withdrawal and Transfer of Authority in the Bakassi Peninsula, 12 June 2006, www.peaceau.org/uploads/cn-agreement-12-06-2006.pdf.

[111] Chidi Odinkalu, 'Stateless in Bakassi: How a Changed Border Left Inhabitants Adrift', *Open Societies Foundation Voices*, https://www.opensocietyfoundations.org/voices/stateless-bakassi-how-changed-border-left-inhabitants-adrift.

The GA should have made provisions for dual nationality or stipulated obligations for documentation in order to enable the Bakassi people to continue to fish and move freely to and from the Peninsula as they have for centuries. It seems that an exodus of migrants was not foreseen during the drafting of the Agreement; the forced migration occurred due to the failure of Cameroon to abide by Article 3. In theory, the bilateral agreement seems like a good idea because it sought to maintain the way of life of the Bakassi people, regardless of the change in administration. However, the Bakassi people are considered non-citizens in Cameroon and are not accorded official documentation in Nigeria; they also face multiple exclusions in the allocation of government resources as well as political representation and participation in both states.

There have been attempts to provide status for Bakassi migrants in Nigeria. In 2007, the government of Cross River State, which shares a border with Cameroon, passed Law No 7 to carve out a new Bakassi Local Government Area (LGA) out of Akpabuyo (an existing LGA) specifically to enable the displaced population to vote and own land in Nigeria.[112] Law No 7 has been ineffective for various reasons. First, by excising the new LGA from an existing LGA, the Bakassi people were imposed on the Akpabuyo LGA, leaving them powerless to fully claim the new LGA.[113] This has created tensions among the Bakassi and has created a split in the resettlement camp in Ikang, which is the New Bakassi LGA. There are also those who claim another location at Dayspring and the Qua Islands (which are said to be uninhabited) as the location where they prefer Bakassi people to settle in Nigeria.[114] The displacement of the people from the Peninsula has created questions and uncertainties regarding where and how they fit into both Cameroon and Nigeria, and, pending resolution, they remain in refugee-like and stateless conditions. Okon Edet argues that the ineffectiveness of Law No 7 was at the root of the dissension with other groups, spurring them to create their own Bakassi LGA and challenge the one created by the state House of Assembly.[115] Edet's view is that the state government did not follow due process because the government was in a rush to create the Bakassi LGA in order to continue receiving federal government funds that stopped coming to the state after the loss of the Peninsula.[116] In other words, Law No 7 failed because it was not created with the intention of protecting Bakassi people and giving

[112] Cross River State Law No 7: Akpabuyo/Bakassi Boundary Adjustment (2007).

[113] A representative elected in 2003 under the Akpabuyo constituency became the representative of the Bakassi constituency in 2007, after Law No 7 was created. As a result, the law created the opposite result of its intention; the political representation of Bakassi people was co-opted by Akpabuyo. See Bassey Inyang, 'Bakassi People: In Quest for a New Abode', *ThisdayLive*, 8 May 2017, https://www.thisdaylive.com/index.php/2017/05/08/bakassi-people-in-quest-for-a-new-abode.

[114] See Okon Edet, *Bakassi Peninsula: The Untold Story of a People Betrayed* (Singapore, Partridge Publishing, 2015). See also Ukpong Cletus, 'Bakassi People "Discover New Island But Nigerian Govt Foot-Dragging" – Leader', *Premium Times*, 22 July 2017, https://www.premiumtimesng.com/news/headlines/237805-bakassi-people-discover-new-island-nigerian-govt-foot-dragging-leader.html.

[115] ibid.

[116] ibid.

them a sense of belonging and identity in Nigeria in the first place. Because of Law No 7, the Bakassi people in Nigeria are divided along political lines; politicians have used this discord to discredit many of the Bakassi people's claims and have co-opted the discussions of where and how they will resettle and participate in Nigerian political life.[117] Additionally, the state government re-adjusted the Akpabuyo LGA without following due process. It did not have the backing of the Independent National Electoral Commission (INEC), which under the provisions in sections 91, 112, 113, 114 and 115 of the Nigerian Constitution is authorised to create or delineate LGA constituencies in Nigeria.[118] The creation of a new LGA by the State House of Assembly also needs to be ordered by the National Assembly, according to the Nigerian Constitution, which states that a bill for a Law of a House of Assembly for the purpose of creating a new local government area shall only be passed if a majority of members support the request and following a referendum in which two-thirds of the people approve the creation of a new LGA.[119] Consequently, displaced Bakassi people have not been able to vote or register as voters and have had no proof of their entitlement to vote since 2007.

In 2011 and 2012, there were two separate litigations between the Bakassi people and the INEC on the implementation of Law No 7.[120] In 2012, the Federal High Court directed the INEC to conduct governorship elections in the new Bakassi wards. The INEC appealed against this judgment, claiming that Law No 7 cannot be implemented without due process,[121] but the state Court of Appeal affirmed the decision of the Federal High Court. The INEC appealed again to the Supreme Court, which finally granted the INEC appeal because only the INEC has the power to delineate local government constituencies.[122] The Court held that even Law No 7 cannot create new constituencies; instead, the law simply adjusted the boundaries of the local governments in the state to create a space to resettle Bakassi migrants. Nevertheless, the Court advised the INEC to create constituencies for Bakassi people in order to generate 'a sense

[117] On the one hand, the Bakassi Peoples General Assembly (BPGA) of Dayspring and the Qua Islands are seeking political leadership and, on the other hand, the Ikang Combined Council of those settled in Ikang are also making political claims. As a result, there are power tussles between the two groups on the representation and resettlement of the Bakassi people in Nigeria.

[118] See Constitution of the Federal Republic of Nigeria, Act No 24, 5 May 1999, ss 91, 112, 113, 114 and 115.

[119] ibid ch 1, pt II, para 8(3).

[120] *Asuquo and Others v INEC*, Federal High Court FHC/CA/CS47/2011 and FHC/CA/CS/21/2012.

[121] *INEC v Asuquo and Others* LPELR-43885 (SC). See also 'INEC Rejects H/Court's Ruling on Bakassi Polls', *The Vanguard*, 11 July 2011, https://www.vanguardngr.com/2011/07/inec-rejects-hcourts-ruling-on-bakassi-polls.

[122] *INEC and Another v Asuquo and Others* LOR (23/2/2018), LPERL-43885 (SC). See also Emmanuel Una, 'Bakassi: Our People May Lose Their Right to Political Representation – Ex-Attorney General', *The Vanguard*, 8 April 2018, https://www.vanguardngr.com/2018/04/b-k-s-s-people-may-lose-right-political-representation-ex-attorney-general; and 'Bakassi: CRSG Tasks INEC on Compliance with S/Court Judgement', *The Vanguard*, 12 April 2018, https://www.vanguardngr.com/2018/04/971903.

of belonging' among them.[123] As the delineation of Bakassi constituencies is advisory, it remains within the purview of INEC to do so or not. For example, in any presidential election, the Bakassi people might still be unable to vote as Nigerians if the INEC does not accept the advice of the Court. We can see that the ICJ decision in 2002 has had a ripple effect from the international level to the regional, the national, the state and the local government levels, with repercussions for the identity and status of the Bakassi people.

In Nigeria, the identity of the Bakassi people is rooted in the power struggles within the Bakassi community for political representation, with the state government for political representation and access to land, and with the Nigerian government at large for documentation, citizenship and residency. The GA was inefficient because the identity of the Bakassi and the obligation to protect their freedom to belong in two different spaces was left unaddressed. The exclusion of the Bakassi people from both Cameroon and Nigeria has become part of the factors shaping the laws and policies affecting them, and even though they share overlapping identities with Nigerian citizens (ethnicity, culture, and religion), they are still othered by not having documentation, land and the ability for full political representation and participation in Nigeria. The failures of the GA and Law No 7 show that the law can indirectly cause or institutionalise exclusions and oppression of individuals and groups. In Cameroon, the ICJ judgment legitimised violence, coercion and discrimination against the Bakassi people by giving their territory away to Cameroon without answering the question of how this change would affect the indigenes of the Peninsula, whereas in Nigeria, it legitimised a political and legal detachment from the protection and resettlement of the Bakassi people.

The lack of access to identity documents in Nigeria and Cameroon excludes the Bakassi people in both spaces from representation and participation, and, as a result, they are not able to protect their interests at the national, state and local levels. In addition, a lack of access to identity documents – whether local government identification or Nigerian passports – means that the Bakassi people are limited in their movement outside borders and/or to carry out other everyday tasks like voting, purchasing property, opening a bank account and obtaining a driver's licence. They also do not have birth certificates proving they are Bakassi, which means that anyone can claim to be Bakassi (an issue that has led to allegations of impersonation at the local level).[124] This indicates that identity is directly tied not only to how the Bakassi people experience the law, but also to the everyday activities of their daily lives. These exclusions in the formal system create a lacuna in terms of justice, access and recognition.

[123] ibid.

[124] Personal conversation with Chief H, former Bakassi Local Government Chairman, Calabar, Cross River State, August 2016; personal conversation with Mr J (n 2); listening session at Ikang Resettlement Camp, Cross River State, Nigeria, June 2016.

In Nigeria, the power struggles that produce oppressive and exclusionary labelling are rooted in the rigidity of colonial imposed borders, which severely limit the existence and presence of the Bakassi people in both Nigeria and Cameroon. I see the artificial borders as an interruption in Bakassi identities, narratives and way of life, and in the space they occupy and exert themselves. Both the ICJ judgment and the GA forced labels upon the Bakassi people. The ICJ judgment labelled the Peninsula as Cameroonian territory, but by not addressing the issue of the identity of its inhabitants further infringed upon Bakassi identity, forcing the Bakassi people to choose between Cameroonian or Nigerian identities and not considering that perhaps Bakassi identity should remain fluid and untouched by colonial boundaries and territorial delimitations. By not considering the opinions of the Bakassi people in the ICJ judgment and the GA, the invisibility and marginalisation of Bakassi people within and across borders was crystallised. The judgment and the GA legitimised violence, coercion and discrimination against the Bakassi people in Cameroon based on their identity as non-Cameroonian inhabitants of the Peninsula, whereas in Nigeria, it legitimises the political and legal detachment of the state from the protection and resettlement of the Bakassi people in Nigeria. Non-citizenship and non-resettlement 'others' the Bakassi people and produce multiple exclusions in their daily lives in Cameroon and Nigeria. While at the international level, Nigeria aspires to receive Bakassi migrants as citizens and resettle them in Nigeria (as evidenced by Nigeria's peaceful acceptance and implementation of the ICJ judgment, the GA and the establishment of the resettlement camp), internal realities place these aspirations in jeopardy.

D. The Intersection of Ethnicity, Socio-economic Status and Militancy among the Bakassi Community in Nigeria

Several layers of oppression have resulted in the failure to protect the Bakassi people at the international level. This includes the failure of the GA to provide safeguards for residency or identity, and the failure of local-level laws like Law No 7 to secure their belonging in Nigeria. The intersection of Bakassi identities has produced multiple types and levels of exclusions that have led to the ineffectiveness of the law. By identifying the Bakassi people as foreigners, the Cameroonian government was able to enforce a number of measures, with requirements to pay for resident permits and pay new taxes, naturalise as Cameroonians, or become undocumented and leave. From the listening sessions in Ikang, Bakassi people stated that they were often stopped and searched for passports, work permits and other things to which fishermen did not have access and were jailed or beaten if they had no documentation.[125] Fleeing to Nigeria

[125] Listening session at Ikang Resettlement Camp (n 124).

was akin to choosing a Nigerian identity and meant that once the Bakassi people left, they could not return to their ancestral lands and properties without Cameroonian residence permits.

Conversely, Nigeria identified the Bakassi as Nigerians, but because there were no obligations created by the GA regarding the documentation, citizenship or resettlement of the Bakassi people should they decide to leave the Peninsula, Nigeria had not been able to offer the protections or privileges of citizenship due to a lack of political will and incentive to do so.[126] Moreover, the Bakassi constituency lost its capacity as an oil-producing and revenue-generating region because the Peninsula was no longer theirs; therefore, their 'value' to the Nigerian government was lost. The Bakassi people were no longer included in the allocation of resources and funds derived from petroleum after they resettled in Nigeria. In resettlement camps, they lost their capacity to practise fishing, which is central to their cultural practices and sense of identity. As a result, in both Cameroon and Nigeria, the Bakassi people lost a sense of belonging, access to economic resources and development funds, economic empowerment and a source of livelihood, their lands and properties, and, most importantly, the freedom to migrate as they had done prior to colonial interference. These multiple layers of marginalisation stem from their new identity as 'not Cameroonian' and as 'displaced persons', 'refugees' or 'returnees' in Nigeria. The borders that resulted from the ICJ judgment limited Bakassi identity by splitting the Bakassi between borderlines: those who remained in Cameroon are now stuck there and those in Nigeria cannot return to the Peninsula freely. As discussed above, even when there were attempts to give access to resources and representation to Bakassi people (Law No 7), these failed because there are no legal obligations for Nigeria and Cameroon in relation to the protection of Bakassi rights specifically.

In both Nigeria and Cameroon, people of Bakassi heritage are ethnic minorities. Efik, Mbo, Orok and other ethnicities are small and have limited political influence – even though they form part of the oil producing regions, politically their minority status does not grant them power to push for greater representation of the Bakassi people at the national level where important legal and policy decisions are being made. Without an understanding of the impact of ethnicity on invisibility, it is difficult to see the ways in which ethnic identity can result in oppression. Ethnic majorities are often amplified in the discussions on power and resource allocation in the Global South, whereas minorities are left out. In the listening sessions in Ikang, people stated that they have been left out of all the legal proceedings during the case at the ICJ,

[126] This is not a discussion about all Bakassi people, as some took, obtained, had Cameroon passports or citizenship. This refers to a subset of Bakassi people that chose to migrate to Nigeria rather than remain on the Peninsula.

during the drafting and signing of the GA, and during many other proceedings relating to their existence.[127] They stated that other majority groups like the Yoruba constituted the legal team from Nigeria and, as a result, none of the outcomes was ever favourable to them. Here, identity was used as a tool by hegemonic power or majority groups to exert power and rob them of their ability to define their own identity. The connection between ethnicity and access to revenue allocations harks back to Hayward's argument that the state shapes ethnic identities and then institutionalises them in laws and policies by distributing resources and opportunities along those lines.[128]

Mr J, one of my respondents, is a lawyer and politician of Bakassi descent who was involved in the advocacy for the Bakassi people during the conflict between Nigeria and Cameroon. According to him, the Bakassi elite settled well in Nigeria and, as a result, it is the poor, mainly the fishing community, who face problems of identification, displacement, unemployment and poverty.[129] The camp leader in Ikang claimed that many of the fishermen cannot read or write and are incapable of processing applications for citizenship or residence, or work permits in Cameroon as they cannot understand or meet the requirements for residency.[130] They are unable to fully participate in the processes to gain representation in Nigeria for the same reasons. Here we see that economic and social class creates another level of vulnerability for the Bakassi people. Within the community, experiences of marginalisation vary. The Bakassi elite can settle in Nigeria due to access to economic status, networks and education, whereas the poorer members of the community face injustices and lack of acceptance. Mr J and other members of the elite I interviewed noted that problems of state-backed exclusion or violence no longer occurred in Nigeria or Cameroon. To Mr J specifically, as soon as people left the Peninsula, the problem was over and those who obtained residence permits in Cameroon were fine. The only problem he felt remained unresolved was the issue of identification documents such as passports and driver's licences. He did not question the accessibility of Cameroonian residence permits for the poorer members of his ethnic group or consider how they were faring in Nigeria without land, resources or security. This perspective is shaped by the privilege of such members of the elite in society.

Militancy and insecurity in Bakassi resettlement areas further complicates the Bakassi identity in both countries. After the ICJ decision and the delimitation of the boundary between Nigeria and Cameroon, militant groups like the Bakassi Movement for Self-Determination, the Movement for the Emancipation of the Niger Delta, the Bakassi Strike Force and the Biafra Secessionist Organisation became active in the region, calling for the secession of Bakassi

[127] Listening session at Ikang Resettlement Camp (n 124).
[128] Hayward and Watson (n 22) 32.
[129] Personal interview with Mr J (n 2).
[130] Listening session at Ikang Resettlement Camp (n 124).

from Nigeria and the protection of the Bakassi people from state-sanctioned violence in Cameroon. The activities of militants have also become a part of the perceived identity of the Bakassi people.[131] The Ikang area has become known for its militancy, as are the waters between Cameroon and Nigeria. During the listening session at the camp in Ikang, the camp leader believed that many people came to rely on militants due to the failure of the international community and the government to provide justice and human rights protection to the Bakassi people. Bakassi resettlement spaces are deemed unsafe as they have been labelled militant hotspots. This has in turn legitimised violence, coercion and discrimination against the Bakassi people, and has left them unprotected from various abuses and forms of insecurity. It has also been used to justify the detachment of the government from these areas. My interviews with the Bakassi local government officials were conducted in Calabar, the capital of the state, which is about 37 km from Ikang, because these officials did not want to engage with the community in Ikang.[132] Interviews with security operatives indicated a similar sentiment that people in the Bakassi community were militants and thus were ungovernable.[133] These perceptions of militancy and insecurity are the reasons behind the area being governed from afar. This distance has led to a clear disconnection between the narratives in Ikang and those in Calabar. People in Ikang felt abandoned by the government and left to face insecurity, poverty and other problems by themselves, whereas in Calabar, the opinions reflected that the idea Ikang was a 'no-go' area overrun by militants. The link between militancy and Bakassi identity has also seen a rise in kidnappings, rapes and other problems in the area, with no protection or engagement from the government or security operatives.[134] These overlapping or separate identities have impacted the manifestations of multiple and simultaneous experiences of oppression and exclusion experienced by the Bakassi people in Nigeria, as well as in Cameroon. People in Bakassi are fishermen and women who are fighting for a space in Nigeria to continue their way of life, even though the structures around them and the labels that come with those structures are constantly at odds with their existence in both Nigeria and Cameroon. In both the case studies in China and Nigeria, displacement, undocumented status or asylum-seeking status does not indicate a total powerlessness or a loss of agency, or overshadow people's resistance, their will to rebuild their lives, to continue to achieve their personal goals and to organise as communities despite the structural forces working against them.

[131] ibid.

[132] Interview and listening session with Bakassi Local Government Chairwoman and officials, Calabar, Cross River State, August 2016.

[133] Interview with Ikang District Police Officer, June 2016.

[134] For example, see Anietie Akpan, '10 Feared Dead as Militants, Kidnappers Clash in Cross River', *The Guardian* (Nigeria), 4 February 2017, https://guardian.ng/news/10-feared-dead-as-militants-kidnappers-clash-in-cross-river.

6

Reclaiming Justice from the Peripheries

Informal Justice in Migrant Communities in China and Nigeria

I. INFORMAL JUSTICE AND THE IMPORTANCE OF CONTEXTUALISATION

INFORMAL JUSTICE COMPRISES numerous systems and frameworks through which justice and law are transmitted. The varying degrees of formality, accountability, recognition, normativity and frameworks make informal justice difficult to define.[1] It may have formal state recognition or not; similarly, it may be facilitated by communities, organisations or traditional structures. From many attempts to define what informal justice means, an initial understanding of the term interpreted it as:

> [A] range of alternative, informal, simpler processes for handling conflicts and disputes. These usually entailed significant participation of the disputants themselves, often with increased involvement for local lay outsiders and less for outside professionals such as lawyers and judges.[2]

This description by JM Fitzgerald fixates on informal justice as a tool for coping with court bottlenecks and minimising the costs of justice. Fitzgerald also discusses the critical legal rationale that informal justice is a tool for the legal autonomy of minorities and the poor because formal law may be an instrument of the dominant class and their agents in the West.[3] This definition focuses on informal justice as the means through which the marginalised in society check injustices and power imbalances, and maintain some form of legal structure

[1] See UNDP, 'Informal Justice Systems: Charting a Course for Human Rights-Based Engagement' (2012), www.undp.org/content/undp/en/home/librarypage/democratic-governance/access_to_justiceandruleoflaw/informal-justice-systems.html.

[2] See JM FitzGerald, 'Thinking about Law and its Alternatives: Abel et al and the Debate over Informal Justice' (1984) 9(3) *American Bar Foundation Research Journal* 637.

[3] ibid at 640.

in their corner of society. Kevin Fandl makes the same argument, but frames it around the informal economy and economic development: individuals in the informal sector may be unwilling, rather than just unable, to resort to formal justice mechanisms to solve their disputes.[4] Fandl discusses the correlations between lapses in the rule of law and underdevelopment on informality (informal justice and informal labour). However, he states that the formal recognition and implementation of informal legal rights has a positive impact on economic development.[5]

On the other hand, in an analysis of customary law and informal justice, Chidi Odinkalu acknowledges the role that colonialism has played in creating legal segregation and hierarchies, as well as radicalising the customary legal systems in Africa.[6] According to him, colonial institutions were often co-opted by the African elites post-independence, resulting in the elites having full access to formal justice systems while the poor were unable to enforce their formal rights even if they wanted to and so were forced to rely on informal justice. This opinion highlights the hierarchies created by colonialism, which have been beneficial not only to the West but also to the elites in developing countries. This means that post-colonial legal systems remain problematic and most often place people at a disadvantage. Likewise, Patrick Akers notes that the perception of formal state justice mechanisms may be tainted by a history of oppression and corruption in developing countries and used as a means through which the elite and ethnic or religious subgroups dominate the poor.[7] He identifies informal justice systems based on either cultural or religious norms, but adds that:

> Other informal justice systems arise from local circumstances and exigencies, such as in urban slums, where community members and criminal gangs effectively maintain social order.[8]

The terms 'local circumstances' and 'exigencies' are key here because the language used makes informal justice a matter of maintaining social order based on the context of a particular community, and specifically poor communities. Akers equates a formal and well-functioning justice system with Western legal structures by quoting Brian Tamanaha that 'developing countries have … defectively trained and disciplined legal officials, a poorly established legal profession, and an inadequately developed body of legal knowledge'.[9] This is a

[4] Kevin J Fandl, 'The Role of Informal Legal Institutions in Economic Development' (2008) 32 *Fordham International Law Journal* 1.

[5] ibid.

[6] Chidi A Odinkalu, 'Poor Justice or Justice for the Poor? A Policy Framework for Reform of Customary and Informal Justice Systems in Africa' (2006) 2 *WBLR: Law and Justice for Development* 141.

[7] See Patrick Akers, 'Establishing Rule of Law through Informal Justice Systems and Development Programs' (2016) 30(1) *Notre Dame Journal of Law, Ethics & Public Policy* 122.

[8] ibid at 119.

[9] ibid at 122.

generalisation of formal justice systems in developing countries and discredits the legal knowledge, training and profession in formal legal systems of the Third World in order to argue for the importance, usefulness or indispensability of informal justice in these spaces. Akers' approach does not take into consideration the impact of colonisation on the practice of law and the experiences of injustice in developing countries, or the fact that the dichotomy between formal and informal is an effect of colonialism, prior to which there were existing and effective systems in place. Colonialism brought about the spread of Western legal practices (eg, civil law), labelled non-Western forms of justice as 'informal' and, by doing so, relegated informal justice mechanisms to the sphere of non-state actors and local rather than state or international interpretations. Akers focuses instead on how foreign development programmes complement informal justice and, by extension, the rule of law in developing countries.

International organisations have extensively tried to engage with the concept of informal justice, particularly based on the international development rhetoric: informal justice is seen as the most suitable way to ensure rule of law – a key ingredient for economic development – in poor countries. The UNDP study on informal justice defines it broadly as:

> The resolution of disputes and regulation of conduct by adjudication or the assistance of a neutral third party that is not a part of the judiciary as established by law and/or whose substantive, procedural or structural foundation is not primarily based on statutory law.[10]

While this definition is comprehensive, it speaks about a specific type of informal justice system. The UNDP study focuses on informal justice systems in countries where they are implemented via recognised traditional frameworks, organisations, individuals and groups, and specifically in post-conflict security and peace-building/reconciliation contexts. These systems have a cultural, religious or historical normative foundation in the countries where they are practised and are generally known, understood and/or accepted. The UNDP study points out the differences between justice mechanisms rooted in customary and tribal/clan social structures, religious authorities, local administrative authorities, specially constituted state customary courts and community forums trained in conflict resolution. However, these classifications are limiting because, first, there are informal justice systems that are rooted neither in customary nor in religious structures, and, second, there are systems that are not run by forums trained in conflict resolution.

All the above definitions are important as they show the discursive conceptualisations of informal justice, but these classifications focus on Western conceptualisations of what informality means and do not consider that informal justice is not always about poverty and economic development or does not

[10] UNDP (n 1) 8.

always happen in traditional settings and contexts. Miranda Forsyth describes informal justice systems as 'normative legal systems operating independently or semi-independently from the state'.[11] Forsyth's definition is more comprehensive. It does not try to specify the sources of the law; rather, it focuses on the degree of independence or semi-dependence of the state on non-state sources of justice. Nevertheless, Forsyth holds that customary law systems and religious-based legal systems are the most studied forms of non-state justice and relies on case studies of village courts and Sharia courts, among others, in her study.[12] Many informal justice mechanisms remain understudied or unobserved because of their informality and how far away they are from formal laws. Forsyth refrains from employing the term 'informal' as a qualifier for justice and instead uses the term 'non-state'. This may be from an understanding that the terminology 'informal' has negative connotations where it delegitimises non-state mechanisms of justice. I prefer to use the term 'informal' because it shifts the focus from the state. 'Informal' for me emphasises the mechanisms that are formed outside of recognised, hegemonic or oppressive legal systems of justice and, as a result, it could be seen as a positive attribute of non-Western approaches to law.

Forsyth clarifies state and non-state systems by designing a spectrum of non-state justice through which we can understand both formal and informal mechanisms.[13] She juxtaposes various forms of non-state justice with levels of state acceptance – on one end of the spectrum is a suppressive relationship between state and non-state systems and, on the other, a total co-opting of non-state mechanisms by the state,[14] as given below:

- Model 1: An extreme of repression of non-state justice systems by the state.
- Model 2: No formal recognition, but tacit acceptance of non-state justice systems by the state.
- Model 3: No formal recognition, but active encouragement of the non-state justice system by the state.
- Model 4: Limited formal recognition by the state of jurisdictions by a non-state system.
- Model 5: Formal recognition of exclusive jurisdiction in a defined area.
- Model 6: State recognition of a non-state system to exercise jurisdiction and the state lends coercive power.
- Model 7: Complete incorporation of non-state justice systems by the state.[15]

[11] See Miranda Forsyth, 'A Typology of Relationships between State and Non-state Justice Systems' (2007) 56 *Journal of Legal Pluralism* 67.

[12] ibid at 68.

[13] This spectrum will be used as a basis when discussing my case studies later on in this chapter.

[14] Forsyth (n 11) 69.

[15] ibid 70.

With each model, Forsyth provides case study examples to contextualise the different possible relationships that informal justice systems may have with the state and the formal justice system. Her study is very important in the literature and in understanding what informal justice signifies. It highlights that, first, there is a spectrum of how these mechanisms function in different countries and contexts. It accepts that in some cases, informal mechanisms can become formalised if they are formally recognised in the exercise of adjudicative power of the non-state system.[16] Informal justice mechanisms can be repressed by the state if it deems it to be in competition with formal justice mechanisms. Informal justice takes different forms and ranges to varying degrees based on historical, political, cultural and other contexts.

Torunn Wimpelmann points to the failure of the justice sector after decades of funding and promotion of the rule of law globally by international organisations in the development community as the backdrop for the rise in popularity of informal justice discourse globally.[17] She discusses the historical and political background from the 1990s leading to the rise of informal justice in the agendas and strategies of aid donors. Her arguments also focus on a specific type of informal justice system – post-conflict-focused justice, where international development and aid donor organisations attempt to 'support' or 'improve' what they perceive is on the ground.[18] In her opinion, the popularisation of informal justice by international organisations taints its very purpose. The fact that foreign organisations define, improve, monitor, intervene in or hold the formal and informal justice mechanisms accountable in developing countries as a form of validating them is problematic. She states that: 'As in colonial times, customary justice processes are measured against standards of civilisation that are ultimately defined by interveners.'[19] This link between Western standards and the conceptualisation of informal justice in the West is very clear. Forsyth also problematises the need for Western scholars and aid organisations to 'recognise, empower and harmonise' between state and non-state systems with very little understanding of and research into what those terms mean.[20] This is the reason why Forsyth focuses on clarifying the different non-state legal arrangements that may exist by degrees of state permission, co-existence or refutation. She uses several case studies in developing countries to show the different possible non-state legal systems on the spectrum, without focusing on the role of Western powers and aid organisations. Using case studies to understand what informal injustice means and how it operates in the daily lives of people in the Global South is more insightful than transposing norms and recommendations from the outside.

[16] ibid.

[17] Torunn Wimpelmann, 'The Informal Justice Paradigm and the Appropriation of Local Reality' (2013) 64(3) *Northern Ireland Legal Quarterly* 398.

[18] Wimpelmann used the case study of the customary justice system in Afghanistan, which has historically been commonplace, well developed and accepted nationally.

[19] Wimpelmann (n 17) 402.

[20] Forsyth (n 11) 67.

A. Linking Informal Justice to TWAIL

A TWAIL perspective contextualises and problematises Third World experiences as they are lived, creating alternative sources of knowledge on global issues and seeking justice for the marginalised in those spaces.[21] The discursive conceptualisations of informal justice at the international level often focus on ideological arguments, reduce the spectrum of informal justice to very specific typologies or use Western blueprints to guide definitions or analysis. As seen above, arguments on the subject of informal justice cover the issue of international development, foreign aid and economic development, as informal justice affects the perception of law in developing countries. The notion of informal justice has been co-opted by neo-liberal institutions who assume they are enhancing or supporting local solutions to local realities, but end up creating more exclusions and marginalisation.[22] This is because informal justice in developing countries is treated as a means to an end (economic development), whereas it might also be an end in itself. From a TWAIL perspective, the international legal system is a tool of domination used by those with vested historical interests in maintaining a status quo in the system.[23] This domination reveals itself in the way in which the law manifests itself at different levels – from who is convicted for international crimes, how treaties are implemented, and dictating what regional and national laws and policies should be and how legal norms develop. As was discussed in Chapter 3, in the case of the ICJ judgment, the local, cultural and historical reality was not used to define who could inhabit the territory instead of colonial treaties and maps between foreigners.[24] This is a perfect example of international law manifesting at different levels and dominating national and local realities of indigenous peoples and communities. International laws stemming from the norms and narratives of the West can be harmful to non-Western peoples when they do not take local, historical, cultural, religious or socio-political contexts into consideration. While international disputes may be resolved at the international level, the impact of this resolution at the local level is often unknown, ignored or understudied.

Informal justice from below presents an opportunity to break away from the chains of international and/or foreign legal norms and laws, and for communities outside those norms and laws to exert legal autonomy and self-expression.

[21] See Ibironke Odumosu, 'Challenges for the (Present/)Future of Third World Approaches to International Law' (2008) 10 *International Community Law Review* 467 at 468.

[22] Wimpelmann (n 17) 401.

[23] See Makau Mutua, 'Critical Race Theory and International Law: The View of an Insider-Outsider' (2000) 45 *Villanova Law Review* 841 at 845; Bhupinder Chimni and Antony Anghie, 'Third World Approaches to International Law and the Individual Responsibility in Internal Conflicts' (2003) 2 *Chinese Journal of International Law* 77 at 79 and 84.

[24] *Land and Maritime Boundary between Cameroon and Nigeria, Cameroon and Equatorial Guinea (Intervening) v Nigeria*, Judgment, Merits [2002] ICJ Rep 303, ICGJ 63 (ICJ 2002), 10 October 2002, UN, ICJ at para 65.

There are very few actual case studies looking at informal justice systems in this light; that is, subaltern counter-publics existing within hegemonic spaces, contributing in unique ways to the development of the rule of law, free from the dictates, influences and judgements of Western interveners. Using a TWAIL perspective and methodology to contextualise informal justice, drawing from lived experiences and narratives in the case studies, is a fitting way of understanding and supporting informal justice mechanisms in migrant communities, particularly those engaged in South-South migrations.

B. Linking Informal Justice to Migrant Communities and Migration

As stated above, current research on informal justice does not speak to systems that are outside recognised traditional or cultural structures – those systems that are formed in alien and foreign spaces. These can be described as ad hoc, temporary spaces like IDP or refugee camps and undocumented migrant communities. Furthermore, studies of informal legal structures do not consider those informal systems that may have no links to formal systems. In 'traditional' informal justice, people can actively choose to resort to informal over formal justice mechanisms because it is cheaper, operated on a voluntary basis, and based on cultural, religious and other beliefs and norms. However, in displaced communities or communities made up of undocumented migrants in developing countries, it is often the only way to achieve justice. Without informal justice in such places, there would be no recourse to justice at all. The absence of the privilege of citizenship means that justice is often difficult to obtain for undocumented migrants. Literature on informal justice either focuses on Western interventions and Western ideals or tends to look at it from a post-conflict, conflict resolution and reconciliation point of view, especially in relation to Africa. Much has been said about the informal justice systems like the Gacaca courts in Rwanda[25] and community post-conflict justice in Liberia,[26] among many other examples. While this is a very key aspect – how communities sustain law and justice during and after armed conflicts – it is limiting to place informal justice only in that sphere. Informal justice exists beyond conflict and post-conflict justice, punishing genocide or war crimes, and the other stereotypes that have shaped the discourse on the African experience. It is applied in the day-to-day lives of undocumented migrant and refugee communities globally. What this means is

[25] See Phil Clark, 'The Rules (and Politics) of Engagement: The Gacaca Courts and Post-genocide Justice, Healing and Reconciliation in Rwanda' in Phil Clark and Zachary Kaufman (eds), *After Genocide: Transitional Justice, Post-conflict Reconstruction and Reconciliation in Rwanda and beyond* (London, Hurst, 2008). See also Sandra F Joireman and Alison Corey, 'Retributive Justice: The Gacaca Courts in Rwanda' (2004) 103 *African Affairs* 73.

[26] See Ezekiel Pajibo, 'Accountability and Justice in Post-conflict Liberia' (2010) 10(3) *African Identities* 301. See also Deborah H Isser et al, 'Looking for Justice: Liberian Experiences with and Perceptions of Local Justice Options' (2009) 63 *United States Institute of Peace* 104.

that informal justice is a living and functioning mechanism in the daily lives of undocumented migrant and refugee communities: the law (in its informal manifestation) is intertwined in the lives of communities that are perceived to be excluded from it.

In Elizabeth Holzer's research on refugee day-to-day experiences of the law in refugee camps, she explores why we must also think of displaced persons and refugees as legal subjects.[27] Holzer conducted the ethnographic research of the Buduburam refugee camp in Ghana, West Africa as a case study on the interaction between refugees and the law in 2012. She argues that these groups of migrants interact extensively with various aspects of international and domestic law in their daily lives. She identifies three dimensions of the experiences of refugees: their development as subjects of international law; their alienation from domestic legal institutions; and their agency in the legal field.[28] These dimensions also apply to undocumented migrants. The three dimensions highlight, first, that the narratives and experiences of migrants who are displaced or seeking asylum have a legal consciousness of their rights that leads them to mobilise, and, second, they show that alienation from domestic legal institutions does not signify that the migrants live without laws at their own level. Holzer's research also shows that the agency of displaced or undocumented migrants leads them to mobilise for justice within their communities; it exposes the link between migration and legal consciousness, and the agency to mobilise and create mechanisms to address injustice and marginalisation in their communities.[29] Holzer's argument significantly explores the inefficiencies of international and domestic law, and the ways in which refugees or displaced persons understand law, legal practices and institutions, and, by extension, how they mobilise to address the injustices they experience. Holzer describes this as a simultaneous engagement with and alienation from the law.[30] This legal consciousness and mobilisation in day-to-day encounters with formal law is what leads to the creation of alternative/informal justice mechanisms in migrant communities. When refugees or displaced persons encounter formal law and experience inefficiencies and exclusion in the system, they become conscious of how the legal system works again them. As a result, they mobilise to find their own solutions to these injustices by forming alternative justice mechanisms to protect their interests.

Holzer states that learning from the lived experiences of refugees and other types of marginalised migrant communities is an important tool in understanding how these communities reach the legal outcomes and interpretations

[27] See Elizabeth Holzer, 'What Happens to Law in a Refugee Camp?' (2013) 47 *Law & Society Review* 837.
[28] ibid.
[29] ibid.
[30] ibid at 839.

that are observable. For example, she highlights that the way in which refugees and migrants experience police corruption shaped their views of the laws of the host country as a 'proprietary resource of citizenship'.[31] In her case study, refugees formed interpretations of the law based on how they were treated by the police – the police did not serve or protect refugees in the same way as citizens were served or protected, and a lack of faith in the ability of the police led to an interpretation that citizens have a 'stronger claim to the law' than non-citizens.[32]

II. INFORMAL JUSTICE IN THE NIGERIAN COMMUNITY IN CHINA

The exponential growth of the Nigerian community in China from the 2000s has crystallised informal justice mechanisms in that community. The informal justice system in the community is well developed, fully functional and respected by members. Sources of injustice and crime in China are often tied to business, unfair arrest and detention by Chinese security operatives, drug trafficking, visa offences and the exploitation of Africans by Chinese locals.[33] The specific problems faced by the community, as well as the local legal and political conditions in the country, influence the kind of informal justice mechanisms that develop within the community.

Figure 6.1 The informal justice hierarchy in the Nigerian community

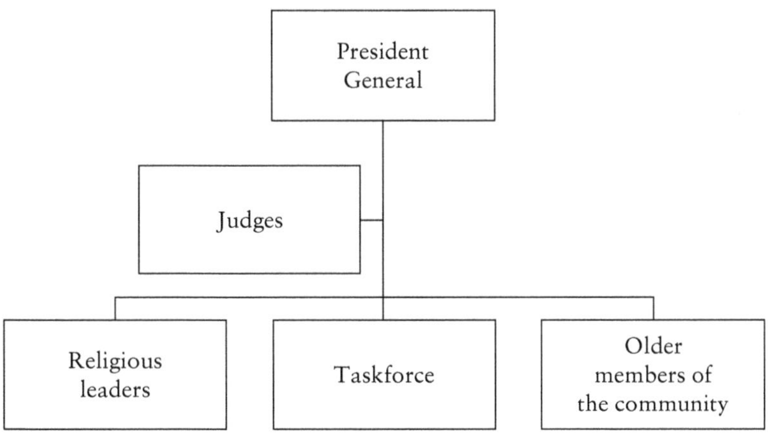

[31] ibid at 840.

[32] ibid at 860.

[33] As was discussed in ch 5, at the local level, all Africans are perceived to be the same, so there is an approach towards Blackness and Africanness, whereas, in reality, there are different national and ethnic communities. Therefore, I switch between the use of 'African' and 'Nigerian' in the China case study.

The community has an elected President General who oversees political organisation, promotes the interests of the community both locally and nationally, and engages in diplomacy with both the Chinese and Nigerian governments on issues that affect Nigerians in China.[34] The President General is at the highest level of the informal justice system and focuses mainly on large-scale issues that need to be resolved beyond the community – for example, the arbitrary arrest, detention and cremation of Nigerians in China.[35] Ethnic group leaders, judges – community executives elected by members to settle cases brought before them – and religious leaders solve disputes at the communal level. Elections help to institutionalise accountability in the informal justice system because the power to remove officials remains in the hands of the members of the community. Due to the undocumented and ad hoc nature of many community members, the judges are elected based on their perceived reputation and respectability. In my research, I found that judges were often businessmen who had lived in China the longest, were there legally and had well-established businesses and investments in China. As a result, the judges' decisions are respected and upheld by Nigerians in China. Mr B, for instance, migrated to China in the late 1990s and is one of the founding members of the Nigerian community in Guangzhou. He is a member of the panel of judges, the Igbo community, as well as the association of Nigerians with Chinese wives. He is also a business mentor in the Nigerian community.

As of the time of my research in 2016, the President General, judges and members of the taskforce were all male. This recalls the discussions on intersectionality in Chapter 5, where maleness and proximity to legality create hierarchies within the community. The informal justice system also has ethnic group leaders who represent the interests of their ethnic groups in conflict resolution, mobilisation for justice and politics. There is an Igbo leader of the Igbo members of the community, and likewise a Hausa leader, a Yoruba leader etc. The leaders in the Nigerian migrant community also liaise with other communities (for example, the Malian community) whenever there is an overlapping of issues. I did not have the chance to find out whether other migrant communities in China have similar structures, but the collaboration between communities indicates that there are at least some leadership structures in other communities that are responsible for solving intercommunal problems. In addition, the Nigerian community has a taskforce – the enforcer or 'police' of sorts. The taskforce implements the decisions of the judges. In two interviews, respondents

[34] Personal interview with Mr B, Baiyun District, Guangzhou, 15 March 2016, on file with the author.

[35] See Onaolapo Delon, 'How Nigerian Citizens are Maltreated in China', *The Vanguard*, 2 April 2014, https://www.vanguardngr.com/2014/04/nigerian-citizens-maltreated-china. In the past, Nigerian prisoners in China who died while in Chinese prisons were cremated by the Chinese government without duly informing the Nigerian government or the families of the prisoners. This has led to tensions in the community as well as a public outcry calling for the Chinese government to stop the cremation of Nigerian prisoners.

noted that the taskforce has collaborated with the Chinese PSB in solving crimes and sharing intelligence on criminality in the community. The community chose to collaborate with the PSB to solve crimes relating to the community as a means of promoting mutualism.[36] Nigerians who have committed crimes such as rape and drug trafficking have been arrested by the taskforce and presented to the PSB. However, collaboration between the community and the PSB does not occur in every case; it is often the crimes that have implications for the wider Chinese community that warrant collaboration between the taskforce and the PSB. Crimes committed at a micro-level are often resolved at that level by the judges, the ethnic group leaders and the taskforce.

The normative framework for the informal justice system in the community stems from China's legal norms and practices. Restitution is not practised in the legal system in Nigeria; it is a Chinese legal norm that has become the practice of the Nigerian community in Guangzhou. In Chinese civil proceedings, restitution is swift and effective.[37] The judges often use this method to resolve communal disputes and remedy injustices. Restitution is the most effective way to ensure that there is justice for victims since members of the community cannot take their grievances to a formal court. Because the Nigerian community is made up of traders, most of the disputes in the community relate to business; as a result, many of the cases and/or crimes that are brought before the judges on business-related disputes are solved by restitution to the victim. In a case where a person defaults on the payment for goods or services, the taskforce either seizes the goods of the offender and presents them to the victim as restitution, or hold the goods until the offender pays what they owe. A leader in the community testified that these measures apply to those who owe within the community and those who owe people in Nigeria as well.[38] As traders, the judges have very strong communication networks in China and Nigeria, and can investigate and verify the details of each case and the claims of all parties.

In addition to investigating and solving crimes and dispute resolution, the community has mechanisms to support community members involved in non-violent crimes like visa violations. The community, through the President General, pools its resources together to negotiate for the release of offenders. However, there are instances where the informal justice mechanisms are not able to protect members of the community from abuse. This is often the case when Chinese citizens are involved in instances of fraud or extortion. One of the migrants I interviewed recounted how he was duped by a Chinese citizen

[36] Personal interview with Mr B (n 34). For example, the taskforce collaborated with the police to track down a suspect in a rape case and handed him over to the PSB. The Nigerian community maintains a strong partnership with the Chinese police, often providing them with valuable information crucial to solving crimes.

[37] Jin Gao Feng, 'The Protection and Remedies for Victims of Crime and Abuse of Power in China', UNAFEI Resource Material Series No 70, (2006) 163–69, https://www.unafei.or.jp/publications/pdf/RS_No70/No70_15PA_Jin.pdf.

[38] Personal interview with Mr B (n 34).

when his immigration status changed.[39] The Chinese citizen took advantage of the fact that the migrant was undocumented and reported him to the authorities after collecting a seed investment from him for a business venture. The migrant in question could not rely on the system in the community for support as there are no provisions made for cases where the offenders are citizens of the state. Another interviewee recounted that his Chinese wife found out that he had a lot of money in savings and decided to report his undocumented status to the PSB. Under the threat of arrest, the interviewee chose to give up his savings in exchange for the withdrawal of the threat.[40] As a result of these loopholes, there are numerous instances of Chinese citizens abusing or exploiting the undocumented status of their Nigerian business partners and acquaintances with no consequences; the Chinese authorities are unable to remedy injustices to non-citizens who are undocumented. In such cases, the Nigerian party will either be arrested and/or deported, go into hiding until the case is forgotten or pay 'compensation' to the extortionist. In each scenario, the Chinese citizen does not face any legal consequences for their actions and there are no remedies from within the Nigerian community. This indicates that regardless of the existence of a well-developed system of informal justice, the privilege of citizenship remains a barrier to justice. In this case study, because undocumented status breaches immigration law, the criminality and corruption of citizens is overlooked and goes unpunished. This illustrates the impact of borders and citizenship on the experiences of injustice that undocumented migrants and refugees face in their daily lives. It appears that the law is skewed in favour of citizens, erasing the criminality of citizens to protect their rights or interests against non-citizens.

Finally, the informal justice mechanisms developed by the Nigerian community in Guangzhou appear to function best when left in the hands of those who created them. For example, on many occasions, the Nigerian foreign mission has tried to interfere in the running and the politics of the Nigerian community with an intention to control the community and erase the negative public opinion of Nigerians in China.[41] In an interview, Mr B disclosed that the Nigerian foreign mission had tried several times to control or disrupt the functions of the Nigerian community. He alleged that the Nigerian foreign mission tried to eliminate the elected President General and install their preferred candidate. He also alleged that the foreign mission had succeeded in halting and/or destroying the political and legal structures built by the community and that the President General as of March 2016 was charged with correcting the impact of the interference and restructuring the community. These interferences have never yielded positive fruits, often setting off further grievances and

[39] Personal interview with Mr T, Baiyun District, Guangzhou, March 2016, on file with the author.
[40] ibid.
[41] Personal interview with Mr B (n 34).

discriminations within the community. Over time, the Nigerian foreign mission has learned to leave the community to solve its image problems as well as other issues.

III. INFORMAL JUSTICE IN THE BAKASSI COMMUNITY IN NIGERIA

The Bakassi community in Nigeria has an entirely different experience of injustice and as a result has a unique informal justice system in place. The communities displaced from the Peninsula in Cameroon already had systems of leadership that handled inter-communal conflict resolution, and these leadership structures survive in the refugee camps in Nigeria. The people displaced from the Peninsula currently reside in two camps in Ikang and Akpabuyo where elders, traditional and political leaders have a role in solving disputes and representing the community's interest to the hosts and the state.[42] In Ikang, community members held that they had lost faith in the capacity of traditional leaders to protect their interests and voice their grievances in Nigeria. This is because leaders had co-opted the Bakassi story and used it for personal gain. In the interview session with leaders in the camp, many accusations were levelled against Bakassi's political leaders ranging from corruption to the theft of funds and supplies meant for the refugees. There were claims that refugees in Ikang were excluded from crucial decisions concerning the relocation of the camp and the resettlement of Bakassi people in Nigeria, and that there is a lack of support from leaders to address the injustices and needs in the camp. The community in Ikang believes that their leadership is not effective in bringing the solutions they need for the problems they face.

Figure 6.2 The informal justice framework in the Bakassi refugee community in Nigeria

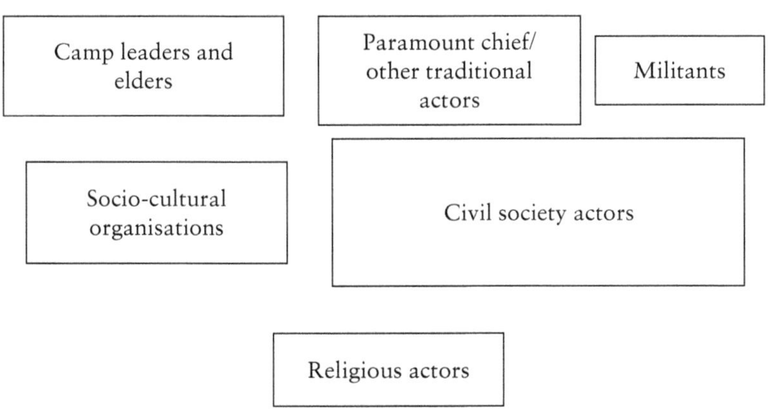

[42] See ch 3 for more background on the Bakassi dispute, the GA, and the camps in Ikang and Akpabuyo.

The Bakassi community faces a different type of injustice in Nigeria stemming from a lack of security and basic amenities like electricity, clean water and food. Poverty and hunger in the camps fuel numerous inequalities that lead to injustices. Injustice also stems from a lack of formal identification in Nigeria; many Bakassi refugees do not have birth certificates, passports and other forms of identification that can help them successfully settle in Nigeria and access services like legal assistance. The main factors influencing the levels of injustice that community members face are insecurity and the overall failure of the justice system in Nigeria. Those interviewed complained about a high level of rape and teenage pregnancy in the camps where young women and girls are often the target of sexual violence. The camp in Ikang faces crimes of rape and lack of access to justice both at the communal and the state levels. Community members stated that many children are attacked and raped when they run errands or go to the stream to fetch water.[43] In these cases of rape, there has been no justice for the victims and the impact of the insecurity in the community has become deeply embedded into the fabric of the society.

The interviews in the refugee settlement in Ikang indicated that because the Nigerian justice system fails refugees who try to rely on the formal justice in the host state, the community is forced to rely on other sources of justice. In addition to relying on the conflict resolution of the community leaders and traditional rulers, the community sometimes relies on militants for justice.[44] A result of the high levels of suffering in the community has been the establishment of militant groups who aim to fight for the rights of the Bakassi community in Nigeria. Though the term 'militant' is politically charged because of the context of militancy in the Niger Delta, I choose to use it because this is the term used by members of the community. Within the community, militants are both a positive and a negative force. Militant groups have put pressure on the state and federal government to address the problems of the community – for example, militants fought against Cameroon Gendarmes who attacked members of the community on the Peninsula[45] – and have also issued warnings to the state and federal governments to keep the promises they made to the refugees on resettlement in Nigeria.[46] Militants have fought for the emancipation of the Bakassi people from both Nigeria and Cameroon in the past.[47]

[43] Group listening session at the Ikang resettlement camp in Cross River State (June 2016), on file with the author.

[44] The militant group is made up of members of the community who may or may not be affiliated with other militant groups in the region.

[45] Estelle Shirbon, 'Up to 21 Cameroon Troops Killed in Bakassi', *Reuters*, 13 November 2007, https://www.reuters.com/article/idUSL1382294.

[46] Anietie Akpan and Julius Osahon, 'Militancy Bakassi Strike Force Overruns Cross River LGAs', *The Guardian* (Calabar), 10 July 2016, https://guardian.ng/news/militancy-bakassi-strike-force-overruns-cross-river-lgas.

[47] George Onah. 'Nigeria: Secession! Militants Declare Bakassi Independent State', *The Vanguard*, 9 July 2006, http://allafrica.com/stories/200607100698.html.

In the absence of local, state and federal government provision of security and justice for rapes and exploitation, the militants have become a viable alternative because they have both the power and the force to implement restitution. The community also depends on the militants for security and sometimes for financial support. This was notable in Ikang, where the refugees have been abandoned by the state, as well as federal government and aid organisations for many years. This reliance may be because the militants are a source of quick justice, often taking immediate (albeit secret) action against offenders. However, they are not a reliable source of justice to the members of the community as their activities are considered by the Nigerian government to be illegal. In addition, their activities have been a source of insecurity locally and are said to have shifted from a role of protection to criminality.[48] Ndifon Neji Obi and Ken Henshaw note that militants extorted members of the community and 'took over the affairs of the communities, replaced the traditional institutions, and presided over court sessions on every matter which involved community members'.[49] These actions had a negative impact on the balance of power and trust in the community.

In my interviews in Ikang and Akpabuyo, it was noted that the camp leaders were most accessible to the members of the community. The camp leaders can mobilise the community very quickly to come together in order to solve problems. For example, when the rape of a refugee occurs, the camp leaders summon a community meeting to find out the facts of the incident and discuss solutions. Whenever an outsider comes into the community, the camp leaders are capable of quickly spotting and interrogating them regarding the purpose of their presence as a means of maintaining law and order in the community. Most of the leaders in the community in Ikang and Akpabuyo were male, highlighting the gendered nature of the informal mechanisms in the community. However, there was a female leader in the Ikang camp who represented the women and raised grievances on their behalf at meetings. During the listening session in Ikang, this woman was only one who spoke along with the leaders and elders of the community. It is unclear how many female leaders exist in the community, but the woman who spoke during the listening session was called by the leaders of the community to give a female perspective on the experiences of displacement in the camp. The overall role of the woman in the community was also unclear, even though her role among the women was that of a leader and elder. Most of the other women who were present (there were about six of them among numerous men) were silent. No woman was called to speak in Akpabuyo. This recalls the discussion in Chapter 5 about intersectionality in the Bakassi community.

[48] Ndifon Neji Obi and Ken Henshaw, 'Insecurity in Cross River State: Issues, Actors and Solutions' in Tarila Marclint Ebiede, Celestine Oyom Bassey and Judith Burdin Asuni (eds), *Insecurity in the Niger Delta: A Report on Emerging Threats in Akwa Ibom, Bayelsa, Cross River, Delta, Edo, and Rivers States* (Abuja, Adonis & Abbey Publishers, 2021) at 199.

[49] ibid.

Civil society, traditional and religious actors intervene to resolve crimes and disputes are resolved at the camp level. If the situation escalates beyond them, militants get involved behind the scenes while camp and traditional leaders try to find solutions in the Nigerian legal system. According to Obi and Henshaw, civil society actors seem to be the most trusted in terms of capacity because traditional rulers rely on the state for power, whereas they do not.[50] Camp leaders also lack the capacity that the CSOs have, which includes their advocacy, networks and quantifiable interventions in peace building, health, and education.[51] Obi and Henshaw also reference the role of socio-cultural organisations like the Ekpe Society, whose:

> [I]nfluence extends beyond the cultural and stretches to the economic and political. Similarly, socio-cultural organizations in Cross River State are created in a manner that ensures they represent ethnic identities across local government areas.[52]

These organisations have political influence at the community level that influence peace and security and play a role in conflict resolution. I was unable to interview members of these socio-cultural organisations to ascertain their engagement in informal paths to justice due to a collapse of security at the time of my research.

Unlike the community in China, the Bakassi community has recourse to legal justice mechanisms; by choosing to migrate to Nigeria, the community became subject to the law and the legal practices in Nigeria. However, access to formal justice is limited because it is costly, time-consuming and requires formal identification documents, which many of the refugees do not have. The cost of formal justice is the main barrier to the community formally challenging the injustice committed by the Cameroonian government in the Peninsula or the enforcement of the GA and the rights that it accords to the community in both countries in the first place. Furthermore, outsiders, including international organisations, the state and federal government agencies and NGOs, focus on interfering in the Bakassi community. For example, government agencies, NGOs and international organisations no longer engage with the refugees in Ikang, where the focus has shifted to those in Akpabuyo because they believe that those in Ikang are supposed to have resettled by now when in fact the problems in the community have simply increased with time. Picking and choosing sides leaves the community in Ikang marginalised and overlooked when important policy measures like the possible allocation of land, cash transfers and skill acquisition programmes arise.

[50] ibid at 181–82.
[51] ibid.
[52] ibid.

IV. APPLYING FORSYTH'S TYPOLOGY OF INFORMAL JUSTICE RELATIONSHIPS

Looking at Forsyth's spectrum on informal justice, we can see where the informal justice systems in the undocumented and displaced communities in China and Nigeria fall. This sheds light on the place these mechanisms occupy within the confines of the state and how these confines affect the function and effectiveness of informal justice. According to Forsyth, in Model 2, the informal justice system has no formal recognition from the state. Here, the state turns a blind eye to the functions of the system, neither encouraging it nor suppressing it.[53] This model aptly describes the informal justice systems in the Nigerian community in China where the Chinese government overlooks the existence of the community justice mechanisms, only relying on them to reach parts of the community to which the government does not have access.

The Chinese government does not suppress or control the informal justice structures directly; the state only punishes members of the community who violate Chinese laws and carries out raids and checks when there is a public outcry or commentary about the Africans in China.[54] Instead of repressing the structures in the community, the PSB has relied on them to prevent and solve crimes or disputes. In other words, the Chinese government allows the Nigerian community to function if it is 'business as usual'; interference occurs when public sentiments are involved or when members of the community are caught violating Chinese laws. Both systems of justice exist side by side, even though one of them is not neither formal nor 'legal' according to Chinese definitions. The mechanisms in the Nigerian community can evolve and thrive to a certain extent (ie, to the extent that the Chinese government permits) due to this co-existence, leading communal justice to evolve and improve over time. Forsyth states that Model 2 on the spectrum has:

> The fluid nature of such a relationship allows both systems to be flexible and guided by local circumstances in their relations with each other ... the non-state justice system is able to define its own norms and procedural framework, allowing it to remain dynamic and legitimate at the grassroots level.[55]

The Nigerian community has built dispute resolution practices and procedures, and protective and investigative measures, as well as diplomatic processes due to the mostly lax attitude of the Chinese government towards the day-to-day activities in the community. Nevertheless, the interaction between the community and the Chinese government is not a mutually beneficial one. This is because of China's political and social characteristics, which are inherently oppressive.

[53] Forsyth (n 11) 75.

[54] Shanshan Lan, 'State Regulation of Undocumented African Migrants in China: A Multi-scalar Analysis' (2015) 50(3) *Journal of Asian and African Studies* 289.

[55] ibid.

The Nigerian community cannot escape this oppressiveness simply by having its own justice mechanisms. We do not know the extent of the Chinese laxity towards the informal justice systems present in migrant communities, mainly because of the undocumented status of most of the members in the community. Already, many Nigerians are in detention in Chinese prisons for various criminal and non-criminal offences and, in these cases, the reach of communal justice is severely limited.

On the other hand the Bakassi community can be said to fall between Model 1 and Model 2 in Forsyth's spectrum. Model 1 is a total repudiation of the informal justice system, an extreme reaction of the state to non-state systems. The mechanisms in the Bakassi community fall between the two models because although Nigeria may acknowledge or allow the communal justice processes put in place by the camp leaders, traditional rulers and/or religious leaders, the government actively represses and rejects the role of militants in the community. Thus, the impact and influence of the militants in the community is underground, hidden from public view. Due to the presence of militants, the development of the informal justice system in the community is stymied. The role that militants play in the community in terms of meting out justice backed by force has replaced other forms of informal justice in a way; it seems to be more effective to rely on militants for protection and justice than on elders, traditional rulers and religious leaders. In my interviews and listening sessions, few of the members of the community had negative perceptions on militancy. In Ikang in particular, interviewees were vocal about their support of the militants. The Bakassi refugee community continues to experience extreme levels of injustice: the camp and traditional rulers are not sufficiently empowered to implement justice because there is no force to back decisions. On the other hand, community members are not sufficiently empowered to utilise the formal justice system. There is also no recognised collaboration between the formal and informal systems, unlike the collaboration that takes place behind the scenes in China. The injustices faced by the Bakassi community have been exacerbated by a lack of belonging in the communities to which they fled. In the listening session in Ikang and the interviews in Akpabuyo, participants felt alienated, ignored or forgotten in Nigeria and could not rely on the Nigerian system to solve their problems. This feeling of alienation and statelessness leads to human rights breaches that are hard to remedy in the Bakassi refugee community, resulting in further marginalisation of community members in the wider society. With ineffective solutions to the injustices in the community, the community is further alienated in Nigeria, and grievances and tensions will continue to mount, which will have implications in the future.

By conceptualising a typology of relationships based on state recognition, Forsyth's spectrum implies that state sovereignty is central in the narrative; informal systems of justice still need some form of approval from the state to function. In terms of the case studies, this means that the Nigerian community in China cannot escape Chinese political, social and cultural realities, even though the community tries to collaborate with the government. Informal justice mechanisms are impacted significantly if the state views these mechanisms as competing with its norms, public opinion etc. These informal justice mechanisms are not traditionally, historically or culturally rooted in the state; they are mechanisms utilised by communities who are outside of the spectrum of citizenship and the protection of formal law. The informal justice systems practised by undocumented and refugee communities have both the potential to protect the most vulnerable members of any society and at the same time are completely at the mercy of the state. When the state feels like there is no competition between its formal system and the informal mechanisms, there is a chance that the informal justice system will be allowed to function, evolve and improve.

V. TEMPORALITY AND THE CRYSTALLISATION OF INFORMAL JUSTICE

In China, and particularly in Guangzhou, the Nigerian community has existed since the late 1990s, after the economic reformation of China.[56] In Nigeria, the Bakassi community has been present before the concept of Nigeria as a country was created in 1914, although the Bakassi refugee community has existed since the early 2000s in Nigeria.[57] Over time, these communities have built structures to enable their survival and to protect their interests in the wider society. Legal structures have appeared and endured in these communities, shaping interactions with their host community (or communities) and the state, and how they encounter the law. Time is a significant factor in the experience of displacement and migration. The longer these communities exist, the more organised they become and the more entrenched informal justice mechanisms will also become – individuals either grow to acclimatise to the host environment or protest against the injustices in the system. In the Chinese case study, we have seen that the community developed mechanisms to mimic the Chinese legal system, as well as other aspects of Chinese society, in order to co-exist and to thrive in the new environment in which they found themselves. The Nigerian community's methods of cooperating and adhering to Chinese rules and norms through informal justice are a strategy of survival given the socio-political realities in China and racism against Africans.

The Chinese case study shows that the existence of the informal justice system reduces the precariousness of the community to a certain degree over time. Collaborations between the community and the police solve crimes at the communal level, but also influence local perspectives on the community, as

[56] Adams Bodomo and Grace Ma, 'From Guangzhou to Yiwu: Emerging facets of the African Diaspora in China' (2010) 5(2) *International Journal of African Renaissance Studies* 283.

[57] Rebecca K LeFebvre, 'Interests and Identities in Peace Negotiations: Nigeria, Cameroon, and the Bakassi Peninsula' (2014) 6(1) *African Social Science Review* 83.

well as how members of the Nigerian community perceive themselves in those spaces. The experiences of injustice faced by members of the community have also changed over time, as have the methods of addressing those injustices. In the early 2000s, it was impossible for Africans to work in China, own homes or mobile phones, or obtain driver's licences. Many of the problems in the community stemmed from a lack of access to these resources and the community focused on solutions to those issues as a result. Much later, after China's visa law and policy reforms, immigration offences became the more prominent problem in the community; issues like visa overstaying and undocumented migration came to the fore. The community is now developing tools to address the impact of migration law and policies on migration. In an interview with one of the leaders in the Nigerian community in Guangzhou, the leader stated that it took many years for the community to consolidate and elect a President General.[58] When this role was created, community members realised that the community needed respected leaders not only to represent them, but also to help them resolve internal disputes; this led to the creation of the positions of elected judges. In addition, they realised that the community needed an enforcement mechanism through which the President General and the judges could effectively implement their decisions. This led to the establishment of a taskforce. Currently, the community is stretching its influence by organising Nigerian student unions in Chinese universities as a means of offering support to Nigerian students in China when they face problems and injustices in China.[59] There are also now Nigerian asylum seekers, which the community did not have in the early 2000s; as such, the community is currently grappling with how to support this growing population.

On the other hand, the Bakassi refugee community has been hindered by multiple factors. First, it does not have the type of economic mobility that the Nigerian community in China has. The community in China is made up of traders and businesspeople who have maintained investments in cities like Guangzhou for decades. Both undocumented and documented members of the community have some level of financial influence in the local economy and, as a result, they can mobilise to protect their interests in ways that the Bakassi community cannot. This shows that undocumented status or 'illegality' does not necessarily mean complete powerlessness. The Bakassi community continues to face precariousness as they grapple with high levels of injustices within the community and in Nigeria. Refugee camps are often considered to be temporary spaces for people in transition, but in the case of the Bakassi refugees, their camp locations have assumed a more permanent status because the Nigerian government has not lived up to its promises of resettlement and empowerment. The Bakassi refugee community is faced with challenges like hunger, lack of access to clean water and electricity, unemployment, illiteracy and teenage pregnancy. Nigeria

[58] Personal interview with Mr C, Baiyun District, Guangzhou, March 2016, on file with the author.
[59] ibid.

is a signatory to the Refugee Convention and its protocol, the ICESCR, the ICRC and CEDAW, among many other international human rights instruments, but the rights enshrined in these instruments have been denied to the Bakassi community.[60] As long as there are shortages of basic necessities, injustices in the community will remain tied to these issues, determining how informal justice in the community develops and how empowered members of the community are to mobilise for their interests. Over time, the justice mechanisms in the Bakassi community can solidify; however, the perception of militancy in the community can become a hindrance to the development of communal responses to issues.

VI. LEGAL CONSCIOUSNESS AND MOBILISATION IN THE CASE STUDIES

In order to understand how these communities mobilise themselves to protect their interests, it is important to first see them as legal subjects that interact with international, domestic and local law in their daily lives. At the international level, the undocumented members of the Nigerian community in China are faced with visa status problems, arbitrary arrest and detention, forced labour in prison,[61] unauthorised executions and cremations,[62] mass deportations etc. In interviews with members of the community, individual undocumented migrants were not aware of their rights in international law because of the general attitude in China towards the human rights of individuals.[63] The conception of group rights as opposed to individual rights in China affects the implementation of international human rights norms, particularly if they are political and civil rights and not economic and social rights.[64] Greater emphasis is placed on the protection of rights which ensure that the basic needs of Chinese citizens are met, like the right to health, education and housing. In terms of civil and political rights, the Chinese government is now trying to improve law enforcement procedures to prevent coercive or punitive measures against citizens, the right to a fair trial, improving religious freedom in accordance with the Chinese Constitution etc.[65] Nevertheless, the Nigerian community is made up of a high percentage of 'overstayers', who by virtue of overstaying have breached the Entry and Exit Law. As a result, though overstaying is a minor offence, the PSB adopts

[60] This was discussed in more detail in ch 3.

[61] See Chiemelie Ezeobi, 'Nigerians Languish in Chinese Jails' *ThisDay*, 17 March 2016, https://www.thisdaylive.com/index.php/2016/03/17/nigerians-languish-in-chinese-jails.

[62] Delon (n 35).

[63] In China, human rights are perceived to be collective rather than individualistic in nature. Moreover, in China, citizens must bear obligations in order to enjoy rights enshrined in the Chinese Constitution. See Sanzhuan Guo, 'Implementation of Human Rights Treaties by Chinese Courts: Problems and Prospects' (2009) 8 *Chinese Journal of International Law* 161.

[64] See Surya P Subedi, 'China's Approach to Human Rights and the UN Human Rights Agenda' (2015) 14 *Chinese Journal of International Law* 437.

[65] See State Council of the People's Republic of China, 'National Human Rights Action Plan of China (2016–2020)', 29 September 2016, http://english.gov.cn/archive/publications/2016/09/29/content_281475454482622.htm.

a law-enforcement approach towards the community. Because the members of the Nigerian community do not see themselves as subjects of international law with individual rights that they can claim in China, they have not been able to mobilise in order to protect their rights at the international level when faced with injustice. At the national level, most of them are undocumented non-citizens and, as such, do not believe that any of the benefits of citizenship in China apply to them. However, as a community, there is a collective interest in protecting themselves. This drives the responses to the realities and exclusions experienced in China as well as the community's engagement with other migrant communities and the Chinese government.

Refugees and asylum seekers in the Nigerian community in China were very cognisant of their rights in international law and this gave them impetus to access the UNHCR in Beijing for support. This may be because as refugees and asylum seekers, they migrated to China with the purpose of seeking refuge. With this specific aim, they have been able to investigate the rules and utilise the rhetoric of international refugee law. In other words, legal consciousness of one's position as subjects of international law requires intention, education and utilisation of the rules and the rhetoric of international law for the purpose of mobilisation. At the domestic level, both documented and undocumented migrants in the community in China experienced forms of alienation from domestic legal institutions and the constant disadvantages of non-citizenship. The domestic legal system simultaneously engages and alienates the community by relying on the community to remedy its own injustices, while allowing Chinese citizens to exploit the undocumented status of members of the community due to the privilege of citizenship. This exclusion from the formal domestic legal mechanisms in the daily lives of the members of the community led to the creation of the parallel/informal justice mechanisms.

An example of the mobilisation of the asylum-seeking population of the community is the information chain that exists between asylum seekers and refugees in different cities. From interviews, I learnt that asylum seekers and refugees share information from Guangzhou, Dongguan, Shanghai and other cities on how to get to Beijing in order to seek asylum. This support system provides asylum seekers with the information and documentation needed in Beijing, including passports, transportation and accommodation on arrival in Beijing. There is also a support system through the asylum application and refugee registration process provided within the community. In addition, undocumented migrants in the community have mobilised by either collaborating with the PSB to solve crimes or to protest against grave injustices in the community. For example, during an immigration raid in 2009, a member of the community was killed when he tried to escape from the police.[66] The community organised

[66] Tania Branigan, 'Africans Protest in China after Nigerian Dies in Immigration Raid', *The Guardian*, 16 July 2009, https://www.theguardian.com/world/2009/jul/16/china-african-protesters-immigration-raid.

the first foreign protests in mainland China to denounce police brutality against its members in 2009.[67] The impact of the community's visibility through this mobilisation was so great that it generated public and international discourse on immigration and racism in China.[68] The community mobilised again in 2012 for the murder of another member of the community in Guangzhou.[69] The community has also mobilised on issues regarding forced cremations, arbitrary arrests and punitive visa policies.[70] In this way, alienation from formal justice has galvanised the agency of the community to mobilise for their interests.

In the Bakassi community, there is a high level of legal consciousness of international law – the source of their displacement and the injustices that have resulted from this. All the individuals interviewed (regardless of their role in the community) were cognisant of international legal norms and practices on borders, statelessness and boundary dispute settlements, as well as the rights accorded to them in Nigeria and Cameroon by the GA. Bakassi refugees are acutely aware that they were subjects of international law because of how directly they were affected by it. From the interviews, it was apparent that the refugees experience alienation from international, regional and domestic laws. At the international level, there has been no implementation of the GA, which states in Article 3 that Cameroon will not force the Bakassi people to change their nationality, culture, language or beliefs.[71] Article 3 affirmed that they have a right to continue fishing and agriculture on the Peninsula, and that their properties and customary land rights are to be protected. Finally, it stipulates that Cameroon should not levy taxes in a discriminatory manner on the inhabitants of the zone, and that the Cameroonian government is responsible for protecting the lives of the Bakassi people from harm and harassment. In addition to these obligations, Nigeria promised to resettle and integrate those who chose to migrate to Nigeria.[72] None of these obligations has been implemented, and the UN and other international bodies have not held the parties to the treaty responsible. The alienation of the Bakassi community from international law has led the community to mobilise to garner international awareness

[67] ibid.

[68] See James Pomfret, 'Out of Africa and into China, Immigrants Struggle', *Reuters*, 21 August 2009, https://uk.reuters.com/article/uk-friction-china-africans/out-of-africa-and-into-china-immigrants-struggle-idUKTRE57K27U20090821.

[69] See 'Africans' Protests Highlight Tensions in Guangzhou', Wall Street Journal, 20 June 2012, https://blogs.wsj.com/chinarealtime/2012/06/20/africans-protests-highlight-tensions-in-guangzhou.

[70] Personal interview with Mr B (n 34). Mr B stated that the community has reached out to both the Chinese government and the Nigerian Embassy in China on different occasions to discuss solutions to these problems in the community. See also Bill Schiller, 'Big Trouble in China's Chocolate City', The Star, 1 August 2009, https://www.thestar.com/news/insight/2009/08/01/big_trouble_in_chinas_chocolate_city.html.

[71] See the Uppsala Conflict Data Program Database, 'Greentree Agreement between Nigeria and Cameroon', New York, 12 June 2006, https://ucdpged.uu.se/peaceagreements/fulltext/Cam-Nig%20 20060612.pdf.

[72] See Relief Web Report, 'Nigeria: Government Unprepared for Returnee Influx', 25 September 2008, https://reliefweb.int/report/nigeria/nigeria-government-unprepared-returnee-influx.

and galvanise change. This is what led to the calls for the independence of the Bakassi people from Cameroon and Nigeria by militants in the past.[73] In addition, members of the community armed themselves with knowledge of international law after experiencing exclusion in the process during the case at the ICJ in The Hague and have utilised this knowledge for activism in the media and in the local political arena. In interviews, members of the community quoted international laws on human rights and humanitarian principles. While these initiatives have not yet been successful in changing their plight, it demonstrates the agency of the members of the community in changing their legal reality and protecting the rights that they are told they have in international law.

At the domestic level, the Bakassi community also experiences exclusion from the protections of formal law. Due to a lack of political will, the Nigerian government has not been able to resettle the Bakassi community in Nigeria properly; levels of formal security in the camps are very low due to the presence of militants in the community, and the formal legal system is hindered by corruption and bottlenecks. The injustices faced in the camps, as well as the inability of the Nigerian government to address these injustices, has created a legal vacuum, which has been filled to some degree by informal justice mechanisms. From the interviews in Ikang and Akpabuyo, the community has been trying to mobilise for justice in Nigeria by organising protests, utilising the media to create awareness on their right to proper resettlement in Nigeria and relying on the militants to attract media attention regarding the levels of insecurity in the camp. The members of the community are greatly limited in agency due to the lack of necessities in the camp, which creates a cycle of exploitation where abuse both within and outside the camp is met with indifference at the local, state, federal and international levels, leading to further injustice and hierarchies and forcing the community to turn to militants for a solution. From the interviews, it appears that those in the camp in Ikang were more aware of their rights in international law and their rights in Nigeria than those in Akpabuyo. This was evidenced in their language and choice of words when discussing the ceding of the Peninsula to Cameroon and the obligations created by the GA towards Bakassi people. For example, leaders in the Ikang camp were quite cognisant of the exact provisions in the GA that accorded them protections in Cameroon (Article 3), the African Union Convention on Refugees etc.[74] All the leaders of the camp were up to date with legal developments in Nigeria and internationally, as well as the treatment of refugees or displaced people in other parts of Nigeria by the Nigerian government, which they used to gauge the treatment of Bakassi people by the state. They were vocal about their opinions on the ICJ and the impact of faraway decisions in The Hague on their lives in Cameroon and Nigeria. They were also

[73] Onah (n 47).
[74] Group listening session in Ikang (n 43).

actively trying to communicate with the Nigerian government by visiting the offices of the NEMA, the Refugee Commission, the Human Rights Commission and political leaders in the Federal Capital to air their grievances.[75]

The community in Akpabuyo was less vocal about their rights and less mobile; this may have been due to their reliance on NGOs, some political leaders and charities as support systems.[76] The community in Ikang had no such support system. These nuances between the two communities of Bakassi refugees indicate that Bakassi experiences of injustice and the law differ. Within the general community, there are different levels of empowerment or disempowerment as well as different levels of acceptance or alienation, recalling the discussion in Chapter 5. This influences the ways in which members of the community perceive themselves in relation to the law and to justice. Just like the Nigerian community in China, the Bakassi community experiences engagement and alienation of the law. Engagement has brought about awareness of rights, while alienation has brought about an awareness of the disadvantage of displacement and statelessness. This has shaped how Bakassi refugees understand law, legal practices and institutions, and, by extension, how they mobilise to address the injustices they experience. Here again, the legal consciousness and mobilisation in day-to-day encounters with formal law is what leads to the creation of alternative/informal justice mechanisms in the community.

VII. GENDER IN INFORMAL JUSTICE SYSTEMS

Gender disparities impact how informal justice mechanisms play out in the day-to-day experiences of undocumented and refugee migrants. When there are no female leaders or decision makers in the community, justice will be gendered. In the case of the Nigerian community in Guangzhou, there were no women involved in any of the decision-making roles of the informal justice system. As a result, men resolved all the cases discussed by the interviewees. Men make up a majority of the population of the Nigerian community, but there are also undocumented and asylum-seeking female members of the community. The lack of female representation in the justice structures leads to the overrepresentation of male opinions and interests in the day-to-day running of the system. For example, there are no support mechanisms in place for Nigerian women who are raped in the community, even though there were consequences for rape when a Nigerian man was accused of raping a Chinese woman. There is no remedy for women who are trafficked, forced into labour or exploited in the community.

[75] The participants in Ikang were also vocal about their communication with the militants and the role of militancy in providing remedies to the injustices in the community.

[76] Group listening session with the Bakassi community in the Akwa Ekot Edem Camp, Akpabuyo, Cross River State, May 2016, on file with the author. The participants in Akpabuyo appealed for support on necessities like food, land and education, and were not as vocal about their opinions and rights.

Trafficking for sex is one of the problems that the Nigerian and other African communities in China face.[77] However, there is no community approach towards sexual violence. Because women are not actively engaged in the informal justice system, they face a deeper level of alienation from international and domestic formal law and exclusion from communal informal justice in China. As a result, remedies are not available for many of the injustices women face. During my research, it appeared that women had no involvement in relation to information sharing, support systems, intelligence sharing, elections and other spaces. In over 36 interviewees, I was only able to speak to two women. While they were able to get support to seek asylum in Beijing, they recounted severe abuse they had experienced in Guangzhou and Dongguan with no access to justice.[78] Both Dongguan and Guangzhou have a high concentration of Nigerians/African communities, and both cities seem to be the location of the highest exploitation and abuse. The two women I interviewed alluded to the incidence of trafficking and forced prostitution in the community and the lack of justice at both the community and the PSB levels.

The Bakassi case study differed slightly in this sense, because women were involved in community decision making and politics. Most of the women I encountered had lost their husbands and sons in the conflict with the Cameroonian Gendarmes and, as a result, there are numerous female-headed households. In addition, women were subject to the worst of the insecurity of the camps. However, the majority of decision makers are still male. As a result, gender has limited the space women occupy in the camps, as well as the space to voice grievances and to mobilise for justice. The lack of representation of women in the informal justice decision-making processes leads to a silencing of women and their experiences of injustice in these communities. This silencing feeds into the hierarchies in these spaces and the further exploitation of vulnerable members. Until both communities include women in the communal justice processes and structures, real justice will unachievable.

VIII. DISMANTLING DISCRIMINATION AND HIERARCHIES

In China, there are multiple layers of injustices that the members of the Nigerian community encounter. First, the Chinese government enforces discriminatory visa laws and policies towards Africans. As discussed above, these injustices chiefly comprise the arbitrary arrests and forceful detention by the PSB, forced labour and the deaths of members of African migrant and refugee communities

[77] Mwita Sosthenes, 'Africa: Human Trafficking Seen Escalating', *Tanzania Daily News*, 21 September 2015, http://allafrica.com/stories/201509210884.html; Polycarp Nwafor, 'Keeping Nigerians away from Jails Abroad', *The Vanguard*, 3 October 2017, https://www.vanguardngr.com/2017/10/keeping-nigerians-away-jails-abroad.

[78] Conversation with A and B, Yanjiao, China, December 2015, on file with the author.

in Chinese prisons. This layer of injustice is rooted in the exclusionary migration law and policy towards Africans practised by the Chinese government. Since the influx of Africans into China in the late 1990s, the Chinese government has progressively focused on reducing the time and spaces that Africans can occupy in China by implementing very stringent visa laws and policies.[79]

The second layer of injustice relates to discrimination and micro-aggressions in the local community. Although China is not monolithic, it presents itself as a racially homogeneous. This narrative of a monolithic culture, as well as the impact of global discourses around migrants and refugees as 'threats', has affected laws and policies towards foreigners in China, particularly Africans.[80] At the local level, members of the Nigerian community face severe discrimination, which limits their access to housing, healthcare, education and other amenities in cities like Guangzhou, where there is a higher concentration of Africans.

At this level, Chinese citizens often use the privilege of citizenship to exploit undocumented members of the Nigerian and African communities, as has been discussed in the case studies above. In my interviews and interaction with Chinese immigration law scholars at the Beijing Institute of Technology, the participants believed that Africans experience discrimination because Africans are radically different from Chinese people in terms of culture, appearance and other characteristics. They opined that perhaps, over time, Chinese people will understand African diversity. Even so, they held that there is a concern that China would develop the same problems that North America and Europe are facing vis-a-vis undocumented migrants from Africa and other parts of the world. This discrimination stems from negative perceptions of Africans and the space they occupy in society. Ms Y, an executive of a community organisation in Guangzhou, stated that local perspectives of Africans are shaped by both Chinese and foreign media sources that often portray Africans as uneducated and poor.[81] Here I would disagree with Ms Y – the media alone does not shape these harmful perceptions. These perceptions are created by the fear of the 'other', of local Chinese communities scared of losing their space to outsiders who look and act differently from them. It is an issue of the space that Africans occupy in China; China is a country where citizens do not have freedom of movement internally and where population pressures shape government law and policies towards their own citizens. Ms M, a researcher in Guangzhou, believed that this was due to the fact that it was at the local level that these population pressures and the presence of Africans were felt more acutely.[82]

[79] Min Zhou, Shabnam Shenasi and Tao Xu, 'Chinese Attitudes toward African Migrants in Guangzhou, China' (2016) 46(2) *International Journal of Sociology* 141.

[80] Listening session with Chinese immigration law scholars at the Beijing Institute of Technology, December 2015.

[81] Interview with Ms Y by email, 29 January 2016.

[82] Skype Conversation with Ms M, a Chinese migration researcher, January 2016, on file with the author.

The impact of harsh immigration laws on Africans (like illegal work and visa violations) further complicates how Africans are seen within local communities. According to Ms Y, locals in Guangzhou saw the media representations of war, famine and underdevelopment in Africa as true representations of Africans. Even though Chinese people are eager and willing to do business with Africans, they are not able to accept African migrants who settle in the community. These perspectives fuel more discrimination that leads to further exclusions and hierarchies in communities where Africans share spaces with Chinese people. For example, many homeowners are unwilling to rent out their houses to Africans and, as a result, access to housing is a problem. In places like Guangzhou, hotels reject African travellers, and immigration policies like the compulsory police registration make it difficult to live outside areas like Xiaobei and Sanyuanli, where most Africans live. At the time of my research, there was a new local policy stating that Africans could only live in designated areas of Guangzhou. These 'hotels' were relatively expensive and monitored by CCTV cameras. Furthermore, the passports of Africans forced to stay there were held as collateral for the payment of hotel fees. I was refused entry into hotels that were not designated for Africans and so stayed in one of these hotels throughout my research in Guangzhou. Without proper access to housing, healthcare and education, the community faces very dire living conditions in China. Communities need to either create or look for an alternative system or networks to access basic amenities, such as health, housing, education and medical care.

During my research, I learned of an underground health system built to exploit the lack of healthcare options available to irregular migrants in places like Guangzhou. Ms M claimed that there were 'black' hospitals specifically for African undocumented migrants who could not access hospitals due to their migration statuses.[83] According to her, these clandestine Chinese hospitals force undocumented migrants to pay for healthcare services in US dollars and at exorbitant rates. A member of the Nigerian community also alluded to the existence of the underground health system, stating that when his visa expired, he fell sick and needed a surgical procedure; he was able to get the procedure done at one such underground hospital by paying in cash.[84] According to both Ms M and Ms Y, Chinese participation in the underground system indicated a tacit permission for their continued existence. These experiences of exploitation are multiplied across other aspects of the lives of the members of the Nigerian community – for example, both Ms M and Mr H at the UNHCR alleged that there were similar covert arrangements for housing undocumented Africans in Guangzhou. Many property owners refuse to accept African renters and the few who do demand for high amounts of money as rent. This is the reason why the Nigerian community has established networks through which members

[83] ibid.

[84] Interview with S, Baiyun District, Guangzhou, February 2016, on file with the author.

can find affordable accommodation with other members of the community. It also explains the inevitable concentration of Africans in places like Xiaobei and Sanyuanli that have come to be associated with African dwellers.

A third layer of injustice is seen at the communal level, where issues like prostitution, human and drug trafficking, and business-related exploitation occur. These problems are rooted in the discrimination and exclusion taking place at the local level, and the hierarchical and discriminatory nature of China's visa policies and laws at the national level. The stringent visa policies force Africans to leave or overstay, and overstaying makes members of the community 'illegal'. Their statuses push them into the underground economy or 'black market', where exploitation leads people into a cycle of human and drug trafficking, forced prostitution and forced labour, which fuels negative perspectives about the community and leads to arbitrary arrests, detentions and other human rights abuses. The Nigerian community's experience of injustice (and, by extension, the broader experiences of undocumented migrants) beyond undocumented status is impacted by the conception of human rights in China. On the one hand, members of the Nigerian community have some understanding and an experience of human rights in Nigeria; on the other hand, in China these rights do not apply to them due to their undocumented status. In several interviews, people stated that the approach of the PSB towards Nigerians and Africans in general was harsher in Dongguan and Guangzhou, and more favourable in places like Shenzhen, for example.[85] They believed that the degree of favourability in Shenzhen was because the size of the undocumented community was smaller than in Guangzhou and Dongguan. Because of the undocumented statuses of majority of the community members in places like Guangzhou, the first response from the PSB is a criminal justice approach. Members of the community who overstay are breaching China's immigration laws, and when there is injustice in the community, there are few formal remedies. Where a legal protection framework is lacking, the informal justice system of the Nigerian community tries to fill in the gaps. As stated above, members of the community who have access to accommodation often offer others housing, the community campaigns for Nigerians who have fallen foul of the Chinese justice system, those who are to be deported, those who have experienced exploitation and fraud etc. For example, Mr B held that every year, the community raises money from its members to pay for the tickets of some Nigerians who were in Chinese prisons in order for them to be able to leave China. The community also has a mentorship programme where the older, successful members of the community act as mentors to younger and newer members.[86]

In Nigeria, the injustices against undocumented individuals are much more complex, as it involves Nigeria, Cameroon and the international community.

[85] Interview of Mr P, a high-level staff member of the IOM, December 2015; personal interview with Mr B (n 34); conversation with A and B (n 78).

[86] Personal interview with Mr B (n 34).

Before the displacement of the Bakassi people from the Peninsula between 2002 and 2013, members of the Bakassi refugee community experienced human rights abuses in Cameroon, including targeted killings, the seizure of their land and property, the threat of the use of force against them, discriminatory taxes, the loss of their right to fish on the Peninsula, the imposition of nationality, name and language changes, sexual violence and discrimination.[87] These abuses did not end when the conflict was resolved with the GA in 2006 and after the majority of Bakassi people fled from the Peninsula between 2009 and 2013; abuses against the Bakassi still occur in Cameroon today.[88] These violations are grave, considering that both Cameroon and Nigeria are parties to both the ICCPR[89] and the African Charter on Human and Peoples' Rights (ACHPR),[90] which require states parties to enforce the rights enshrined in those conventions in good faith. There has been no attempt to hold Cameroon responsible for its breaches of Article 3 of the GA, which offers protections in relation to the political, economic, social, and cultural lives of the Bakassi people both regionally and internationally.[91] The militants in the Bakassi community attempted to fight for the justice of the community in Cameroon, and members of the community have attempted to attract international attention to their treatment within Cameroon's borders.[92]

This layer of injustice is rooted in colonialism and the interference of France and Great Britain, and through the ICJ in territorial determinations in the region. Backed by international law and the ICJ, colonial decisions were upheld in the ceding of the Peninsula to Cameroon.[93] The injustices are also rooted in the lack of monitoring or implementation of the GA by the UN Mixed Commission, the Commission that oversaw the ceding of the Peninsula to Cameroon and the GA.[94] The informal justice system in the refugee community was established because of refugee experiences in Cameroon. The oppression of the Bakassi people in Cameroon has affected how they see themselves in relation to the state, formal law and access to justice in Cameroon and Nigeria. The perception that formal law is not on their side has influenced the rise in militancy as a tool to fight against injustice. The second layer of injustice and

[87] Group listening session in Ikang (n 43).

[88] See Editorial, 'Travails of Nigerians in Bakassi', *ThisDay*, 17 July 2017, https://www.thisdaylive.com/index.php/2017/07/17/travails-of-nigerians-in-bakassi.

[89] UN General Assembly, International Covenant on Civil and Political Rights, 16 December 1966, Treaty Series, vol 999, p 171, UN Doc A/6316 (1966).

[90] Organization of African Unity (OAU). African Charter on Human and Peoples' Rights ('Banjul Charter'), 27 June 1981, CAB/LEG/67/3 rev 5, 21 ILM 58 (1982).

[91] See Centre for Treaties of the Federal Republic of Nigeria (n 71) art 3.

[92] See Hindatu Maigari Yerima and Ranjit Singh, The Bakassi Dispute: People's Dynamics and the Rise of Militancy' (2017) 22(1) *IOSR Journal of Humanities and Social Science* 67.

[93] The background on the ceding of the Bakassi Peninsula to Cameroon was discussed in ch 2. Cameroon relied on colonial-era agreements between France and Great Britain on the ownership of the Peninsula, whereas Nigeria relied on pre-colonial, historical and cultural links to the Bakassi people.

[94] Group listening session in Ikang (n 43).

human rights violations comes from the response of the Nigerian government to the displaced community in Nigeria. In the listening session conducted in the Ikang camp in August 2016, community members stated that Nigeria did not live up to any of the resettlement promises made to those who fled from Cameroon.[95] The lack of basic amenities – access to education, electricity, clean water, a source of livelihood etc – in the camps since 2008 has fuelled other injustices like insecurity and crime in the community, which the informal justice mechanisms in the community attempt to resolve. The leaders in the camp in Ikang allege that the funds earmarked for the resettlement and development of the community have been stolen by government parastatals, federal and state government officials, and traditional rulers.[96] The poor conditions in the camp testify to this allegation. In addition, the state government promised a conditional cash transfer to the members of the community and, each year, the state government budget earmarks the funds without releasing them to the community.[97] According to the interview with participants in Ikang, the cash transfer was agreed when the refugees first arrived in Nigeria, but has not been released since 2013. The members of the community lost faith in their political leaders due to this high level of corruption, and rely on non-state and non-customary sources of justice and mobilisation.

Many members of the community have no birth certificates, no local government identification papers or passports that link them to Nigeria; as a result, they cannot vote or run for office in Nigeria. Discrimination based on a lack of political representation, as well as exclusion from the benefits of local, state and national identification limit the spaces of cultural, social, political and economic expression of the Bakassi community. Exclusion from local and state-level politics affects the protection of their interests at the local, state and federal levels. Because they are no longer inhabitants of an oil-producing area, they are also denied the benefits that other oil-producing communities have.[98] In addition, not having access to their ancestral lands and a land of their own in Nigeria limits their cultural and social lives. These injustices are rooted in Nigeria's disengagement from the refugee community. The state has prioritised the refugee crisis in northeast Nigeria over other groups. Government officials opined that Bakassi refugees have resettled and no longer need government support.[99]

[95] ibid.

[96] ibid.

[97] For example, see Cross River State Government, '2022 Approved Budget Summary', https://budgetpedia.ng/Download/390/cross-river/7797/crs-2022-approved-budget-print, at 56. The 2022 budget mentions a conditional cash transfer for COVID-19 and not specifically for Bakassi returnees.

[98] Group interview with Ms I, the Bakassi Local Government Chairwoman, and members of the Local Government, August 2016, on file with the author.

[99] Personal interview with State Emergency Management Agency staff in Calabar, Cross River State, June 2016, on file with the author; phone interview with NEMA staff in June 2016; personal interview with a former Bakassi Local Government Chairman in Calabar, Cross River State, August 2016, on file with the author; personal interview with Mr J at University of Calabar, Cross River State, June 2016, on file with the author.

Despite pre-conceived assumptions of what marginality and agency are, both case studies show that while these communities faced different types of discrimination and even harassment by the state, they are not powerless. Undocumented and displaced people are often characterised as lacking power to protect their interests on their own because of their lack of status. However, instances of legal consciousness and mobilisation show that despite the vulnerabilities imposed, undocumented migrants and refugees still have agency; even though it may not be powerful enough to grant unhindered access to rights and resources, it gives them access to some level of justice, resistance to oppression and cohesion within their communities (and may, over time, help forge a community identity).

IX. INFORMAL JUSTICE SYSTEMS AND THE PROMISE OF JUSTICE

According to Keebet von Benda-Beckmann, globalisation creates and changes complex legal structures.[100] Both China and Nigeria have long-running formal and informal legal systems. However, the impact of global connectedness created by the migration of Africans looking for business opportunities in China and the international legal decisions on the Bakassi community in Nigeria has created new communities of migrants. In China, most of the members of the Nigerian community (particularly in Guangzhou) do not have Chinese visas or permission to reside in China. Similarly, the Bakassi refugee community in Nigeria does not have proof of citizenship both in Nigeria and Cameroon. As a result, both communities live on the fringes of society. Because of the undocumented nature of these communities, their members also live outside the formal justice system and, as a result, there are justice lacunae that create the need for communal justice mechanisms. While states may have the power to accept or suppress the existence of non-state or informal law, numerous informal justice systems exist not because of the state, but in spite of it. This is the situation in the two case studies, where communal justice frameworks are necessary and crucial to the existence of the community, whether the state approves it or rejects it. The state is not at the centre of the narrative on informal justice systems; rather, indigenous communities and individuals are central to their very existence.

The existence of informal justice mechanisms demonstrates that communities in the Global South contribute to the rule of law, the protection of rights and interests, and justice without the influence, approval or support of the state. Undocumented and displaced persons in developing countries have significant roles to play in the development of the law in ways that the state

[100] Keebet von Benda-Beckmann, 'Globalisation and Legal Pluralism' (2002), 4 (1) *International Law Forum du droit international* 19 at 20.

and international organisations cannot. We can find Third World approaches to the law in these communities: communities of the undocumented, displaced, asylum seekers and the stateless and those engaging in South-South migrations. Communities made up of these groups and individuals are key to understanding the role and significance of Third World contributions to the law and justice because these communities live on the fringes of formal law. They establish and operate informal justice mechanisms despite the state and the international community. These mechanisms allow for conflict resolution at the communal level, thereby enabling communities to address injustices and uphold rights in the community on their own terms. These communities, while being marginalised and excluded, aspire to the rule of law and justice, characteristics that are often not accorded to them. Such communities are contributing in their own way to the body of law, the rule of law, justice, the protection of human rights and legal mobilisation.

Nevertheless, informal justice systems have their own limits and problems. As demonstrated in the case studies, informal justice is hindered by gender exclusions, a lack of accountability (for example, regarding the activities of the militants in the Nigerian case study) and the impending threat of politics, public opinion and illegality. Another limit on the influence of informal justice systems is the lack of the power to enforce decisions in the community. These threats to informal justice are severe, but, as discussed in the introduction to this chapter, they cannot be remedied by intervention from outsiders or engagement with the state alone.

Informal justice mechanisms are not a panacea for all injustices in these communities; instead, they bear the promise of justice[101] to communities who are on the fringes of society. They create a desire for and an optimism about justice, human rights and the rule of law, and give members of the community an opportunity to live their daily lives with dignity. The fact that the hands of the marginalised construct informal justice makes it an even more powerful tool in domestic and international law. According to Sionadh Douglas-Scott, the law in the hands of the vulnerable is the law we aspire to because in their hands, it targets oppression and marginalisation immediately when it occurs.[102]

The existence and functionality of informal justice systems in both case studies is a testament to the significance of legal pluralism and the fact that the law exists even in the most excluded communities. Scholars like Douglas-Scott state that legal pluralism may lead to many forms of injustice and abuse due to the multiplicity of the law and that a proliferation of legal regimes does not particularly guarantee the protection of the most vulnerable individuals in the world.[103] This is because the multiplicity of the law complicates its rigidity and protects

[101] Jonathan Crowe, 'The Limits of Legal Pluralism' (2015) 24(2) *Griffith Law Review* 330.
[102] Sionaidh Douglas-Scott, *Law after Modernity* (Oxford, Hart Publishing, 2013) at 147.
[103] ibid at 196.

the interests of states and powerful corporations as opposed to those of communities and individuals.

In other words, an abundance of laws will create more hierarchies and exclusions, hindering the vulnerable from access to justice and creating more benefits for the privileged and the powerful.[104] This is true of any legal system; I have seen the impact of complex international and domestic laws on both migrant communities in Nigeria and China. However, the informal justice systems in place in these spaces attempt to remedy the injustices caused by the rigidity and complexity of formal law. According to Douglas-Scott, we need to focus on aspirations of justice, human rights and the rule of law, particularly because of the injustice that legal pluralism causes. Informal justice mechanisms focus on remedying abuses and concrete injustices created by the law in the daily lives of the most vulnerable people, and, by so doing, these mechanisms 'save the day'.

Members of these communities mobilise and rally together for remedies immediately whenever an abuse or injustice occurs. The immediacy of legal mobilisation is what makes informal justice frameworks crucial in these spaces. These actions on the ground are more impactful than drawn-out discussions, international organisation interventions, international calls to action, social media publicity or any other 'outside' responses to the injustices that occur in communities on the fringes. Ultimately, informal mechanisms dismantle injustice, exclusions and hierarchies created by the legal, the formal and the normative.

[104] ibid at 170.

7

Final Thoughts

I. REFLECTIONS ON THE RESEARCH PROJECT

IN DOCUMENTING THE narratives of communities and individuals engaging in different forms of South-South migrations, as TWAIL-oriented work, this connects with the ideas of Luis Eslava[1] in studying the continuities and discontinuities between the law and the lived experiences of migrants in the Global South. The purpose of this book has been to understand the local specificities and trends of South-South migrations from below, the structures in migrant communities imagined to be outside the fringes of the law, and the hierarchies within those communities that are evolving and shaping how migrants in the Global South experience norms and decisions coming from the international level and from the state. Most importantly, beyond specificities and trends, the aim was to understand legal realities from the narratives of people and everyday life.

With South-South migrations foremost in mind, I reflected on the significance of discussing experiences from below. I found out that a lot of TWAIL work focused on theory: the works of Sundhya Pahuja, Antony Anghie, Makau Mutua, Balakrishnan Rajagopal, James Gathii, Obiora Chinedu, Ibironke Odumosu, Sujith Xavier and many others took on the TWAIL theoretical project. If I wanted to discuss lived experiences, I needed more than theory.[2]

[1] Luis Eslava, 'TWAIL Coordinates', *Legal Critical Thinking* (2019), http://criticallegalthinking.com/2019/04/02/twail-coordinates.

[2] See Luis Eslava and Sundhya Pahuja, 'Between Resistance and Reform: TWAIL and the Universality of International Law' (2011) 3 *Trade Law and Development* 103; Makau Mutua, ''Critical Race Theory and International Law: The View of an Insider-Outsider' (2000) 45 *Villanova Law Review* 841; Antony Anghie, 'Finding the Peripheries: Sovereignty and Colonialism in Nineteenth Century International Law' (1999) 40 *Harvard International Law Journal* 1; Balakrishnan Rajagopal, 'International Law and Social Movements: Challenges of Theorizing *Resistance*' (2003) 41 *Columbia Journal of Transnational Law* 397; James Thuo Gathii, 'TWAIL: A Brief History of its Origins, its Decentralized Network, and a Tentative Bibliography' (2011) 3 *Trade Law & Development* 26; Obiora Chinedu Okafor, 'Critical Third World Approaches to International Law (TWAIL): Theory, Methodology, or Both' (2008) 10 *International Community Law Review* 371; Ibironke T. Odumosu, 'Challenges for the (Present/)Future of Third World Approaches to International Law' (2008) 10 *International Community Law Review* 467; Sujith Xavier, 'Learning from below: Theorising Global Governance through Ethnographies and Critical Reflections from the Global South' (2016) 33 *Windsor Yearbook of Access to Justice* 229.

The work of Eslava on the law of the everyday, as well as his use of legal ethnography to document the impact and the manifestations of international law at a micro-level in Latin American communities, was a blueprint for what I wanted to do on South-South migrations. I chose to contribute to discussions of migration in the law of the everyday and TWAIL not because it is a trendy topic, but because migrants (particularly the undocumented, asylum seeking or displaced) are often discussed as objects of international law rather than subjects who are centred in their experiences of the law. Their acts of resistance against different forms of hegemony and oppression are habitually overlooked. Undocumented, displaced and asylum-seeking migrants are often thought to live at the fringes of the law. Research that centres on their resistance and their experiences achieves some of the aims of TWAIL, which is to diversify sources of knowledge about law, to infuse the study of international law with the realities of people whose lives it affects daily and their realities on the ground, to challenge ideas of marginality and power and hegemony, and to critique the reconstitution or repackaging of imperialist or hegemonic practices in the Global South.

II. REVISITING MY SUBSTANTIVE CHAPTERS, ARGUMENTS AND CONCLUSIONS

Chapter 1 set out the definitions of broad terms that I use in the book, including 'Global South', 'Global North', 'South-South' and 'peripheries', as well as the types of migrations that the research focuses on. The terms I used were far from perfect or complete, but they captured the idea of global asymmetries of power within and outside different regions; there is a difference between conceptions of the Global North and the Global South, but also in the Global South, there are peripheries within, with people classified as undocumented, stateless, refugees, asylum seekers etc. As Eslava opines, the categories of North and South are not absolute or fixed realities, but can be constituted and reconstituted in response to what Eslava terms local specificities, as well as regional trends to understand the inequalities between and within communities, states and regions.[3]

I chose to study communities engaging in multiple forms of migration within the Global South because this reflects reality: migrants move in diverse ways for a variety of reasons and do not have one-dimensional or fixed realities, and even these categories fail to capture how migrants see themselves or the complex situations shaping their decisions to migrate. I also laid out the reasoning behind my choice to study Nigeria and China for an understanding of South-South migrations. They represent two hegemonies in Africa and Asia: China's position as both a world power and a country with significant

[3] Eslava (n 1).

inequalities, the imperialistic dynamics in Sino-African relations, as well as Nigeria's position in Africa as a regional power made both countries great case studies on South-South migrations. In terms of the significance of this study, beyond shifting the focus from North-South migrations, it contributes not only to the budding area of South-South migrations – linking it to concepts such as intersectionality – but it also expands discussions on TWAIL into areas in migration and informal justice. In addition, it is a contribution to TWAIL methodology, which I discussed in Chapter 2.

I used legal ethnography as a tool to map out the continuities and discontinuities of legal relations from the international level to the everyday life minutiae of migrants in the Global South and to explain the significance of the case studies as methodological tools. My case studies were not selected because I thought there would be any similarities; in fact, similarities were not of any significance at all. Instead, the research was centred on understanding different ways in which people encounter the law in the Global South and on framing research on South-South migrations in China and Nigeria within international law discourse with the aim of unpacking the knowledge found there. A commonality between the two case studies is that they focus on predominantly Nigeria-related communities, which is due to my positionality as a Nigerian researcher. I believe that the research I do should be related to or contribute to knowledge about where I come from and should reflect the realities I see every day. Moreover, being a Nigerian and of an ethnic minority gave me a certain level of access and perspective as I interacted with the respondents in both China and Nigeria. My case studies and experience of research on the ground took me outside of all the theoretical discussions I had studied to see the ways in which people are impacted by international norms and legal decisions in their daily lives.

During my research in both countries, respondents always expressed surprise that a person like them (African, Black, Nigerian, Nigerian of ethnic minority) was carrying out research about their legal realities. It was telling that in places as far away from each other as Beijing/Guangzhou and Ikang/Akpabuyo, people were not used to seeing people like them coming as researchers and documenting their stories. Respondents in Guangzhou complained about being treated like objects of curiosity by many researchers from the West who come taking photos of them without their permission, treating them like oddities and telling stories about them to audiences that they do not know. As a Nigerian, even though I was not experiencing the exact same struggles as members of that community, I experienced what it was to be Black/African/Nigerian in Guangzhou, and sharing something in common with them made it a different experience. Respondents in Bakassi complained about similar experiences of being treated like distant objects for scrutiny, because none of the foreign researchers ever came back after taking their photos and writing their notes. None of them was Bakassi, Nigerian or even African – they came, asked their questions, got the data they needed and left forever. Members of the community were filled with anger at being constantly used for news stories and analysis without any long-term engagement with or continued activism for the community. Even though my research was not going to change their struggles or solve their problems, I was connected at some level to what they were experiencing. Yet, I questioned how I would be different from the researchers who came, gathered data and moved on. This was one of the eye-opening aspects of the realities I found on the ground: research on the Global South is a larger and longer project than unpacking hidden or ignored narratives and knowledge; it is about representation, occupying space and resisting norms, laws, policies and other things that silence or misrepresent people in the Global South, to do research on something and partake in the experience at some level at the same time, and to continue until there is reform or a change. One of the assumptions I made before embarking on my research was that my core objective was to contribute to knowledge and discourse, but meeting people in real life during the research phase made me realise that it was much larger than that.

This raises questions about who the audience or readership of research on the Global South is, how the audience shapes the processes of research, how knowledge from these sites is represented, and the ultimate goals or motivations of the researcher and the research itself. The challenge of research is to engage with people in those spaces not as sources of data, but as people confronting and challenging hegemony and asymmetries of power in their daily lives, to represent these confrontations accurately and to be committed to using the knowledge in ways that those who responded or were interviewed would approve of. This is the reason why the combination of TWAIL, legal ethnography, intersectionality and case studies were important, and, I would argue, the most appropriate tools I could use to discuss South-South migrations. TWAIL enables me to think about long-term engagements with this research and ways to keep the narratives of the communities in China and Nigeria alive in the discussions of the law of the everyday. Legal ethnography enables me to use narratives and personal accounts to understand legal realities, and intersectionality enables me to see the layers of oppression which have become institutionalised in legal, economic and social structures, the power at play in these communities, and the diverse realities of individuals in these communities. Case studies make it possible for me to study different perspectives and lived experiences within one project.

I discussed research methodology limitations in Chapter 3. However, in addition to challenges, including the expansiveness of the context of both case studies, the risk of forgoing theoretical discourse due to the focus on legal ethnography and the danger of fetishising the Global South and the 'informal' over the formal, there were other limitations. Finding scholarly resources from purely Third World-focused scholars and articles was a challenge. I initially intended to base my analysis solely on the theoretical framework of scholars in the Global South as part of my TWAIL methodology. Is it possible or necessary to use only resources that are written by scholars from developing countries or by scholars with a similar attention to Third World case studies or narratives?

I asked myself this question throughout the process of writing this book. The difficulty in accessing the work of scholars in the Global South is a testament to one of the contentions that TWAIL scholars focus on challenging and changing. Academic work, most of which focuses on issues affecting people in the Global South, remains overwhelmingly tied to institutions or scholars based in the Global North, and this impacts how knowledge about the Global South is produced, disseminated and interpreted. It was also challenging to find scholarly resources on international law that focused on my case studies; I often found more political, economic or anthropology-focused work. This indicates that in international law scholarship, there remains a lot of work to be done to reflect the perspectives from the Global South and to make those perspectives part of the mainstream.

The research questions changed numerous times during the project. Initially, I thought I would focus on state sovereignty and the exclusions that come about because of it. I also considered the impact of globalisation on migration regimes in the Global South. However, the research led me to other themes that reflected the realities I did not know existed. I encountered narratives that raised questions about informal law and justice, how refugee and migration regimes from the top affect the daily lives of people, and narratives of discrimination that showed the complexity and entangled nature of identity and changed my understanding of what marginality is. The project morphed into becoming broadly about how migrant communities and individuals in the Global South are encountering the law at their level and what the ramifications of these encounters are. My subquestions evolved to be about the hierarchies and power struggles migrants encounter because of structural violence, what regional and local specificities say about approaches and interpretations of international law in China and Nigeria, and, finally, about the narratives of intersectionality, informal justice and the problem of non-responsibility of states towards certain types of migrants. This book deals with three levels of analysis: the impact of international and regional legal regimes, of state-level rules and policies, and of local-level, 'informal' forms of law in communities. This shaped the way in which I arranged the chapters of the book. Chapters 1, 2 and 3 dealt with the frameworks of the book, Chapter 4 focused on international and regional-legal approaches and the impact on the experiences of migrant communities, Chapter 5 focused more on the state-level and how legal structures enhance certain forms of discrimination that are complicated by identity and intersectionality, and Chapter 6 analysed the legal structures developed in these migrant communities as a result and in response to international, regional and state-level structural issues. The aim was to look at these three levels and come up with conclusions on South-South migrations.

Chapter 4 delved into the disengagement of states from human rights obligations towards certain classifications of migrant status – undocumented, asylum-seeking and displaced migrants – and how this affects the way in which these groups and individuals experience refugee and human rights laws. I aimed to use my case studies, juxtaposed with theoretical and other evidence, to reach some conclusions on the impact of state responsibility (or the lack thereof) to protect the human rights of undocumented and asylum-seeking groups and individuals engaging in South-South migrations. Bhupinder Chimni's discussion of selected bad practices of Western states that have been imbibed by states in the Global South, from *non-entrée* policies to the lack of burden sharing, have become normalised.[4] In addition, doctrines like the responsibility to protect do not apply to non-citizens. The Committee of the ICESCR agrees that states have a responsibility to protect migrants, even if they are undocumented, refugees or asylum seekers; however, as highlighted, the Committee deferred to the protection of citizens first and the discretion of states on the matter. As was discussed in Chapter 4, state responsibility towards refugees and asylum seekers is not clarified in the Refugee Convention, and state responsibilities towards non-citizens remains a grey area. This has become an excuse to avoid full responsibility for the well-being of refugees and asylum seekers. As the case studies showed, leaving the discretion of burden sharing to states impacts how refugees and asylum seekers are treated. Because of the burden of internal migration and population control, which remains a major problem, China leaves the entire responsibility of refugees and asylum seekers to the UNHCR. Also, for a long time, China has seen refugee protection as something that is a Western value and responsibility; however, Lili Song highlights how this is changing now.[5] All of Song's examples of the changes in China towards refugees were external: China has increased funding and pledges to support refugees in other countries and not those within its territory. This means that it may take time to see the internal manifestations of the commitment that China is developing externally. Beyond the practices of Western states, Chimni's myth of difference also comes into play in China, where it has been known to grant refugee status only to people who are of Chinese descent because it is perceived as easier to accept people who have a shared history and culture in common with the receiving state. Beijing remains the only place where asylum seekers can seek refuge in China, which severely limits the UNHCR's access to places where refugees might be present, like airports and borders. It also forces migrants into dangerous situations where they are trafficked in the process of trying to get to Beijing from their ports of entry to seek asylum.

China limits how the UNHCR engages with other UN bodies and organisations that work with refugees and other migrants in irregular situations due to a suspicion of international interference in internal matters. Because the PSB, which is the police, is the main government body that works with migrants,

[4] Bhupinder Chimni, 'Reforming the International Refugee Regime: A Dialogic Model' (2001), 14 Journal of Refugee Studies 151.

[5] Lili Song, 'Strengthening Responsibility Sharing with South-South Cooperation: China's Role in the Global Compact on Refugees' (2018), 30 *International Journal of Refugee Law* 687.

the approach towards asylum seekers, refugees or undocumented migrants is often a criminal justice-oriented one. Lack of communication due to language skills within the PSB means they are often unable to engage with non-Chinese migrants at all. In addition, Chinese immigration law discriminates against people of African descent specifically, making it harder for African migrants to have opportunities in both the formal and informal job markets. International frameworks to protect these groups of migrants have not been subsumed under national law, and regional frameworks that encourage responsibility towards undocumented or asylum-seeking migrants are lacking. These and many more realities reflect China's lack of responsibility towards non-Chinese asylum seekers, refugees and undocumented migrants. This lack of responsibility in turn affects how different groups of these migrants' experience life and the law in China. Narratives of migrants showed that the lack of protection from China meant that the processes of seeking asylum were wrought with dangers (for instance, trafficking (as mentioned above), forced labour, hostility at the PSB and an overstretched UNHCR).

Nigeria, on the other hand, is not lacking in terms of national and regional frameworks for responsibility towards refugees and undocumented migrants. In fact, as was explored in Chapter 4, Nigeria is known for actively providing refugee status to people from Liberia and Sierra Leone. However, when it comes to the Bakassi people, lack of responsibility is rooted in a lack of political will to live up to promises made to protect and resettle them in Nigeria, as well as a lack of implementation of the international and regional obligations. I discussed how this stems from the vagueness in the GA about responsibilities towards the Bakassi people if they leave the Peninsula, as well as the politicisation of the Bakassi narrative in Nigeria. Within the obligations created by the GA, none addressed the provision of legal documentation in Nigeria. This presents a conundrum for the Bakassi people, who are considered citizens but do not benefit from the privilege of citizenship. Furthermore, due to global pressures/agendas of the War on Terror, Nigeria has prioritised the Boko Haram conflict and so has temporarily deprioritised the protection of the Bakassi people. Responsibility towards the Bakassi people has been perceived to be a short-term obligation (ie, after the ruling and the GA) and not a long-term commitment to resettlement. Internal laws like Law No 7, which would have enabled the Bakassi people to belong and to participate in processes such as voting in Nigeria failed woefully because of a lack of due process, as well as the fact that within Nigeria, the Bakassi do not have their own land. Any land assigned to them already belongs to other groups (as was with Ikang), and this created clashes and tensions between locals and the Bakassi people. All these issues create problems for the Bakassi people in their everyday lives, including the capacity to continue practising fishing, which is their primary source of livelihood. China and Nigeria have similar yet divergent contexts, frameworks and approaches towards migrants engaging in South-South migrations. Both states rely on local organisations and the UNHCR to take responsibility for the migrant communities in question. In terms of differences, China bases acceptance of refugees on political reasons (eg, rejection of North Korean refugees) and a shared history and culture. In that context, African migrants cannot enjoy the same protections as some Asian migrants (as is the case concerning Indonesian refugees, for example). Nigeria has a more open understanding of its obligations towards these groups of migrants, but is not conscientious in the implementation or enforcement of these. In the case of the Bakassi people, Nigeria has not been responsible due to the loss of its economic and political interests in the Peninsula to Cameroon. State responsibility towards migrants is affected by national, economic and political interest, and its moral obligation to citizens to the detriment of non-citizens. The case studies show that regardless of which frameworks and perspectives on burden sharing exist, a state must be willing to act responsibly.

Chapter 5 built on Chapter 4 and looked at the impact of discrimination and the intersectionality of identities on the experiences of migrants. The failures of these states to be responsible has an impact on the migrants' daily lives and contribute to the creation of hierarchies and exclusions in the state and within migrant communities. I try to understand what identity means and why it is significant in understanding asymmetries of power and resistance in relation to migrants. Eilleen and Emma Pittaway, Osamudia James, Tayyab Mahmud and other discussions of identity give an insight to the different conceptualisations of identity and power struggles in relation to non-citizens and minority groups. These discussions of identity provide a background for later discussions on intersectionality. As was discussed in Chapter 5, migrants in the Global South challenge notions of state and nation, the cohesion of citizenship, the sacrosanctity of borders, and the territorial sovereignty and jurisdiction of the state.[6] I also examined how migration from and within the Global South challenges citizenship and is used to justify structural violence. Most importantly, I used intersectionality as a framework to make sense of the complexity of migrant identities in the Global South, in line with Mutua's conceptualisation of how CRT tools like intersectionality can be used in TWAIL research to unpack multiple oppressions in the experience of the law and to critique the distribution of power and justice in the Global South. Intersectionality not only shows the ways in which legal structures reinforce discrimination on multiple and simultaneous levels, but also the areas in which resistance and reform are ongoing or possible. As was discussed in Chapter 5, without intersectionality, I stand the risk of treating the migrant communities in my research as monoliths, which is contrary to the aims of this research project. I use the work of Kimberlé Crenshaw for a background of intersectionality both as a methodology, but also as a theory in the understanding of identity and experiences

[6] Tayyab Mahmud, 'Migration, Identity & the Colonial Encounter' (1997) 76 *Oregon Law Review* 633.

of marginality. I also look at critiques of intersectionality from scholars like Jennifer Nash and Nira Yuval-Davis for a better understanding of the gaps in intersectionality and how best to use this tool in my research; the challenge of broadening intersectionality discourse beyond race and gender alone to ethnicity, language, class, nationality and sexuality, as well as the challenge of complicating the experiences of minorities to resist the temptation of presenting them as monolithic in their experiences of marginality. Nash argues that intersectionality should be broadened as a general theory of identity for these reasons.[7] This perspective is reflected in some discussions on the problems with international human rights law and nationality, for example.

According to Homi Bhabha, Article 27 of the UDHR provides protection to minorities, but in declaring that their identities are to be 'preserved', the UDHR unwittingly prioritises national identity and foregrounds minority identities as an 'excess' of national identity.[8] Because the UDHR prioritises national identity, it maintains the power status quo and hierarchies that exclude minority groups and the rights of migrants, particularly undocumented migrants. Even though minority rights are in many ways the predecessors to human rights, the precedence of national identity in human rights law is said to be because international human rights agreements are between states and, as a result, there is no escape from national identity in the experience of human rights and the protections they afford.[9] Human beings cannot escape national identity in attaining the privileges and protections they offer, which automatically means that those who fall out of that national identity, whether they are undocumented, stateless, asylum seeking or displaced, are deprioritised by the law that was created to protect them in the first place. Hence, national identity remains an important category that we can use to understand intersectionality, in addition to race, gender and other categories. I keep these critiques of intersectionality in mind to bring intersectionality into South-South migration research, but also to mark where there are differences in marginality or privilege in my studies. I use the case studies to demonstrate the interplay of race, nationality, class, ethnicity and immigration status, and how it affects the participants in my research on South-South migrations in China and Nigeria. One of the main arguments I make through the case studies is that intersectionality is necessary for a deeper and more true-to-reality understanding of the realities of South-South migrating individuals and groups, revealing why things are the way they are and why people resist power imbalances in the way that they do so.

Looking at the case studies and my respondents' narratives, some key elements about intersectionality are raised. In China, I discuss how perceptions

[7] Jennifer C Nash, 'Rethinking Intersectionality' (2008) 89 *Feminist Review* 1 at 4.

[8] See Homi K Bhabha, 'On Minorities: Cultural Rights' (2000) 100(6) *Radical Philosophy* 3.

[9] Yussef Al Tamimi, 'Human Rights and the Excess of Identity: A Legal and Theoretical Inquiry into the Notion of Identity in Strasbourg Case Law' (2018) 27(3) *Social & Legal Studies* 283 at 287.

of Blackness and African-ness shape how migrants in the case study experience life in China, as well as legal and policy developments at the local and national levels. Blackness in the context of China is distinct from Blackness elsewhere due to China's unique history and internal realities, and its relationship with the African continent. At the local level, there are no distinctions between different Africans based on nationality or ethnicity. My respondents come to terms with what Blackness and African-ness mean in that context in their daily lives. Their perception of self – ie, as their ethnic identity and national identity within the larger African community – does not match how Chinese locals perceive them, which is under the broad brush of Blackness and African-ness. This manifests in labels like *san fei* becoming the institutionalisation of anti-Black and anti-African migrant laws and policies. It also manifests in discrimination in the job market against African people. On the surface, all Africans experience the same struggle, but with intersectionality, variations of experience became evident. Nationality complicates experiences of discrimination particularly in the Nigerian community, because due to the size of the community in relation to other migrant communities, there is a growing stereotype that Nigerians commit the most crimes. As such, the Nigerian experience of stringent migration laws and policies, as well as experiences of injustice and incarceration, was on a different scale. Proximity to Chinese citizens also created hierarchies within the Nigerian community: the experiences of respondents who were married to Chinese citizens differed from those who were either unmarried or married to members of the community. Intersectionality revealed that economic status/class created varying degrees of exclusions within the Nigerian community: rich, educated or documented members of the community enjoy a level of privilege denied to those who are poor, uneducated or undocumented. Gender and sexuality also create variations of experience; female respondents were exposed to gender-based violence, trafficking, forced labour and forced prostitution. Nevertheless, the all-encompassing label of Blackness/African-ness affects every member of the community; even those with privilege still face discrimination and oppression at a certain level.

Similarly, in the Nigerian case study, intersectionality showed the manifestations of asymmetries of power in the Bakassi community. The history of colonialism, the formation of borders between Nigeria and Cameroon, and the decision of the ICJ set the context for the complexity and the questions relating to Bakassi identity and belonging. As was discussed in Chapters 3 and 5, prior to the exodus of some Bakassi people from the Peninsula, discrimination against them was institutionalised by Cameroonian laws and policies. Both international law (through the ICJ decision) and regional agreements (through the GA) failed to protect the Bakassi people from oppression in Nigeria and Cameroon. National identity justified state-backed violence and coercion in Cameroon. The Bakassi people who fled this structural violence in Cameroon faced discrimination based on the intersection of ethnicity and ethnic minority status with economic class and gender, leading to different manifestations of oppression in Nigeria. First, due to ethnicity, the Bakassi people as ethnic minorities in Nigeria have not been able to push for visibility at the national level for the protection of their interests; ethnic majorities are often empowered to shape political will at the national level and, by so doing, to impact law and policy development. Within the Efik ethnicity, which is already a minority in Nigeria, Bakassi people are on the periphery. After the loss of the Peninsula and its oil-generating revenue capacity, Nigeria's interest in the people and the region waned. The Bakassi people were denied access to their primary sources of livelihood; they not only lost oil revenue for development, but also access to the ocean – a vital necessity for a fishing community. The Nigerian government's failure to successfully resettle the Bakassi in Nigeria, as reflected in the failure of Law No 7, compounds asymmetries of power because the Bakassi people have no land and no local government; as such, they cannot access the necessary documentation. The lack of land also creates power struggles within the community relating to where and how the Bakassi people should be resettled and who should lead that push for resettlement. It leads to conflict and disputes with local communities where the Bakassi people have settled in Nigeria. These aspects of the impact of the ICJ decision are not discussed at all in mainstream discourse about international law.

Within the Bakassi community, intersectionality also reveals different experiences of oppression or marginality. Ethnic minority status affects all Bakassi people, but the Bakassi elite can participate in local-level politics in ways that those who are poorer cannot; ethnicity and class intersect to create this range of experience. The Bakassi elite settled easily in Nigeria by virtue of their economic privilege, maintaining proximity to Nigerian citizenship in ways that poorer members of the community were unable to – they had access to passports and driver's licences, and they were able to build a sense of belonging with the greater Nigerian elite. Poorer Bakassi people are faced with the problems of documentation highlighted above. Moreover, poorer Bakassi who used to fish now face struggles in the job market that richer and educated people in the community do not. Militancy and insecurity compound the experiences of marginalisation among poorer members of the community; due to the increase in militancy as a response to marginality, state-backed coercion, violence and exclusion in places like Ikang have become institutionalised. Gender creates further privilege for men in places like Ikang, where rape and gender-based violence severely impact and limit opportunities for women in the community. Women experienced exclusion from the job market, the impact of poverty and lack of identification documents more acutely than men.

Comprehensively, Chapter 5 challenges the idea that marginality is experienced in the same way or that communities engaging in South-South migrations are monolithic. People can gain justice, access or recognition within the spaces in which they find themselves in vastly different ways based on different factors and contexts. More than race and gender, nationality, economic class and sexuality also shape asymmetries of power. Intersectionality exposes diverse hierarchies created outside and within these communities. This chapter also shows the need to centre gendered experiences of migration in migrant communities, especially when those communities are male-dominated. Finally, these case studies reveal some of the areas where resistance is already ongoing: in China, the Nigerian community has protested against institutionalised violence against Africans and stringent migrations laws and policies on different occasions. These actions are of significance in a country like China – that a community of mainly undocumented migrants can call for justice and dignity is an indication of the power and agency this community has in the face of oppression. In Nigeria, the litigation springing from the failures of Law No 7 highlights the ongoing resistance against the state's lukewarm attitude towards the plight of the Bakassi people and the push for true resettlement regardless of the many challenges that structural violence has created for the Bakassi people.

Chapter 6 was constructed upon the frameworks of Chapters 4 and 5, and focused on informal justice mechanisms as the ultimate resistance of undocumented, displaced or asylum-seeking migrant communities. Through the case studies, we see how migrant communities exert their agency by confronting asymmetries of power and oppressive structures imposed from the international, regional, national and communal levels, creating their own definitions and structures of law and justice. Informal justice in this chapter is not conceptualised in the 'traditional' sense, which came from neoliberal, Western institutions focused on economic development, post-conflict peace building and resolution, humanitarian intervention etc. I critique the assumptions that informal justice must be related to Western interventions and international development policies, as well as Western definitions of its characteristics, parameters and aims. I also critique assumptions that informal justice mechanisms must be structured around traditional leaders and settings. In my understanding, informal justice is present in communities that have been excluded from formal structures, which includes undocumented, refugee and asylum-seeking communities engaging in South-South migrations. Informal justice is not just for post-conflict resolution and peace building; it is also woven into the daily lives of community members in the periphery and is a crucial component of life in those communities where formal law is often out of reach. This chapter has expanded the discussion on the ways in which informal justice manifests in real life as forms of resistance to hegemony and exclusions while also seeking to understand and critique those manifestations. As Chidi Odinkalu argues, colonialism created forms of segregation in the legal systems that elites in the Global South co-opted in the post-independence era.[10] Formal legal structures are inaccessible to the poor

[10] Chidi A Odinkalu, 'Poor Justice or Justice for the Poor? A Policy Framework for Reform of Customary and Informal Justice Systems in Africa' (2006) 2 *WBLR: Law and Justice for Development* 141.

for this reason, forcing them to rely on informal justice systems. The case studies demonstrate this: for example, the Bakassi elite rely on the formal justice system in Nigeria, whereas the poorer members of the community are unable to enforce their formal rights in that system. I use Forsyth's spectrum of informal justice to argue that informal justice mechanisms are mutative.[11] This illustrates the different dimensions of informal justice, from semi-formalised to completely repressed by the state depending on the context. The case studies show this range: in China, the state allows the mechanisms in the Nigerian community to exist and sometimes even relies on those mechanisms. This does not affect the oppressive relationship between the state and the migrant community, but it shows that the state acknowledges the importance of informal justice in that community. On the other hand, in Nigeria, the state allows camp leaders, traditional or religious rulers to implement communal justice while repudiating the role of militants in the community and exerting control over all the actors involved in justice and conflict resolution. I discuss how temporality determines the structure of informal mechanisms, as well as how much acceptance those systems have within the state. As seen in the Chinese case study, over time the delicate framework in the early 2000s has become sturdy as the community evolved in response to each unique challenge faced. The Bakassi community has not experienced the same changes due to the unstable nature of their existence in Nigeria; they still live in refugee-like conditions and their obstacles have not changed since their migration to Nigeria.

I discuss legal consciousness and mobilisation in both case studies to show that different communities utilise their awareness of their rights in varying ways to achieve the goal of recognition, access and justice. On the one hand, the Nigerian community in China cannot exert the same rights as are claimed in Nigeria due to the context of human rights in China. Asylum seekers were more cognisant of the language and the rules of international law, which I believe is because their migration is for the specific purpose of seeking refuge. Other members of the community focus more on personal economic and financial development, but have a shared interest in protecting the community from issues like police brutality and mass incarceration. On the other hand, the Bakassi community is cognisant of all the details of the ICJ ruling, the laws and jurisprudence behind it, the details of the GA and the obligations stemming from that agreement. This awareness has shaped the activism in the community and its use of the language of international law to fight for the rights of its members in Nigeria. This shows how these communities negotiate the obstacles placed on the path to justice by international, regional and national structures; they confront obstacles with agency. The case studies have shown that informal justice has many faces: the hegemonic model defined and monitored by

[11] Miranda Forsyth, 'A Typology of Relationships between State and Non-state Justice Systems' (2007) 56 *Journal of Legal Pluralism* 67 at 69.

international neoliberal organisations, the post-conflict, traditionally driven model and the model emerging from local realities from below in communities on the fringes of formal law, acceptance and recognition. None of these models is perfect. As was discussed in Chapter 6, the mechanisms in my case studies remain gender-discriminatory, further enhancing exclusions within the community for women and remaining inefficient in addressing the injustices that women face. The full participation of women is crucial for a more efficient informal justice system. The case studies also show that within communities, the elite benefit from maintaining hierarchies and asymmetries of power that are harmful to justice. Accountability of leadership, illegality, lack of enforceability and politics also threaten the efficiency of informal justice system. The solutions to these problems must come from within and cannot be remedied by the state or the international community, given that the actors institutionalise the same hegemonic structures that informal justice aims to resist.

Finally, the case studies show that these South-South migrating communities are involved in the creation of law. They are shaping the subjects of their own laws, their own interpretation of justice, different forms of authority, accountability and enforcement. Therefore, militants can play a role, even though on the surface they seem at odds with the concept of justice. In the Ikang and Akpabuyo communities, militants have been a part of the struggle against hegemony and, as a result, are also stakeholders in the community. They are a part of the process of force and justice, whether their methods are acceptable to the state or not. These forms of law making are borne out of necessity, and in communities of undocumented or stateless people, it is often the only available path to justice. It is arguable that informal justice mechanisms fill the lacunae between formal law and people in the periphery, and, in so doing, are a part of the tapestry of law and the development of law. International law should recognise informal justice for the role it is already playing, which is to correct some of the wrongs created by certain international rules and norms that have been imbibed by states and the elite in the Global South to the detriment of communities at the fringes of society. In addition to recognising the validity, significance and power of these mechanisms in creating legal change in peripheral spaces, international law and states must not intervene in these processes; rather, the challenge is to learn from them and understand how the subaltern create law, and to use this knowledge to create a more equal international system.

III. KEY PROJECT CONCLUSIONS AND CONTEMPLATING AREAS FOR FUTURE RESEARCH

There has been a lot to unpack and learn in studying migrant communities in Nigeria and China. Several key points emerge from observing different communities and their paths to justice. First, the case studies indicate that resistance is happening in multiple simultaneous ways. From protests against police brutality in Guangzhou to litigation for inclusion in elections in Cross River State, migrants who are usually silenced by a lack of status, poverty and other structural issues are exerting themselves, demanding recognition and justice, and showing that they are aware of their rights within the state. The ways in which migrants resist marginalisation and injustice in their daily lives is an area where future research could develop. What other case studies can we learn from? In what ways are migrant communities confronting and changing asymmetries of power? How are migrant communities mobilising to protect their interests within the state? So many questions arise as a result of these case studies that can contribute immensely to the discourse on resistance in the Global South.

Second, my conceptualisation of marginality and what marginality means has changed significantly because of this resistance. The case studies show that marginality is complex; it is not black and white as it may appear on the surface and contains many grey areas. Before embarking on my research, I assumed that because of undocumented status or displacement, the people I would encounter would be powerless given the structures set up against them. Power and oppression are opposite sides of the same coin. In China, for example, it is arguable that the respondents in the Nigerian community are capitalist subjects; they are empowered by their success in business and wealth, and this success has created some recognition for them in China. In that sense, they are not helpless – in fact, wealth and maleness empowers them in particular ways. Marginality does not rob individuals and communities of their ability to forge their own paths or to thrive in spite of the limitations of undocumented status, statelessness or displacement, as discussed in terms of the levels of legal consciousness and mobilisation ongoing in Nigeria and China. At the same time, racism, gender-based violence and other factors create vulnerabilities and injustice. This is where there is potential for more intersectional work on South-South migrating communities: there is a need to understand the different levels of privilege and power that affect migrant communities. There is also room to study legal consciousness in other migrant communities – for example, among stateless people – to contribute to challenging conceptualisations of marginality in the Global South. The case studies on Nigeria and China unpacked citizenship and non-citizenship as a means of understanding marginalisation and empowerment. The Global South has imbibed bad practices from the international level in terms of dealing with migrants and non-citizens. Citizenship remains one of the central aspects of international migration law, and the impact of non-citizenship on people in the Global South is an area which needs to be developed. Future research can build on this by using other case studies to understand the links between non-citizenship and marginalisation or empowerment.

Informal justice is fundamental to the survival of people on the periphery of the state, it is mutative and it is a positive attribute in the lives of members of the migrant communities that I encountered. However, it is imperfect, as some of the very structures that have excluded the community are part of the communal system. Hierarchies based on gender, corruption and other factors can weaken the transformative power of informal justice. Nevertheless, more research needs to be done in order to expand the knowledge of informal justice mechanisms in the Global South that challenge the traditional understandings of that field. Informal justice does not need to be coupled with Western-driven economic development in the Third World, as neoliberal organisations often push for. It is necessary for everyday living, and in communities at the fringes of formal legal systems. As was discussed in Chapter 6, informal justice is not confined to post-conflict resolution or international development rhetoric, but manifests itself in the daily lives of people who are excluded from formal legal systems for a wide range of reasons. It would be interesting to see how other informal legal systems fit into Forsyth's typology of informal justice relationships and how this impacts upon the space and the processes that these systems occupy. The gendered nature of informal justice in South-South migrant communities and its impact on women is yet another area of discussion that can be developed from this project.

Fourth, this volume highlights the crucial fact that the Global South is not monolithic. As the case studies have shown, context and history shape the unique ways in which states engage with international law, as well as how people below respond to it. Different communities and people demonstrate the law of the everyday and paths to justice in multiple ways. This evokes Eslava's thoughts on TWAIL co-ordinates, which highlight that local specificities and regional trends, as well as changes to global economic and political systems, deepen disparities not only between regions and states but also within states – and, I should add, disparities within communities.[12] It is for this reason that Mutua believes intersectionality will unveil the disparities and the places where law is in need of reform in relation to different regions, states and communities in the Global South. Intersectionality as a broad theory of identity can be applied to understand the realities of undocumented, stateless or displaced migrants in the Global South, expanding the application of the concept and looking at what it means in an African context.

Finally, South-South migrations hold a wealth of knowledge about the law, informal justice, asymmetries of power, resistance to hegemony and undocumented migrants as legal subjects, among many other things. As a result, generally, this is an area that has the potential to contribute to our understanding of international law and the contributions of the Global South to the reform of the law. This area of study is growing, and I foresee further case studies on South-South migrations and law in the future.

[12] Eslava (n 1).

Bibliography

BOOKS AND BOOK CHAPTERS

Al Kalwas AM and Ndumbe AJ (eds), *Case Studies of Conflict in Africa: The Niger-Delta, the Bakassi Peninsula and Piracy in Somalia* (New York: Edwin Mellen Press, 2012)

Appadurai A, *Modernity at Large: Cultural Dimensions of Globalization* (Minneapolis: University of Minnesota Press, 1996)

Arendt H, *The Origins of Totalitarianism* (New York: Schocken Books 2004)

Asiwaju AI, 'Partitioned Culture Areas: A Checklist Africans' in AI Asiwaju (ed), *Ethnic Relations across International Boundaries 1884–1984* (London: C Hurst & Co, 1985)

Balakrishnan R, *International Law from Below: Development, Social Movements and Third World Resistance* (New York: Cambridge University Press 2003)

Bodomo A, *Africans in China: A Socio-cultural Study and its Implications on Africa-China Relations* (New York: Cambria Press, 2012)

Buchanan A and Golove D, 'Philosophy of International Law' in Jules Coleman and Scott Shapiro (eds), *The Oxford Handbook of Jurisprudence and Philosophy of Law* (Oxford: Oxford University Press, 2002)

Castles S, and Miller M, *The Age of Migration: International Population Movements in the Modern World* (Basingstoke: Palgrave Macmillan 2003)

Charlesworth H and Chinkin C, *The Boundaries of International Law: A Feminist Analysis* (Manchester: Manchester University Press, 2000)

Chen HYA, *An Introduction to the Legal System of the People's Republic of China* (Hong Kong: LexisNexis Butterworths, 2004)

Clark P, 'The Rules (and Politics) of Engagement: The Gacaca Courts and Post-genocide Justice, Healing and Reconciliation in Rwanda' in P Clark and Z Kaufman (eds), *After Genocide: Transitional Justice, Post-conflict Reconstruction and Reconciliation in Rwanda and beyond* (London: Hurst, 2008)

Collins PH, *Black Feminist Thought: Knowledge, Consciousness, and the Politics of Empowerment* (Boston: Unwin Hyman 1990)

Dauvergne C, *Making People Illegal: What Globalization means for Migration and Law* (Cambridge: Cambridge University Press, 2008)

Derrida J, 'Differance' in P Kamuf (ed), *A Derrida Reader: Between the Blinds* (New York: Columbia University Press, 1991)

Dittmer L and Yu G (eds), *China, the Developing World, and the New Global Dynamic* (Boulder: Lynne Rienner, 2010)

Douglas-Scott S, *Law after Modernity* (Oxford: Hart Publishing, 2013)

Edet O, *Bakassi Peninsula: The Untold Story of a People Betrayed* (Singapore: Partridge Publishing, 2015)

Eggli AV, *Mass Influx of Refugees and the Limits of Public International Law* (The Hague: Martinus Nijhoff Publishers, 2002)

Eslava L, *Local Space, Global Life: The Everyday Operation of International Law and Development* (Cambridge: Cambridge University Press, 2015)

Filesi T, *China and Africa in the Middle Ages*, David L Morison (trans) (London: Frank Cass in association with the Central Asian Research Centre, 1972)

Glenn Evelyn N, 'The Social Construction and Institutionalization of Gender and Race: An Integrative Framework' in M Ferree (ed), *Revisioning Gender* (Thousand Oaks, CA: Sage Publications, 1999)
Golove D and Buchanan A, 'Philosophy of International Law' in J Coleman and S Shapiro (eds), *The Oxford Handbook of Jurisprudence and Philosophy of Law* (Oxford: Oxford University Press, 2002)
Goodwin-Gill GS, *The Refugee in International Law* (Toronto: Oxford University Press, 1983)
Gordon A, *Nigeria's Diverse Peoples: A Reference Sourcebook* (Santa Barbara, CA: ABC-CLIO, 2003)
Hall S, 'Cultural Identity and Diaspora' in J Rutherford (ed), *Identity: Community, Culture, Difference* (London: Lawrence & Wishart, 1990)
Hill Collins P, *Black Feminist Thought: Knowledge, Consciousness, and the Politics of Empowerment* (Boston: Unwin Hyman, 1990)
Harnois EC, 'Age and Gender Discrimination: Intersecting Inequalities across the Life Course' in V Demos and M Texler Segal (eds), *At the Center: Feminism, Social Science and Knowledge* (Bingley: Emerald Group Publishing, 2015)
Holzgrefe JL and Keohane R (eds), *Humanitarian Intervention: Ethical, Legal and Political Dilemmas* (Cambridge: Cambridge University Press, 2003)
Joppke C, *Challenge to the Nation State: Immigration in Western Europe and the United States* (Oxford: Oxford University Press, 1998)
Koo VK, *The Status of Aliens in China* (New York: AMS Press, 1968)
Koser K, *International Migration: A Very Short Introduction* (New York: Oxford University Press, 2007)
Laclau E, *New Reflections on the Revolution of Our Time* (London: Verso 1991)
Liu G, *The Right to Leave and Return in Chinese Migration Law* (Dordrecht: Martinus Nijhoff Publishers, 2007)
——, *Chinese Immigration Law* (Farnham: Ashgate, 2011)
Mallia P, *Migrant Smuggling at Sea: Combating a Current Threat to Maritime Security through the Creation of a Cooperative Framework* (Leiden: Martinus Nijhoff, 2010)
Mastoureh F, *Intersectionality, Class and Migration: Narratives of Iranian Women Migrants in the UK* (New York: Palgrave Macmillan, 2017)
Muntarbhorn V, *The Status of Refugees in Asia* (Oxford: Clarendon Press, 1992)
Ndifon N and Henshaw K, 'Insecurity in Cross River State: Issues, Actors and Solutions' in TM Ebiede, CO Bassey and JB Asuni (eds), *Insecurity in the Niger Delta: A Report on Emerging Threats in Akwa Ibom, Bayelsa, Cross River, Delta, Edo, and Rivers States* (Abuja: Adonis & Abbey Publishers, 2021)
Nesiah V, 'Theorizing Transitional Justice' in A Orford and F Hoffman (eds), *Oxford Handbook of International Legal Theory* (Oxford: Oxford University Press, 2016)
Preston D, *The Boxer Rebellion: The Dramatic Story of China's War on Foreigners That Shook the World in the Summer of 1900* (New York: Berkley Books, 2001)
Sassen S, *Losing Control? Sovereignty in an Age of Globalization* (New York: Columbia University Press, 1996)
Soguk N, *States and Strangers: Refugees and Displacements of Statecraft* (Minnaeapolis: University of Minnesota Press, 1999)
Stevens J (ed), *Access to Justice in Sub-Saharan Africa: The Role of Traditional and Informal Justice Systems* (London: Penal Reform International, 2000)
Wang G and Mo J (eds), *Chinese Law* (The Hague: Kluwer Law International, 1999)
Whitehouse B, 'Overcoming the Economist Fallacy: Social Determinants of Voluntary Migration to the Sahel from the Congo Basin' in A Kane and T Leedy (eds), *African Migration Patterns* (Bloomington: Indiana University Press, 2013)

ARTICLES

Achiume T, 'The Fatal Flaw in International Law for Migration: Model International Mobility Convention Commentary' (2017) UCLA School of Law, Public Law Research Paper No 17-35

——, 'Reimagining International Law for Global Migration: Migration as Decolonization' (2017–18) 111 *American Journal of International Law Unbound* 142

Ahmad N, 'State Responsibility, Country of Origin and Human Rights' (2009) 10 *Asia-Pacific Journal on Human Rights and Law* 1

Akers P, 'Establishing Rule of Law through Informal Justice Systems and Development Programs' (2016) 30(1) *Notre Dame Journal of Law, Ethics & Public Policy* 122

Alden C and Large D, 'On Becoming a Norms Maker: Chinese Foreign Policy, Norms Evolution and the Challenges of Security in Africa' (2015) 221 *China Quarterly* 123

Al Tamimi Y, 'Human Rights and the Excess of Identity: A Legal and Theoretical Inquiry into the Notion of Identity in Strasbourg Case Law' (2018) 27(3) *Social & Legal Studies* 283

Alobo EE et al, 'The ICJ's Decision on Bakassi Peninsula in Retrospect: A True Evaluation of the History, Issues and Critique of the Judgement' (2016) 6(10) *International Journal of Humanities and Social Sciences* 108

Anghie A, 'Finding the Peripheries: Sovereignty and Colonialism in Nineteenth Century International Law' (1999) 40 *Harvard International Law Journal* 1

Azgaku BC, 'The Role of Nigeria in Peace Building, Conflict Resolution, and Peacekeeping since 1960', Conference Paper, Ahmadu Bello University, Zaria, 2005

Banks K and Kohn-Wood L, 'Gender, Ethnicity and Depression: Intersectionality in Mental Health Research with African American Women' (2002) 8 *African American Research Perspectives* 174

Bassey JR, 'Anglo-German Treaty of 1913 and its Influence on World Court Decision in the Nigeria v Cameroon Case Concerning Bakassi' (2014) 6(11) *International Journal of Current Research* 9832

Becker Lorca A, 'Alejandro Alvarez Situated: Subaltern Modernities and Modernisms That Subvert' (2006) 19 *Leiden Journal of International Law* 879

——, 'Universal International Law: Nineteenth-Century Histories of Imposition and Appropriation' (2010) 51(2) *Harvard International Law Journal* 475

Benvenisti E and Harel A, 'Embracing the Tension between National and International Human Rights Law: The Case for Discordant Parity' (2017) 15(1) *International Journal of Constitutional Law* 36

Berman PS, 'Global Legal Pluralism' (2007) 80(6) *Southern California Law Review* 1155

Bhabha H, 'On Minorities: Cultural Rights' (2000) 100(6) *Radical Philosophy* 3

Bhabha J, 'International Gatekeepers: The Tension between Asylum Advocacy and Human Rights' (2002) 23 *Immigration and Nationality Law Review* 159

Bodomo A, 'The African Trading Community in Guangzhou: An Emerging Bridge for Africa-China Relations' (2010) 203 *China Quarterly* 693

Bodomo A and Grace Ma, 'From Guangzhou to Yiwu: Emerging Facets of the African Diaspora in China' (2010) 5(2) *International Journal of African Renaissance Studies* 283

Bürkner H, 'Intersectionality: How Gender Studies Might Inspire the Analysis of Social Inequality among Migrants' (2012) 18(2) *Population, Space and Place* 181

Burton E, 'Why We Need Comparative Legal Studies' (1984) 8 *Resource News* 9

Campbell H, 'Remilitarisation of African Societies: Analysis of the Planning behind Proposed US Africa Command' (2008) 3(1) *International Journal of African Renaissance Studies* 6

Carmody P and Kragelund P, 'Who is in Charge: State Power and Agency in Sino-African Relations' (2016) 49 *Cornell International Law Journal* 1

Castillo R, 'Feeling at Home in the "Chocolate City": An Exploration of Place Making Practices and Structures of Belonging amongst Africans in Guangzhou' (2014) 15(2) *Inter-Asia Cultural Studies* 235

Chan E and Schloenhardt A, 'North Korean Refugees and International Refugee Law' (2007) 19 *International Journal of Refugee Law* 215

Chan K, 'Is China Abolishing the Hukou System?' (2008) 195 *China Quarterly* 582

Charlesworth H, 'International Law: A Discipline of Crisis' (2002) 65 *MLR* 377

Charlesworth H, Chinkin C and Wright S, 'Feminist Approaches to International Law' (1991) 85 *American Journal of International Law* 613

Cheng T and Selden M, 'The Origins and Social Consequences of China's Hukou System' (1994) 139 *China Quarterly* 644

Chimni BS, 'The Geopolitics of Refugee Studies: A View from the South' (1998) 11 *Journal of Refugee Studies* 350

——, 'Marxism and International Law: A Contemporary Analysis' (1999) 34(6) *Economic and Political Weekly* 337

——, 'Reforming the International Refugee Regime: A Dialogic Model' (2001) 14 *Journal of Refugee Studies* 151

——, 'Third World Approaches to International Law: A Manifesto' (2006) 8 *International Community Law Review* 3

——, 'Prolegomena to a Class Approach to International Law' (2010) 21(1) *European Journal of International Law* 57

——, 'The World of TWAIL: Introduction to the Special Issue' (2011) 3(1) *Trade, Law and Development* 14

Chimni BS and Anghie A, 'Third World Approaches to International Law and the Individual Responsibility in Internal Conflicts' (2003) 2 *Chinese Journal of International Law* 77

Chongfu L, 'National Identity in the Course of Globalization: The Marxist Theory of the State and National Identity' (2014) 35(2) *Social Sciences in China* 124

Chow Pok Yin S, 'Has Intersectionality Reached its Limits? Intersectionality in the UN Human Rights Treaty Body Practice and the Issue of Ambivalence' (2016) 16 *Human Rights Law Review* 453

Collins PH, 'The Tie That Binds: Race, Gender and US Violence' (1998) 21(5) *Ethnic and Racial Studies* 917

——, 'Social Inequality, Power and Politics: Intersectionality and American Pragmatism in Dialogue' (2012) 26(2) *Journal of Speculative Philosophy* 442

Corri Z, 'Islamic Contributions to International Humanitarian Law: Recalibrating TWAIL Approaches for Existing Contributions and Legacies' (2015) 109 *AJIL Unbound* 271

Crenshaw K, 'Demarginalizing the Intersection of Race and Sex: A Black Feminist Critique of Antidiscrimination Doctrine, Feminist Theory and Antiracist Politics' (1989) 1 *University of Chicago Legal Forum* 139

Crowe J, 'The Limits of Legal Pluralism' (2015) 24(2) *Griffith Law Review* 330

Dada JA, 'Impediments to Human Rights Protection in Nigeria' (2002) 18(1) *Annual Survey of International & Comparative Law* 67

——, 'Human Rights under the Nigerian Constitution: Issues and Problems' (2012) 2(12) *International Journal of Humanities and Social Science* 33

Dada OF, 'The Justiciability and Enforceability of Women's Rights in Nigeria' (2014) 14(5) *Global Journal of Human Social Science: Economics* 49

Dauvergne C, 'Sovereignty, Migration and the Rule of Law in Global Times' (2004) 67 *MLR* 588

Dehm J, 'Post-Paris Reflections: Fossil Fuels, Human Rights and the Need to Excavate New Ideas for Climate Justice' (2017) 8(2) *Journal of Human Rights and the Environment* 280

De Lombaerde P, Guo F and Neto H, 'Introduction to the Special Collection: South-South Migrations: What is (Still) on the Research Agenda' (2014) 48 *International Migration Review* 103

De Souza P, 'Evaluating Access to Justice in Informal Justice Systems: A Suggestive Framework' (2015) 19(1) *Max Planck Yearbook of United Nations Law* 469

Dickinson R, 'Transformation of the Modern State: State Sovereignty and Human Rights in the Internet Age' (2013) 29 *Connecticut Journal of International Law* 51

Doering K, 'The Relationship between State Sovereignty and Human Rights' [1979] *Acta Juridica* 77

Dokubo C and Abiodun JO, 'Nigeria's Role in Conflict Resolution: A New Paradigm' (2011) 3(3) *Journal of Alternative Perspectives in the Social Sciences* 551

Donnelly, J, 'International Human Rights: A Regime Analysis' (1986) 40 *International Organization* 599

Dzur AW and Olson SM, 'Revisiting Informal Justice: Restorative Justice and Democratic Professionalism' (2004) 38(1) *Law & Society Review* 139

Eberle EJ, 'Comparative Law' (2007) 13 *Annual Survey of International & Comparative Law* 93

Ekhator O, 'The Impact of the African Charter on Human and Peoples' Rights on Domestic Law: A Case Study of Nigeria' (2015) 41(2) *Commonwealth Law* Bulletin 253

Eslava L and Pahuja S, 'Between Resistance and Reform: TWAIL and the Universality of International Law' (2011) 3 *Trade Law and Development* 103

Eze O, Elimian A and Uchenna C, 'The Politics of State Creation and National Integration in Nigeria' (2015) 8 *Journal of Politics and Law* 113

Fandl K, 'The Role of Informal Legal Institutions in Economic Development' (2008) 32 *Fordham International Law Journal* 1

FitzGerald, JM, 'Thinking about Law and its Alternatives: Abel et al and the Debate over Informal Justice' (1984) 9(3) *American Bar Foundation Research Journal* 637

Fitzpatrick P, 'The Impossibility of Popular Justice' (1992) 1 *Social & Legal Studies* 199

Foerstel K, 'China in Africa' (2008) 2(1) *CQ Global Researcher* 1

Forsyth M, 'A Typology of Relationships between State and Non-state Justice Systems' (2007) 56 *Journal of Legal Pluralism* 67

Gander M, 'The Intersection of Gender and Age: An Exploration' (2014) 18(1) *Perspectives: Policy and Practice in Higher Education* 9

Gant L, 'Intersectional Contexts of HIV/AIDS: Global Examples' (2017) 16(1) *Journal of HIV/AIDS & Social Services*

Gathii J, 'TWAIL: A Brief History of its Origins, its Decentralized Network, and a Tentative Bibliography' (2011) 3 *Trade Law & Development* 26

Goodwin-Gill G, 'Refugees and Responsibility in the Twenty-First Century: More Lessons Learned from the South Pacific' (2003) 12(1) *Pacific Rim Law & Policy Journal* 23

Griffiths J, 'What is Legal Pluralism?' (1986) 24 *Journal of Legal Pluralism & Unofficial Law* 1

Grosfoguel R, Oso L and Christou A, '"Racism", Intersectionality and Migration Studies: Framing Some Theoretical Reflections' (2015) 22(6) *Identities* 635

Guirardon V and Gallya L, 'A Reappraisal of the State Sovereignty Debate: The Case of Migration Control' (2000) 33 *Comparative Political Studies* 163

Guo S, 'Implementation of Human Rights Treaties by Chinese Courts: Problems and Prospects' (2009) 8 *Chinese Journal of International Law* 161

Hallett K, 'Intersectionality and Serious Mental Illness: A Case Study and Recommendations for Practice' (2015) 38(1–2) *Women & Therapy* 156

Hameiri S and Jones L, 'Rising Powers and State Transformation: The Case of China' (2016) 22(1) *European Journal of International Relations* 72

Hampton A, 'Population Control in China: Sacrificing Human Rights for the Greater Good' (2003) 11 *Tulsa Journal of Comparative and International Law* 321

Harley T, 'Regional Cooperation and Refugee Protection in Latin America: A South-South Approach' (2014) 26 *International Journal of Refugee Law* 22

Hasan M, 'South-South Migration and Security Risks: Political Islam and Violent Extremism in the Shadow of Globalisation in Bangladesh' (2017) 73(3) *India Quarterly* 312

Haugen HO, 'Nigerians in China: A Second State of Immobility' (2012) 50(2) *International Migration* 65

Huang G, 'Policing Blacks in Guangzhou: How Public Security Constructs Africans as *Sanfei*' (2018) 45(2) *Modern China* 171

Hayward CR and Watson R, 'Identity and Political Theory' (2010) 33 *Washington University Journal of Law & Policy* 9

Henkin L, 'That "S" Word: Sovereignty, and Globalization, and Human Rights, et Cetera' (1999) 68(1) *Fordham Law Review* 1

Holzer E, 'What Happens to Law in a Refugee Camp?' (2013) 47 *Law & Society Review* 837

Horwitz P, 'Uncovering Identity' (2007) 105 *Michigan Law Review* 1283

Isser DH et al, 'Looking for Justice: Liberian Experiences with and Perceptions of Local Justice Options' (2009) 63 *United States Institute of Peace* 104

Jacobson D, 'New Border Customs: Migration and the Changing Role of the State' (1998) 3(2) *UCLA Journal of International Law and Foreign Affairs* 443

James O, 'Valuing Identity' (2017) 102 *Minnesota Law Review* 127

Johnston L, 'Intersectional Feminist and Queer Geographies: A View from "Down-Under"' (2018) 25(4) *Gender, Place & Culture* 554

Joireman S and Corey A, 'Retributive Justice: The Gacaca Courts in Rwanda' (2004) 103 *African Affairs* 73

Kennedy DW, 'New Approaches to International Law Bibliography' (1994) 35 *Harvard International Law Journal* 417

Kiyani GA, 'Third World Approaches to International Criminal Law' (2015) 109 *American Journal of International Law Unbound* 255

Kiyoteru T and Wotipka C, 'Global Human Rights and State Sovereignty: State Ratification of International Human Rights Treaties, 1965–2001' (2008) 23(4) *Sociological Forum* 724

Knopp K, 'Re/Statements: Feminism and State Sovereignty in International Law' (1993) 3 *Transnational Law and Contemporary Problems* 293

Knowles A, 'Implementing International Refugee Law in the People's Republic of China' (2018) 9 *Beijing Law Review* 67

Kolawole B, 'African Immigrants, Intersectionality, and the Increasing Need for Visibility in the Current Immigration Debate' (2017) 7 *Columbia Journal of Race and Law* 373

Kong Q and Ping X, 'International Law in International Institutions: Implications for a Rising China' (2015) 1 *Chinese Journal of Global Governance* 157

Lacombe-Duncan A, 'An Intersectional Perspective on Access to HIV-Related Healthcare for Transgender Women' (2016) 1(1) *Transgender Health* 137

Lan S, 'State Regulation of Undocumented African Migrants in China: A Multi-scalar Analysis' (2015) 50(3) *Journal of Asian and African Studies* 289

Landauer C, 'Things Fall Together: The Past and Future Africas of TO Elias's Africa and the Development of International Law' (2008) 21 *Leiden Journal of International Law* 351

LeFebvre R, 'Interests and Identities in Peace Negotiations: Nigeria, Cameroon, and the Bakassi Peninsula' (2014) 6(1) *African Social Science Review* 83

Legrand P, '*A Modern Approach to Comparative Law* by Peter de Cruz' (1995) 58(2) *MLR* 262

Lerner N, 'Group Rights and Legal Pluralism' (2011) 25(2) *Emory International Law Review* 829

Lenzerini F, 'Asylum, Human Rights and State Measures against Immigration Flows: State Prerogative or Disguised Refoulement' (2004) 4 *ISIL Yearbook of International Humanitarian and Refugee Law* 11

Lewis H, 'Transnational Dimensions of Racial Identity: Reflecting on Race, the Global Economy, and the Human Rights Movement at 60' (2009) 24 *Maryland Journal of International Law* 296

Liasidou A, 'Intersectional Understandings of Disability and Implications for a Social Justice Reform Agenda in Education Policy and Practice' (2013) 28(3) *Disability & Society* 299

Lim CL, 'Neither Sheep nor Peacocks: TO Elias and Post-colonial International Law' (2008) 21(2) *Leiden Journal of International Law* 295

Ling W, 'Decentralization and Hukou Reforms in China' (2013) 32(1) *Policy and Society* 33

Liu G, 'Legislation, Impacts and Deficiencies of the Law of Exit and Entry Administration of China 2013' (2014) 4(4) *International Journal Public Law and Policy* 381
Mahmud T, 'Migration, Identity & the Colonial Encounter' (1997) 76 *Oregon Law Review* 633
Matthews G and Yang Y, 'How Africans Pursue Low-End Globalization in Hong Kong and Mainland China' (2012) 41(2) *Journal of Current Chinese Affairs* 95
Mawdsley E, 'Human Rights and South-South Development Cooperation: Reflections on the Rising Powers as International Development Actors' (2014) 36 *Human Rights Quarterly* 630
Merril K, 'China's National Resident Identity Card: Identity and Population Management in Transition' (2005) 23 *UCLA Pacific Basin Law Journal* 212
McCall L, 'The Complexity of Intersectionality' (2005) 30(3) *Signs* 1771
Michelson K, 'Rhetoric and Rage: Third World Voices in International Legal Discourse' (1997) 16 *Wisconsin International Law Journal* 353
Miller D, 'National Responsibility and Global Justice' (2008) 11(4) *Critical Review of International Social and Political Philosophy* 230
Min Z, Shabnam S and Tao X, 'Chinese Attitudes toward African Migrants in Guangzhou, China' (2016) 46(2) *International Journal of Sociology* 141
Mitsilegas V, 'Immigration Control in an Era of Globalization: Deflecting Foreigners, Weakening Citizens, and Strengthening the State' (2012) 19(1) *Indiana Journal of Global Legal Studies* 3
Moodley J and Graham L, 'The Importance of Intersectionality in Disability and Gender Studies' (2015) 29(2) *Agenda* 24
Munck R, 'Globalisation, Governance and Migration: An Introduction' (2008) 29(7) *Third World Quarterly* 1227
Mutua M, 'Critical Race Theory and International Law: The View of an Insider-Outsider' (2000) 45 *Villanova Law Review* 841
Mutua M and Anghie A, 'What is TWAIL?' (2000) 94 *American Society of International Law* 31
Nagel T, 'The Problem of Global Justice' (2005) 33 *Philosophy and Public Affairs* 113
Nash J, 'Rethinking Intersectionality' (2008) 89 *Feminist Review* 1
Nawyn S, 'Migration in the Global South: Exploring New Theoretical Territory' (2016) 46(2) *International Journal of Sociology* 81
Ng H, 'Intersectionality and Shared Decision Making in LGBTQ Health' (2016) 3(5) *LGBT Health* 325
Odinkalu CA, 'Poor Justice or Justice for the Poor? A Policy Framework for Reform of Customary and Informal Justice Systems in Africa' (2006) 2 *WBLR: Law and Justice for Development* 141
Odumosu I, 'Challenges for the (Present/)Future of Third World Approaches to International Law' (2008) 10 *International Community Law Review* 467
Ogunnubi O and Okeke-Uzodike U, 'Can Nigeria Be Africa's Hegemon?' (2016) 25(2) *African Security Review* 110
Ojarukotu V and Ndlovu-Gatsheni S, 'Surveillance over a Zone of Conflict: Africom and the Politics of Securitisation of Africa' (2010) 3(6) *Journal of Pan African Studies* 94
Ojukwu Nelson C, 'Enforcement of the African Charter on Human and Peoples Rights as a Domestic Law in Nigeria' (2000) 25 *International Legal Practitioner* 140
Oklopcic Z, 'Beyond Empty, Conservative, and Ethereal: Pluralist Self-Determination and a Peripheral Political Imaginary' (2013) 26 *Leiden Journal of International Law* 509
Okafor OC, 'Critical Third World Approaches to International Law (TWAIL): Theory, Methodology, or Both' (2008) 10 *International Community Law Review* 371
Opasina Oladapo K, 'Legal Pluralism in Contemporary States: Between Traditional and Formal Justice Mechanisms in Nigeria and Cote d'Ivoire' (2017) 1 *Glocalism: Journal of Culture, Politics and Innovation* 1
Pajibo E, 'Accountability and Justice in Post-conflict Liberia' (2010) 10(3) *African Identities* 301
Parmar P, 'TWAIL: An Epistemological Inquiry' (2008) 10 *International Community Law Review* 363

Peters A, 'Humanity as the A and Ω of Sovereignty' (2009) 20(3) *European Journal of International Law* 515

Peterson G, 'The Uneven Development of the International Refugee Regime in Post-war Asia: Evidence from China, Hong Kong and Indonesia' (2012) 25(3) *Journal of Refugee Studies* 326

Pickering S, 'Border Terror: Policing, Forced Migration and Terrorism' (2004) 16(3) *Global Change, Peace & Security* 211

Pittaway E and Pittaway E, 'Refugee Woman: A Dangerous Label' (2004) 10(1) *Australian Journal of Human Rights* 119

Purkayastha B, 'Intersectionality in a Transnational World' (2012) 26(1) *Gender & Society* 55

Purvis T and Hunt A, 'Identity versus Citizenship: Transformations in the Discourses and Practices of Citizenship' (1999) 8 *Social & Legal Studies* 457

Rajagopal B, 'International Law and Social Movements: Challenges of Theorizing *Resistance*' (2003) 41 *Columbia Journal of Transnational Law* 397

Reitz J, 'How to Do Comparative Law' (1998) 46(4) *American Journal of Comparative Law* 617

Riles A, 'A View from the International Plane: Perspective and Scale in the Architecture of Colonial International Law' (1995) VI(1) *Law and Critique* 39

Rodrigues Rios J, 'Tension between Sovereignty and Human Rights in International Migration' [2015] *Conferinta Internationala de Drept, Studii Europene si Relatii Internationale* 538

Ruddick E, 'The Continuing Constraint of Sovereignty: International Law, International Protection, and the Internally Displaced' (1997) 77 *Boston University Law Review* 429

Ryburn M, 'Living the Chilean Dream? Bolivian Migrants' Incorporation in the Space of Economic Citizenship' (2016) 76 *Geoforum* 48

Sangroula Y, 'The Scope of Informal Justice Mechanisms in Criminal Justice System: Critical Observations on Principles, Theories and Prospects' (2013) 2 *Kathmandu School of Law Review* 9

Saul M and Pelican M, 'A New Research Perspective on Contemporary African Migration' (2014) 43(1–3) *Urban Anthropology and Studies of Cultural Systems and World Economic Development* 2

Sautman B, 'Anti-Black Racism in Post-Mao China' (1994) 138 *China Quarterly* 413

Schauer F, 'Community, Citizenship, and the Search for National Identity' (1986) 84 *Michigan Law Review* 1504

Schindlmayr T, 'Sovereignty, Legal Regimes and International Migration' (2003) 41(2) *International Migration* 109

Shanhe J, Lambert E and Wang J, 'Correlates of Formal and Informal Social/Crime Control in China: An Exploratory Study' (2007) 35(4) *Journal of Criminal Justice*

Shelton D, 'On Identity' (2016) 49 *George Washington International Law Review* 1

Song L, 'Who Shall We Help? A Refugee Definition in a Chinese Context' (2014) 33(1) *Refugee Survey Quarterly* 44

——, 'China and the International Refugee Protection Regime: Past, Present, and Potentials' (2018) 37(2) *Refugee Survey Quarterly* 139

——, 'Strengthening Responsibility Sharing with South-South Cooperation: China's Role in the Global Compact on Refugees' (2018) 30 *International Journal of Refugee Law* 687

Subedi S, 'China's Approach to Human Rights and the UN Human Rights Agenda' (2015) 14 *Chinese Journal of International Law* 437

Sunter AF, 'TWAIL as Naturalised Epistemiology' (2007) 20(2) *Canadian Journal of Law and Jurisprudence* 475

Talib M, 'Numbers versus Rights: State Responsibility towards Asylum Seekers and the Implications for the International Refugee Regime' (2013) 27 *Georgetown Immigration Law Journal* 405

Tay A, 'China and Legal Pluralism' (1984) 8(3) *Bulletin of the Australian Society of Legal Philosophy* 14

Thomas C, 'Critical Race Theory and Postcolonial Development Theory: Observations on Methodology' (2000) 45 *Villanova Law Review* 1195

Toufayan M, 'When British Justice (in African Colonies) Points Two Ways: On Dualism, Hybridity, and the Genealogy of Juridical Negritude in Taslim Olawale Elias' (2008) 21(2) *Leiden Journal of International Law* 377

Valdes F, 'Sex and Race in Queer Legal Culture: Ruminations on Identities and Inter-connectivities' (1995) 5 *Southern California Review of Law and Women's Studies* 25

Volsky A, 'Reconciling Human Rights and State Sovereignty, Justice and the Law in Humanitarian Interventions' (2007) 3(1) *International Public Policy Review* 44

Von Benda-Beckmann, K, 'Globalisation and Legal Pluralism' (2002) 4(1) *International Law Forum du droit international* 19

Warner J, 'Nigeria and "Illusory Hegemony" in Foreign and Security Policymaking: *Pax-Nigeriana* and the Challenges of Boko Haram' (2017) 13(3) *Foreign Policy Analysis* 638

Webber J, 'Legal Pluralism and Human Agency' (2006) 44 *Osgoode Hall Law Journal* 1

Wexler L, 'The Role of Human Rights in Migration Regional Consultative Processes' (2012) 106 *American Society of International Law* 65

Widlak HT, 'Sovereignty vs Human Rights: A Case of the Relation between Order and Justice in International Society' (2009) 3 *Journal of Philosophy of International Law* 7

Wihtol de Wenden C, 'New Migrations' (2016) 23 *SUR – International Journal on Human Rights* 17

Wimpelmann T, 'The Informal Justice Paradigm and the Appropriation of Local Reality' (2013) 64(3) *Northern Ireland Legal Quarterly* 398

Windrow H and Guha A, 'The Hukou System, Migrant Workers and State Power in the People's Republic of China' (2005) 3 *Northwestern Journal of International Human Rights* 1

Woolford A and Ratner RS, 'Disrupting the Informal–Formal Justice Complex: On the Transformative Potential of Civil Mediation, Restorative Justice and Reparations Politics' (2010) 13(1) *Contemporary Justice Review* 5

Xavier S, 'Learning from below: Theorising Global Governance through Ethnographies and Critical Reflections from the Global South' (2016) 33 *Windsor Yearbook of Access to Justice* 229

Xue H and Jin Q, 'International Treaties in the Chinese Domestic Legal System' (2009) 8(2) *Chinese Journal of International Law* 299

Yerima H and Singh R, 'The Bakassi Dispute: People's Dynamics and the Rise of Militancy' (2017) 22(1) *IOSR Journal of Humanities and Social Science* 67

Young MA, 'Smuggling and Trafficking of Refugees and Asylum Seekers: Is the International Community Neglecting the Duty to Protect the Persecuted in the Pursuit of Combating Transnational Organized Crime?' (2004) 27 *Suffolk Transnational Law Review* 101

Yuval-Davis N, 'The "Multi-layered Citizen"' (1991) 1(1) *International Feminist Journal of Politics* 119

——, 'Intersectionality, Citizenship and Contemporary Politics of Belonging' (2007) 10(4) *Critical Review of International Social and Political Philosophy* 561

——, 'Theorizing Identity: Beyond the "Us" and "Them" Dichotomy' (2010) 44(3) *Patterns of Prejudice* 261

Yuval-Davis N and Arat Z, 'The Politics of Belonging: Intersectional Contestations' (2014) 16(3) *International Feminist Journal of Politics* 515

Zhou M, Xu T and Shenasi S, 'Entrepreneurship and Interracial Dynamics: A Case Study of Self-Employed Africans and Chinese in Guangzhou, China' (2016) 39(9) *Journal of Ethnic and Racial Studies: Ethnic Entrepreneurship in Intersectional Perspectives* 1573

——, 'Chinese Attitudes toward African Migrants in Guangzhou, China' (2016) 46(2) *International Journal of Sociology* 141

Zhu G and Price R, 'Chinese Immigration Law and Policy: A Case of Change Your Direction, or End up Where You are Heading' (2013) 26 *Columbia Journal of Asian Law* 1

Zumbansen P, 'Transnational Legal Theory' (2010) 1(2) *Transnational Legal Theory* 141

OTHER ARTICLES

Bakewell O, 'South-South Migration and Human Development: Reflections on African Experiences' (International Migrations Institute, University of Oxford, MPRA Paper No 19185, 2009)

Campillo-Carrete A, 'South-South Migrations: A Review of the Literature' (International Institute of Social Studies, Erasmus University of Rotterdam, 2013)
Chukwuma N, 'The Banjul Charter and Universal Human Rights: A Comparative Analysis' (African Law Report, 2016)
Cisse D, 'South-South Migration and Trade: African Traders in China' (Centre for Chinese Studies at Stellenbosch University, 2013)
Ginsburg S, 'Counter-terrorist Mobility: Shaping an Operational Strategy' (Migration Policy Institute, 2006)
Hirono M, 'Exploring the Links between Chinese Foreign Policy and Humanitarian Action: Multiple Interests, Processes and Actors' (Humanitarian Policy Group Working Paper, 2018)
Hossack K, 'Duties of Virtue and Justice: Rethinking Responsibility in the Global Refugee Regime' (PhD thesis, Brandeis University, 2016)
Jin G, 'The Protection and Remedies for Victims of Crime and Abuse of Power in China' (UNAFEI Resource Material Series No 70, 2006)
Juma M, 'The Role of Nigeria in Peace Building, Conflict Resolution, and Peacekeeping since 1960' (conference paper, Ahmadu Bello University, Zaria, 2005)
Phuong C, 'Identifying States' Responsibilities towards Refugees and Asylum Seekers' (ESIL, 2005)
Sceats S and Breslin S, 'China and the International Human Rights System' (Royal Institute of International Affairs, 2012)
Yip J, 'Stranded amidst Resettlement Applications: A Case Study of Pakistani Refugees in China' (MA thesis, Central European University, 2011)
Yun S, 'Africa in China's Foreign Policy' (Brookings Institute, John L Thornton China Cente, Washington DC, April 2014)
Zhu Z, 'China's New Diplomacy in Africa' (conference paper, International Studies Association 48th Annual Convention, Chicago, 2007)

INTERNET/NEWS SOURCES

'Africans' Protests Highlight Tensions in Guangzhou', *Wall Street Journal*, 20 June 2012
Adeniji G, 'Nigeria Tried for Us But We Need Help to Return Home – Oru-Ijebu Ex-refugees from Sierra Leone, Liberia', *Punch*, 28 January 2018
Ajayi O, 'Bakassi People on Verge of Becoming Stateless, UNHCR Warns', *The Vanguard*, 6 October 2016
Akpan A, '10 Feared Dead as Militants, Kidnappers Clash in Cross River', *The Guardian* (Nigeria), 4 February 2017
Akpan A and Osahon J, 'Militancy Bakassi Strike Force Overruns Cross River LGAs', *The Guardian* (Nigeria), 10 July 2016
'Bakassi: CRSG Tasks INEC on Compliance with S/Court Judgement', *The Vanguard*, 12 April 2018
'Bakassi Residents to Pay Tax under Cameroon Sovereignty', *BBC News*, 15 August 2013
Beech H, 'A Nigerian Dies in China – and Racial Tensions Heat Up', *TIME*, 20 June 2012
Branigan T, 'Africans Protest in China after Nigerian Dies in Immigration Raid', *The Guardian*, 16 July 2009
'President Xi Attends Nuclear Security Summit, Visits Europe', *China Daily*, 2 April 2016
Delon O 'How Nigerian citizens are maltreated in China', *The Vanguard*, 2 April 2014
Eslava L, 'TWAIL Coordinates', *Legal Critical Thinking*, 2 April 2019
Ezeobi C, 'Nigerians Languish in Chinese Jails', *ThisDay*, 17 March 2016
'INEC Rejects H/Court's Ruling on Bakassi Polls', *The Vanguard*, 11 July 2011
Inyang B, 'Bakassi People: In Quest for a New Abode', *ThisDay*, 8 May 2017
Koestse M, 'Chinese Netizens on World Refugee Day: "Don't Come to China"', *WhatsonWeibo*, 23 June 2017

Lee A, 'China Refuses to Give up "Developing Country" Status at WTO Despite US Demands' *South China Morning Post*, 6 April 2019

'Liberian, S. Leonean Refugees to Settle in Nigeria', *Reuters*, 7 August 2007

'Nigeria–China Relations Deepen as Senator David Mark Visits Chinese Parliament', *Africa Independent Online*, 15 May 2014

Nwafor P, 'Keeping Nigerians away from Jails Abroad', *The Vanguard*, 3 October 2017

Odinkalu C, 'Stateless in Bakassi: How a Changed Border Left Inhabitants Adrift', *Open Societies Foundation Voices*, 2 April 2012

Onah G, 'Nigeria: Secession! Militants Declare Bakassi Independent State', *The Vanguard*, 9 July 2006

Pomfret J, 'Out of Africa and into China, Immigrants Struggle', *Reuters*, 21 August 2009

Ryburn M and von Berlo P, 'South-South Migration: Law, Procedure, and Exclusion in Under-explored Contexts', *Leiden Law Blog*, 16 November 2016

Sam-Duru P and Anyagafu V, 'Nigerians in China Cry out, Drug Traffickers Robbing Us of Privileges', *The Vanguard*, 7 January 2017

Schiller B, 'Big Trouble in China's Chocolate City', *The Star*, 1 August 2009

Shi J, 'China Willing to Open Pockets Not Borders to Middle East Refugees', *South China Morning Post*, 26 June 2017

Shirbon E, 'Up to 21 Cameroon Troops Killed in Bakassi', *Reuters*, 13 November 2007

Sosthenes M, 'Africa: Human Trafficking Seen Escalating', *Tanzania Daily News*, 21 September 2015

Ukpong Cletus, 'Bakassi People "Discover New Island But Nigerian Govt Foot-Dragging" – Leader', *Premium Times*, 22 July 2017

Una E, 'Bakassi: Our People May Lose Their Right to Political Representation – Ex Attorney General', *The Vanguard*, 8 April 2018

Wang X, 'China Raises Humanitarian Profile Globally', *China Daily*, 19 March 2019

'Why Many Nigerians are in Chinese Prisons', *The Vanguard*, 26 February 2018

Zhai I, 'Africans Protests in Guangzhou after Nigerian Feared Killed Fleeing Visa Check', *South China Morning Post*, 16 July 2009

Appendix: List of Interviews (Chronological)

China

Personal conversation with A and B Yanjiao, China, November 2015

Personal conversation with Mr P, a high-level staff member of the IOM, November 2015

Email interview with Mr P from the International Organisation of Migration in Beijing, December 2015

Listening session with Chinese immigration law scholars at Beijing Institute of Technology, December 2015

Skype conversation with Gary C, an expert in Chinese immigration law, December 2015

Email conversation with Ms Y, a staff of a Chinese community organisation working with African migrants by email, January 2016

Personal conversation with Mr H at the UNHCR Headquarters in Beijing, China, January 2016

Skype conversation with Ms M, a Chinese migration researcher, January 2016

Personal conversation with Mr S in Baiyun District, Guangzhou, February 2016

Personal conversation with Mr B in Baiyun District, Guangzhou, March 2016

Personal interview with Mr N in Yuexiu District, March 2016

Personal conversation with Mr T in Baiyun District, Guangzhou, March 2016

Personal conversation with Mr C in Xiaobei, Guangzhou, March 2016

Personal conversation with B and T, staff of a Chinese community organisation working with migrants in Xiaobei, Guangzhou, March 2016

Nigeria

Listening session with the Bakassi community in Akwa Ekot Edem Camp, Akpabuyo, Cross River State, May 2016

Personal conversation with State Emergency Management Agency staff, June 2016, Calabar, Cross River State

Phone Conversation with National Emergency Management Agency staff, June 2016

Listening session with the Bakassi Community in at the Bakassi Returnee Camp, Ikang, Cross River State, June 2016

Interview with Ikang District Police Officer, June 2016

Listening session with Bakassi Local Government Chairwoman, Ms I and officials in Calabar, Cross River State, August 2016

Personal conversation with Chief H, former Bakassi Local Government Chairman, Calabar, Cross River State, August 2016

Personal conversation with Mr J, University of Calabar, Cross River State, Nigera, August 2016

Personal interview with the Nigerian Police Commissioner of Cross River State, August 2016

Personal interview with Ms O, an activist, Calabar, August 2016

Index

www.ingramcontent.com/pod-product-compliance
Ingram Content Group UK Ltd.
Pitfield, Milton Keynes, MK11 3LW, UK
UKHW020815290926
15470UKWH00003B/1163

9 781509 958184